CARE, GENDER, AND JUSTICE

CARE, GENDER, AND JUSTICE

DIEMUT ELISABET BUBECK

CLARENDON PRESS · OXFORD

1995

Oxford University Press, Walton Street, Oxford OX2 6DP
Oxford New York
Athens Auckland Bangkok Bombay
Calcutta Cape Town Dar es Salaam Delhi
Florence Hong Kong Istanbul Karachi
Kuala Lumpur Madras Madrid Melbourne
Mexico City Nairobi Paris Singapore
Taipei Tokyo Toronto
and associated companies in
Berlin Ibadan

Oxford is a trade mark of Oxford University Press

Published in the United States
by Oxford University Press Inc., New York

British Library Cataloguing in Publication Data
Data available

Library of Congress Cataloging-in-Publication Data
Bubeck, Diemut Elisabet.
Care, gender, and justice / Diemut Elisabet Bubeck.
Includes bibliographical references
1. Housewives. 2. Caring—Moral and ethical aspects. 3. Sex
discrimination against women. 4. Sexual division of labor.
5. Feminist theory. 6. Social justice. I. Title.
HD8039.H84B8 1995
305.43'649—dc20 95–18020
ISBN 0–19–827990–6

1 3 5 7 9 10 8 6 4 2

Typeset by Graphicraft Typesetters Ltd., Hong Kong
Printed in Great Britain
on acid-free paper by
Biddles Ltd., Guildford and King's Lynn

PREFACE

Philosophy, according to one of the many accounts of itself, has its origins and its motivation in the bemused or awed amazement of those who refuse to take for granted what everybody else takes for granted.[1] Amazement, though, does mostly not occur 'naturally': it is often an achievement which has to overcome the combined pressures of history, social context and individual habits of thought, all of which lead to certain things being taken for granted. In fact, it may be the fundamental task of philosophy to elicit amazement in its readers or listeners where there was none before, and a proof of its quality if it succeeds. In my own case, it took me years of studying philosophy before I felt comfortable enough—or maybe, rather, driven enough—to start turning my often unacknowledged and certainly pre-philosophical frustration and anger into a more productive amazement at certain aspects of society which most philosophers seemed to take for granted even if they questioned much else. Having been steeped in marxist theory and analytical philosophy and subsequently in marxist and socialist feminist theory, none of which helped me in the end to articulate quite what it was I wanted to question, it took me a long time to work out the particular amazement that I felt deeply and wanted to elicit in others, as well as the answers I wanted to give to the questions posed.

The working out spanned several years as a doctoral student and lecturer and its results materialized finally in my doctoral thesis. Hence I would like to start off by expressing my special gratitude to the two supervisors who, in their own and very different ways, saw a slow and ever changing doctoral thesis and a rather unhappy doctoral student through to a happy end. Jerry Cohen started off very unconvinced, forcing me to question my own ideas to the point of despair, but surprised me in the last stages by having changed some of his ideas and being as

---

[1] This idea has always been with me and is probably the one that enticed me to become a philosopher eventually. I must have come across it either as a pupil in an evening course on philosophy or as an undergraduate student in one of the philosophy lectures or seminars at the University of Bochum (Germany). Unfortunately, I could not trace a written source for this account.

supportive, encouraging and reliable as anyone could wish for. Sabina Lovibond joined in after a year with characteristically tentative but spot-on comments, a general conviction that whatever it was I was trying to do was worth doing, and a belief in me which helped carry me through periods of complete self-doubt. Being now involved in Ph.D. supervision myself, with the nature of Ph.D. supervision in the UK changing toward a much more directive style and strict time limits, I appreciate greatly the freedom I had to change my mind as often as I did and that I could take my time to develop my ideas. The initial years of working on the thesis were supported by a grant from the Studienstiftung des Deutschen Volkes (Scholarship Foundation of the German People) which gave me not only the material means, but also some confidence to persist in my academic work.

Special thanks also go to Andy Mason, who commented on some version of all of the chapters of the thesis and who was one of the very few men in the male-dominated and male-biased academic environment of Oxford to be interested; and to David Beetham, who not only encouraged me and commented on work in progress, but also saved me from exam marking in my first year as a lecturer so that I could get down to some work on my thesis: I did, and came up with a then path- and paralysis-breaking draft of the central part of this book. Janet Coleman and Rodney Barker have taken an interest in, commented on, and encouraged my work since my arrival at the London School of Economics. John Charvet, Brian Barry, Diana Coole, Anne Sellers, Elisabeth Kondal and Julie George also commented variously and at various stages.

Elizabeth Frazer and Richard Norman, my thesis examiners, Tony Skillen and Vicky Randall, who read the thesis for OUP, and Tim Barton at OUP, helped with the crucial stage of turning the thesis into a book with comments and suggestions for rewriting.

Last, but not least, I am deeply grateful to Wendy Ayotte and Aleine Ridge whose care in difficult times sustained me and taught me a lot of what I know about care. If I have not been able to weave into the argument of the book all that is important about care—all that we should be amazed about when thinking about it—this is partly because of bad timing, and partly because academic writing and materialist theory are not very hospitable contexts for the expression of certain kinds of knowledge.

CONTENTS

PART III

ABBREVIATIONS

The following abbreviations are used for texts by Karl Marx.
Dates in parentheses indicate locations in the References.

Cap.	*Capital* (vols. i, iii) (1976a, 1981)
CGP	'Critique of the Gotha Programme' (1969c)
EPM	'Economic and Philosophical Manuscripts' (1975)
GR	*Grundrisse* (1973)
Preface	'Preface to the *Critique of Political Economy*' (1969d)
'Results'	'Results of the Immediate Process of Production' (1976b)
TSV	*Theories of Surplus Value* (parts i, iii) (1969a, 1972)
WLC	'Wage Labour and Capital' (1969b)

Texts by Karl Marx and Friedrich Engels are abbreviated:

CM	'Manifesto of the Communist Party' (1969a)
GI	*German Ideology* (1965)

In addition, Aristotle's *Nicomachean Ethics* is cited with the abbreviation *NE*.

Introduction

(i) Amazement: social justice and gendered reality

Social justice, according to John Rawls's famous formulation, is 'the first virtue of social institutions'.[1] In his theory, principles and considerations of social justice apply to 'the basic structure of society',[2] comprised of the basic social institutions. Thus the principles of justice 'are to govern the assignment of rights and duties in these institutions and . . . are to *determine the appropriate distribution of the benefits and burdens of social life'*.[3] Thus far, I have no qualm with Rawls. In fact, I more than agree. I find his formulations very helpful, and so have many others: his theory has been immensely stimulating for political philosophy as a whole. If Rawls has got these very basic ideas about justice right, however, how is it possible that he could not see, along with many others, that his theory applies equally to a social institution which he never even acknowledges: the sexual division of labour? If, more generally, theorists of social justice are interested in spelling out how societies have to be structured to be just, how can they possibly not address the obvious and persistent inequalities between men and women?[4] How could they not see what is staring them in the face, and how could they not realize its relevance?

Many facts could be cited here to illustrate these inequalities, but the statistic originating from the UN Decade of Women puts most succinctly the kind of facts that should have worried all theorists of social justice and that capture the fundamental concern informing this book: women, it states,

---

[1] Rawls 1971: 3.   [2] Ibid. 54.
[3] Ibid. (my emphasis).   [4] See Okin 1989, ch. 1.

constitute *half* the world's population,
perform nearly *two-thirds* of its work hours,
receive *one-tenth* of the world's income
and own less than *one-hundredth* of the world's property.[5]

Now even if it is true that the statistics for the Western industrialized countries, to which my argument is restricted, are less
scandalous, they would nevertheless bear witness to persistent
material inequalities between men and women. Since other forms
of inequality have scandalized political and social philosophers—
notably those of class and to some extent race in the recent discussion of social justice—why, on the whole, have they not been
scandalized by the inequalities of gender?[6] And how exactly are
we to understand these inequalities?

The main inequality I am concerned with in this book is the
fact that it is still mainly women who do most of the unpaid
work performed in any home which goes towards the meeting
of needs in others. Part of the problem with this work, which I
take the first three chapters to grapple with, is its complete mis-
conception in the history of social and political philosophy until
the present. So it is, on the one hand, not surprising that this
work has not really troubled the heads of philosophers on the
whole. On the other hand, however, if social justice concerns the
distribution of burdens and benefits in a society, it should: work
is one of the main burdens anybody faces in their lives—if they
have to face it—and even if it is not always burdensome, it is
usually burdensome enough to have to be paid or usher in other
benefits for those who work actually to engage in it. Hence even
on its own terms, Rawls's conception of justice should have led
him and many others after him to discuss the distribution of
work as an important, if not the most important, instance of the
distribution of burdens, hence also the sexual division of labour.

The most obvious reason why what I shall call 'women's work'[7]
has not been discussed in social and political philosophy is that

[5] Quoted after Pahl 1988: 349.
[6] Green 1985 is a notable exception, but the topic of his book is democracy
rather than social justice.
[7] By 'women's work', I do not mean to imply that this kind of work is necessarily or 'naturally' done by women. Rather, I use the term descriptively and
as a useful shorthand for the particular kinds of work that, traditionally and in
most if not all societies, women have been responsible for and taken on more
or less as a matter of course.

philosophers on the whole still do not take into account the issues or problems raised for their own topics by a gendered reality. (This is not really a reason, but simply a reference to a general pattern which itself remains unexplained.) Feminist philosophers have criticized gender bias in its various manifestations over the last twenty years. The feminist critique of theories of justice in particular has recently been much advanced by Okin's *Justice, Gender, and the Family*.[8] My own work shares with Okin's a preoccupation with the sexual division of labour—more specifically the gendered distribution of work in and between the public and private spheres—and the material inequality that results from it. As should be obvious from the preceding paragraphs, I agree with Okin and her critique of Rawls that the sexual division of labour poses important questions with regard to the distribution of benefits and burdens for any theorist of social justice: if social justice at its most basic is about the distribution of benefits and burdens, questions about the differential distribution to women and men of work and material benefits that may or may not be linked to their performance of work are central to any feminist conception of social justice.[9] In contrast to Okin, however, who remains loyal to the liberal, Rawlsian framework, seeing herself as rectifying its gender bias, I approach the issue of social justice from a materialist perspective. I also focus

---

[8] Okin 1989.

[9] Another feminist, Iris Young, has provided us with a sustained discussion of social justice in her *Justice and the Politics of Difference* (1990). This is a fascinating book in many respects, especially in its reach beyond distributive considerations, but her critique of too narrow a concern of theorists of justice with what she calls the 'distributive paradigm' is mistaken. Most unfortunate in this respect is her unquestioned assumption that divisions of labour do not fall within the scope of distributive considerations. It is, of course, true that the liberal distributive theorists whom she discusses have not looked at divisions of labour, but she is wrong in concluding that this throws a bad light on the distributive paradigm. Rather, what the example of liberal distributive theorists shows up is the limited scope or interpretation which they have given to the 'distributive paradigm'. Instead of criticizing this limited scope and thus widening the distributive paradigm, Young concurs with this interpretation. As a result, she perceives social divisions of labour—which are nothing but unequal distributions of labour, and as such very much within the scope of distributive considerations—as falling outside the distributive paradigm, and then criticizes the distributive paradigm itself as too narrow. Furthermore, and very unfortunately given her feminist provenance, the only division of labour she is seriously interested in is that between mental and manual work. The sexual division of labour, by comparison, is not discussed at any length.

on the more preliminary question of conceptions of work and exploitation in the first part of the book. These two points of difference are systematically connected. I shall explain them in the next section by first looking at the centrality of work in the materialist tradition of thought and then at the notion of exploitation.

(ii) *The materialist perspective: work, exploitation, and social justice*

Nothing hinders liberal theorists from concerning themselves with the work people do, but they usually do not,[10] and Okin's discussion of the sexual division of labour represents a notable exception to the rule. By contrast, it is typically writers from within the materialist tradition of thought who have been most interested in work and the social structures which underlie and systematically reproduce specific distributions of work among different groups in society. Work has such a central place in the materialist tradition of thought for at least two reasons. First, Marx, as the most influential thinker in this tradition, makes it central throughout his work. Whilst the early Marx tended to focus on the quality of work as a result of social conditions, notably the many ways in which work could be alienated, the later Marx was more interested in the social distribution of work and the conditions which create particular distributions of both work and the goods produced by it, especially the exploitative conditions which are characteristic of class-divided societies. It is this focus on the distribution of work and material benefits deriving from work, and specifically the notion of exploitation, which makes Marx and the materialist perspective more generally interesting for anybody working on social justice. This focus also presents itself as an obvious starting-point for anybody interested in looking at women's work in relation to social justice. Secondly, writers in this tradition also typically believe that facts about the work people do—what type of work they do, how they do it, and under what constraints, how work is distributed,

---

[10] Skillen (1977) takes various mainstream political philosophers, including Rawls, to task for their lack of attention to work in their theories.

how technologically developed it is—explain or at least caus-
ally constrain all other social phenomena including history and
the sphere of ideas and values. In the words of the early Marx
and Engels, materialist theory starts with and focuses on 'the
representation of practical activity, of the practical process of
development of men'.[11] Work, then—practical activity, or 'material production'[12] or 'the production and reproduction of immediate life'[13] in roughly equivalent formulations—plays a very
prominent role in the materialist tradition of thought.[14]

It follows from this centrality of work that a materialist approach
to social justice—in so far as this is thought possible[15]—will

[11] *GI* 38.   [12] *GI* 38 and *passim*.

[13] Engels's often quoted formulation from the Preface of his *Origin of the Family*
. . . (Engels 1972: 71).

[14] This is one among many possible interpretations of materialist theory, and
certainly not the most orthodox one. But it is the most productive one for my
own purposes, and I also think it captures a very basic aspect of Marx's own
thought which has been obscured by narrowly economic interpretations, which
also purport to be more 'scientific'. Moreover, as will be seen from my argument in the first two chapters, a concentration on the paid (and hence visible)
work performed as part of what is officially and theoretically recognized as a
society's economy is in itself inherently gender biased. Hence it is absolutely
vital for anybody interested in gender from a materialist perspective to distinguish a focus on work or material practice from a focus on the 'material basis'
or the economy and to take the former rather than the latter as the basic characteristic of their approach. Note also that this interpretation differs radically
from that of two feminists whose theories are heavily influenced by marxist
thought: Firestone's reinterpretation of historical materialism focuses on the sexually differentiated human biology and its transcendence through technological
progress (Firestone 1971), whilst MacKinnon (1989), rather categorically, claims
that 'sexuality is to feminism what work is to marxism', thus giving up a focus
on work altogether, but retaining a reinterpreted materialist analysis of social
and political institutions. For yet another interpretation of materialist theory and
explanation see Mason 1993, chs. 4 and 5.

[15] There is an extended debate about whether Marx himself had a conception
of social justice and whether, more specifically, he thought capitalism was unjust.
Arguably, Marx does think that capitalism is unjust despite his explicit denial
mainly because the concept of exploitation is a normative as well as an economic concept and is used as such by Marx despite himself. Hence the fact that
capitalism as an economic system is based on the systematic exploitation of wage
workers establishes the injustice of capitalism as an economic and social system.
But I want to side-step this debate here. (Geras 1986 gives an admirably clear
presentation of the evidence and the arguments on both sides of this debate; see
also his 'Addendum and Rejoinder' in Geras 1992.) Even if Marx did not have
a conception of justice himself and used the concept of exploitation only in its
technical, economic sense, there is still an argument to be made that materialist
theory, if not Marx himself, provides us with a distinctive perspective on social
justice.

include work as one of the main entities that are socially distributed and that can therefore be justly or unjustly distributed.
Thus notice the contrast between two different conceptions of
who in any given society might be badly off, or even worst
off, and hence most likely to be unjustly treated. Rawls, on the
one hand, defines the 'worst off' in terms of their access to primary social goods[16]—benefits consisting of 'rights and liberties,
powers and opportunities, income and wealth'[17]—while their
share of burdens does not play a role in determining their position, even though principles of justice apply to the distribution
of both benefits and burdens. Furthermore, Rawls's very limited
discussion of burdens includes only duties and obligations, such
as the duty of justice and the more specific duties to contribute
one's share of the tax to finance social redistribution and the
duties related to political office or public functions, but not work.
Marx and Engels, on the other hand, say of the proletariat that
it is the class which 'has to bear all the burdens of society without enjoying its advantages'.[18] What makes the proletariat badly
off, as far as Marx and Engels are concerned, is a particularly
striking combination of high burdens and low benefits: not only
is it most burdened with work, but it also enjoys little in terms
of material resources and goods.

Marx and other materialist theorists after him have used the
notion of *exploitation* to point to this particular combination of
being burdened with work whilst not receiving many benefits
in return. The notion of exploitation implies reference to both
benefits and burdens in that it compares the work people do,
their burden, with the material benefits they enjoy in their lives.
Those who are exploited are burdened more than they benefit,
while exploiters benefit without being burdened (or are burdened less than they benefit). Furthermore, these different combinations of burdens and benefits in exploiters and the exploited
arise because exploiters 'extract' work, or the products of work,
from those they exploit, hence there is a one-sided transfer of
benefits combined with a one-sided performance of work.[19]
According to a materialist perspective, then, wherever there is

---

[16] Rawls 1971: 396.   [17] Ibid. 62.   [18] *GI* 85.
[19] This characterization of exploitation is sufficient for the purposes of the
introduction, but obviously very vague. I discuss the concept of exploitation at
length in Ch. 2 sect. vi and Ch. 3.

exploitation there is an uneven distribution of the burden of work and the benefits deriving from that work. What is thus distinctive about a materialist approach to social justice is its focus on work or people's material activity and on the conditions and constraints under which they engage in it, notably exploitative conditions.

Since the materialist perspective has a peculiarly powerful grasp on a combination of distributive facts about both burdens and benefits, it is in a good position to indict such distributive patterns and their systematic reproduction in society with regard to their injustice: it seems obvious that those who are comparatively heavily burdened, whilst also being comparatively little benefited, are treated unjustly. I do not have any elaborate argument to establish this last point, but if it were disputed, it seems to me that the burden of proof lies on those who want to say that those who are exploited are being treated perfectly justly, hence that there is a presumption that, unless shown otherwise, exploitation is unjust. Hence I shall presume for the rest of the book that those who are exploited are on the whole unjustly treated.

Given this focus on work and exploitation in the materialist approach to social justice, this approach seems to lend itself perfectly to looking at the work women do, and specifically to discussing the question whether women are exploited and hence treated unjustly in doing all the unpaid work they do. Unpaid work, more than any work that is paid but nevertheless exploitative, seems to be a perfect candidate for work that is exploitative: anybody who does a lot of unpaid, unremunerated work, or any social group or class which shoulders a large part of the work that is done unpaid or unremunerated in a society, is likely to be exploited because they are burdened without receiving any benefits in return. Looking specifically at the above-quoted UN statistic which indicates women's collective high work burdens and appallingly low control of material benefits, it is all the more astounding that materialist theorists have not been more forthcoming with discussions of the exploitation of women.

In the first part of the book, I explore the reasons why even a tradition of thought which would have been an obvious place to look for a discussion of women's work and women's exploitation has either been completely gender blind or else obstructive of any real insight. This exploration contributes only indirectly to the discussion of social justice: it deals with, and clears away, certain misconceptions which stand in the way of a clear perception of what exactly the problem is with respect to women's work. My discussion in this part is about conceptions of work and specifically of women's work and about conceptions of exploitation. The guiding assumption throughout this first part is that women are exploited by doing the work they do, and its theoretical and conceptual task lies in pinpointing the misconceptions which obstruct the recognition of this fact. In the process of working through these unsatisfactory conceptions—as Locke would have said, in the process of 'clearing the ground a little, and removing some of the rubbish, that lies in the way to knowledge'[20]—I make way for my own conception of women's work as care and for my own argument as to why and how women's work raises questions of social justice.

The conceptions of work and women's work I discuss in this first part are the following. In Chapter 1, I look at Marx's thought about work, especially about what he called necessary labour. I argue that women's work is necessary labour according to his conception of it, but nevertheless very different from that work which he focused on in his discussion. This can be seen in his conception of the communist utopia, but also in his conception of the dialectic of labour. Marx's thought about work thus cannot be applied in any straightforward way to women's work. It represents a beginning, but gives no answers. In Chapter 2, I analyse two main positions within what has come to be known as the domestic labour debate. Unlike Marx's thought about work, this debate focused explicitly on women's unpaid work in the home, with the intention of analysing it within marxist political economy. The debate, however, proved to be a complete dead end not only because it did not even allow for the possibility of using the notion of exploitation in the context of a conception of women's unpaid work, but also because it was generally riddled with orthodox marxist assumptions which frustrated feminist attempts to get ahead with their enquiry about women's work. Nevertheless, in pinpointing what went wrong I am also able to retrieve Marx's conception of exploitation from the orthodox lion's den. In Chapter 3, I discuss the only sustained

[20] Locke 1975: 10.

conception of women's exploitation that can be found within the
materialist tradition: Delphy and Leonard's theory of women's
exploitation as wives.[21] Although their approach is basically on
the right track, their theory of women's exploitation is unfortunate in so far as it is based on a reinterpreted notion of exploitation which has ceased to be about exploitation in the materialist
sense they start off by endorsing. It is also based on a model of
family relations and obligations which is either outdated already
or fast in the process of becoming so. In discussing Delphy and
Leonard's theory, I also point out the difficulties anybody faces
in developing a theory of women's exploitation. Having found
only unsatisfactory conceptions of work, women's work, and exploitation, I proceed in the second part of this book to develop
my own theory of women's work as care and of women's exploitation as carers.

(iii) *Care, the ethic of care, and justice*

Women's work—especially women's unpaid work in the domestic sphere, but by extension also a lot of women's paid work—
is best understood not as production, as in the materialist tradition,
but as care. I define care as an activity or practice aimed at the
meeting of needs in others.[22] As such, it is fundamentally other-
directed and beneficial to others, whilst involving an investment
of the carer's time and energy. In this last respect, it is like material production, or any type of work, and can be regarded as a
burden, as much as work can. In its other-directed and other-
beneficial aspect, however, it is very unlike any of the work that
is usually discussed, and it involves very different virtues and
values for those engaged in such care, as well as a particular
urgency and motivation in those receptive to the demands of
need. As I shall argue, the reasons why women do most or
all of the caring that needs to be done in any society, and why
women are exploited as carers, are manifold. There are material and social constraints, but also, and more interestingly, reasons

---

[21] Delphy and Leonard 1992.
[22] This basic definition needs to be qualified: see my discussion in Ch. 4
sect. i.

deriving from the peculiar logic that care as an other-directed practice exhibits: given the skills and virtues of attentiveness and responsiveness to others which are required in any good carer, it makes those who care vulnerable to exploitation in a very specific way. It is thus this new understanding of women's work as care that allows us also to understand how it is that women are exploited, hence unjustly treated.

The second part of this book, in which I present this theory of women's work as care, is pivotal in several senses. First, and most simply, it connects the seemingly unconnected first and third parts of the book. Secondly, and more importantly, it marks the transition from critique to constructive discussion: having rejected unsatisfactory conceptions of work, women's work, and women's exploitation in Part I, I develop an account of women's work as care which allows me not only to capture some of the aspects of women's work that I found missing in the conceptions I discussed in Part I, but also to give an account of how it is that women are exploited as carers. Hence Part II represents a positive response and narrative closure to the amazement at the silence about women's work in discussions of social justice with which I started off and which motivated and guided my discussion in Part I. At the same time, this theory opens up new questions, specifically about the link between the ethic of care—which forms part of women's practice of care—and considerations of justice, which are then discussed in Part III. Thirdly, then, Part II connects the materialist perspective focusing on women's work and exploitation of Part I with the seemingly unrelated discussion of the ethic of care in Part III. The 'missing link' between the two parts is questions that arise from the peculiar combination of the materialist perspective I endorse and the ethic of care as it has been presented in much of the recent discussion. I shall explain how these questions arise after a quick reference to the ethic of care.

The ethic of care is best understood as an ongoing collective research project which, based on Gilligan's classic research presented in her book *In a Different Voice*,[23] is aimed at working out the form and content of the ethic of care, what concepts, considerations, values, and virtues would be characteristic of it, and

---

[23] Gilligan 1982.

how it relates to traditional moral theory.[24] Gilligan's original claim was that she could detect a 'different moral voice', the ethic of care, mostly in women, which contrasted with the 'ethic of rights and justice', endorsed by modern moral philosophers and psychologists in various versions as the only game in town, as *the* moral theory as such. This contrast between the two ethics, juxtaposing care and justice, has been both embraced and disputed in the last decade, and much of the ensuing ethic of care debate can be understood as an attempt to spell out, refine, or resist this juxtaposition. Some have even claimed that care and justice are fundamentally incompatible moral theories, perspectives, or frameworks.[25]

If it were true that care and justice were incompatible perspectives, it would seem as if I had to choose between my original interest in social justice and my theory of care including the ethic of care, but that I could not possibly combine the two. This question is all the more intricate because I came to talk about women's work as care precisely because I was looking for a way of understanding how and why women are exploited. The theory of women's work *as care*, in other words, is my final and positive response to the challenge of showing how women are unjustly treated. Even more interestingly, since I approach this whole topic from a materialist perspective, I am committed to—and at any rate want to—endorse the ethic of care as a system of concepts, values, and ideas, arising from the practice of care as an organic part of this practice and responding to its material requirements, notably the meeting of needs. As a materialist endorsing a theory of women's work as care, in other words, I am committed to endorsing the ethic of care.

In fact, once the (typically, but not exclusively, materialist) move from the level of looking at care as a practice to the level of conceptual discussion is made, it is possible to understand

---

[24] Literature on and within this field is growing exponentially (see Tronto 1991*a*). Classic, but relatively dated collections of papers are Kittay and Meyers 1987 and Hanen and Nielsen 1987 (see also Card 1991); Larrabee 1993 contains a recent collection of 'classic' papers in psychology and philosophy; Noddings 1984 and Ruddick 1989 are two path-breaking book-length versions of the ethic of care and mothering, respectively; Held 1993 presents her own perspective on and synthesis of much of the ethic of care discussion; Tronto 1993 uses the ethic of care perspective for interesting new arguments in political theory. See also my discussion in Ch. 5 and Ch. 6 sect. ii.   [25] See Noddings 1984.

and use the theory of care much more broadly as a general perspective or standpoint which allows feminists not only to theorize the hitherto untheorized or wrongly theorized, that is, women's work, but which provides a much more wide-ranging and overarching new approach to social and political theory and philosophy in general.[26] Thus care could be seen as a paradigm or model of social interaction, and *persona carans* could replace *homo economicus* as the individual theorized in social and political theory.[27] The motivation for such a switch would be the consideration that care is a deeply human practice and certainly more basic than production, exchange, or contracting, or engaging in one's life projects: in suitable conditions, humans can exist without any of these, but we cannot even survive the first days of our life without being cared for by others. Furthermore, we cannot grow up to be healthy, strong, responsible, and caring adults without being able to rely and prosper on the right kind of care, aimed at meeting our ever changing and developing physical, emotional, and intellectual needs as children and adolescents. That we are so dependent on others' care throughout our lives, even as adults if we are to live well, may be a painful, worrying, and ultimately humbling fact to realize, but its recognition may have beneficial effects in our own lives as much as in our theories. Recognizing the importance of care theoretically thus not only means recognizing the importance of, and including in our theories, what has traditionally been women's work, it may also mean rewriting a lot of social and political theory with a completely new approach. This process of rewriting can be seen to be happening implicitly if not explicitly in much feminist writing in this field.[28]

Unfortunately, I cannot pursue the possibility of using the theory of care as a standpoint or perspective, neither in this introduction, nor in the rest of the book, although it seems to me as if much work is waiting to be done in this direction.[29] Instead, I spend most of my time in the third part addressing myself to the more specific question whether a concern with justice is

---

[26] For a discussion of standpoint theory see Harding 1987, 1991.

[27] Held (1987*b*, 1993) has argued for mothering as a new paradigm. I find mothering too specific, but Held provides some interesting arguments for nevertheless using it in this vein (Held 1993, ch. 10).

[28] For a critical assessment of care and mothering in political theory see Dietz 1985.   [29] See Ch. 6 sect. ii.

incompatible with the ethic of care, arguing—as I would have to —that considerations and even principles of justice can be seen to inform care as a practice, and are therefore a valid part of the ethic of care. I argue, in other words, that the choice between care and justice is a false choice and that, in fact, considerations of justice have to form part of an ethic of care if it is to be acceptable at all. Not all considerations of justice can be accommodated within the ethic of care, however. In the last chapter, I discuss the most difficult question arising from the practice and the ethic of care, that is, to what extent the endorsement (of any version) of the ethic of care makes those who endorse it vulnerable to exploitation. I argue that such vulnerability is unavoidable in carers since they will always give considerations of care more weight than considerations of justice if the two conflict and this, in turn, implies that they will continue to care even in situations which are clearly exploitative. It is this vulnerability, then, which lies at the heart of women's exploitation as carers as long as the sexual division of labour persists which assigns most or all of the unpaid care to women. We need not conclude, however, that women ought to stop caring, since in a just society such vulnerability would be prevented from occurring through suitable social institutions. The incompatibility of considerations of care and considerations of justice as far as exploitative caring situations are concerned does, however, reflect back on the possibility of developing an all-embracing, very general ethic of care: the ethic of care, whilst a promising route to pursue, does have real limits which need to be recognized as much as its potential.

Last, but not least, the systematic inclusion of justice in the discussion of the ethic of care is also important in feminist theory because many feminists express unease about 'celebrating women's difference', in this instance celebrating women as carers, precisely because women are put in their place, and exploited, as such. It is undeniable—as I argue below—that there is, in social reality as much as in prevalent ideas, an oppressive association of women and care. A vivid sense of justice, and an explicit and integral treatment of questions of social justice in a theory of care, are needed, first, to resist any suggestions that women should do what they are good at doing anyway and leave the rest—the 'real stuff'!—to the men, and, secondly, to argue for a fairer, universal distribution of care. They are needed,

thirdly, to insist at the same time that women are given credit
and real social recognition for what they have been doing for
so long and are on the whole better at doing. On the other hand,
however, the project of theorizing care (including more specific forms such as mothering) has so far proved to be an immensely stimulating and productive new development in feminist
theory which should not be stopped in its tracks by misguided
worries about the continuation and reinforcement of gender
stereotyping on the basis of the oppressive association of women
with care. A materialist theory of care meets these worries by
situating care in a broader social context, and it makes the concern with care strategically and politically robust by introducing considerations of justice into the theory. Hence feminists can
relax, sit back, have our cake and eat it, too: if my argument is
correct, we can both criticize women's exploitation as carers and
use the theory of care as the basis for distinctive new work in
social and political theory. After care, theories of justice will
hopefully never be the same again.

(iv) *Ways through the jungle*

Since the readership of this book is probably varied, and interests will inevitably be varied, too, not everybody will want to
read everything. Those interested in care in a more practical vein
may just want to read Part II and the last chapter where I return
to more practical conclusions. Those interested in a critical discussion of Marx and marxist theory should read Part I, but would
be well advised also to read Part II, just so as to get a taste of
what marxists miss out on. For those interested in theories of
women's work, including women's exploitation and women's
oppression, Parts I and II are the most obvious places to go to,
but the last chapter may offer a challenging twist to the story.
Those interested in the ethic of care debate may want to start
with my theory of care in Part II, but my analysis and discussion of the ethic of care debate itself is to be found in Part III,
especially Chapter 5. Finally, those wonderful readers whose ap-
petite has been whetted by this introduction and all those who,
like me, find it hard not to read a book from cover to cover are
welcome to the whole of the book: I hope it won't disappoint.

PART I

1

Marx's Utopias and Women's Work

Marx's writings are a rich source of thought about work. As will emerge from this chapter, however, his thought does not lend itself easily to feminist purposes. I shall argue that his vision of abundance in the communist utopia, which is one of the solutions he sees to the necessary labour problem (section i), could only occur to him as a solution because he did not consider women's work (section ii). Marx's alternative distributive solution to the problem is more fruitful and interesting, however, since it poses the question of how necessary labour (including women's work) is to be distributed and what constraints can be imposed on the distribution of work (section iii). Finally, his conception of the dialectic of labour, although in tension with his thought about necessary labour, can be used to imagine more concretely who would do women's work in the utopia derived from the dialectic of labour, and under what circumstances (section iv).

(i) *The necessary labour problem*

The necessary labour problem results from the conjunction of two theses which Marx held, the *distributive thesis* and the *metaphysical thesis*. I shall present and discuss the two theses in turn and then indicate how the problem derives from them.

The distributive thesis characterizes the distribution of freedom or free development[1] under communism as universal and equal. Marx endorses this thesis implicitly in his statement in the *Communist Manifesto* that communism is a society where the 'free development of each is the condition for the free

---

[1] I use the two expressions interchangeably since nothing in my argument hinges on a distinction between the two terms. My discussion of the metaphysical thesis elucidates the intended meaning further.

development of all'.[2] It is not clear exactly what Marx meant to say in this conditional formulation over and above the simple claim that under communism, free development would be equally possible for all members of society. What seems fairly safe to say, however, is that if the free development of all is conditional on the free development of each in communist society (whatever this means), then freedom under communism, in so far as it is achieved, implies the universal and equal distribution of freedom. This interpretation is further supported by the contrast drawn in Marx's argument between communism and the 'old, bourgeois society, with its classes and class antagonisms'[3] which the communist association is to replace, and in which the achievement of freedom and free development for some—the ruling class—is conditional on the oppression and exploitation of, and hence the denial of freedom and free development to, others—the working class.[4] Freedom under communism, then, will for the first time in history be realized equally and for all, instead of for some at the expense of others as in all class-divided societies hitherto.[5]

Marx's metaphysical thesis divides human activities into free and unfree ones. Unfree activities, according to this distinction, are activities which are determined by a combination of human needs and circumstances, while free activities are not thus determined. Thus Marx stresses in a famous passage from *Capital* iii that

[t]he realm of freedom really begins only where labour determined by necessity and external expediency ends; it lies by its very nature beyond the sphere of material production proper. Just as the savage must wrestle with nature to satisfy his needs, to maintain and reproduce his life, so must civilized man, and he must do so in all forms of society and under all possible modes of production.[6]

Thus, for example, given our nature as warm-blooded animals, we have to burn up more or fewer calories depending on the

---

[2] CM 127.   [3] Ibid.   [4] Cf. *Cap*. i. 667; *Cap*. iii. 958.
[5] There has been much debate about whether freedom is a moral or non-moral value in Marx's thought (see, among many others, Wood 1981, Brenkert 1983, Lukes 1985, Geras 1986). I side-step this debate by presenting Marx's distributive thesis as a claim about freedom in communist society, which Marx certainly did endorse, regardless of whether he also believed that freedom was morally or non-morally desirable.   [6] *Cap*. iii. 958-9.

temperature we find ourselves in in order to retain a constant body temperature, hence eat more or less, and depending on social as well as other natural circumstances, we may have to do more or less work to get the food we need. Regardless of these variations in circumstances, however, we have to eat a certain amount of food and certain types of foodstuffs simply because our biological make-up is such that we have these needs. Activities which we have to engage in to satisfy these needs, then, are unfree because we do not have a real choice about satisfying our needs (short of illness or death):[7] they are, as it were, dictated by our nature as human beings. These unfree activities make up the 'realm of necessity'[8] and are also identified by Marx as 'necessary labour', by which he understands that labour which is necessary to 'maintain and reproduce' the worker and/or his labour power.[9]

True freedom, by contrast, is to be found in the 'realm of freedom' and lies in activities which are not thus necessitated by our nature: 'The true realm of freedom, the development of human powers as an end in itself, begins beyond [the realm of necessity], though it can only flourish with this realm of necessity as its basis. The reduction of the working day is the basic prerequisite.'[10] True freedom, according to this passage, consists of the free development of our human faculties, and such development is not possible whilst we are engaged in necessary labour: it takes place 'beyond' and thus outside the sphere of necessity.[11] Furthermore, for free development to be possible the

---

[7] We may, of course, have a choice about how to satisfy them, but free choice about the mode of satisfying them does not imply free choice about satisfying them.   [8] *Cap*. iii. 959.

[9] Necessary labour is also that part of a worker's work, or working day, that goes into his own maintenance and reproduction, as opposed to surplus labour, which is that part which is appropriated by his oppressor. (See *Cap*. i, chs. 6, 7, 9, 18 and my discussion of exploitation in Ch. 3.) It seems to me that this identification of necessary labour with a part of the working day, which Marx clearly makes as a central part of his economics, specifically his labour theory of value, is one of the reasons why he neglected women's work: it locates necessary labour exclusively in material production and thus obscures the fact that some forms of necessary labour might take place outside the production recognized by economists as such. See sect. ii and Ch. 2 for an argument that women's work is a case in point.   [10] *Cap*. iii. 959.

[11] These characterizations in spatial terms are not necessarily very helpful and may even be misleading, but since Marx used them himself, it is important to realize that he may have fallen under their spell. (See also n. 16.)

working day—by which Marx obviously refers to that part of the day where necessary labour is performed—has to be reduced as much as possible.[12]

Now Marx does acknowledge that some kind of freedom can be achieved in the realm of necessity through the transformation of necessary labour from an activity determined by social and natural circumstances into an activity which is under the conscious control of those who engage in it: first, by rationally regulating and distributing it among producers, that is, by taking control of the social constraints under which it is performed, and, secondly, by applying science to the process of production and thus mastering nature instead of being mastered by it.[13] In the same passage, however, Marx is nevertheless very clear that this gain in freedom does not 'add up to' the true freedom which is found in the realm of freedom, beyond the sphere of necessity. Whilst Marx is not very explicit about why this is so, the best guess, it seems to me, is that he insists on the distinction because necessary labour remains unfree in the sense that it remains dictated by our needs. Thus even if some external constraints on necessary labour can be overcome through conscious control, the basic constraints set by our own nature remain, and it is those which oppose it to activities that are truly free.[14]

---

[12] *Cap.* iii. 959, and my next paragraph.

[13] See *Cap.* iii. 959, and a very similar earlier formulation in *GR* 611–12. The *Grundrisse* passage, more elaborate than the very terse formulations in *Cap.* iii, very much revolves around the imposition of conscious control on nature and the process of production as that factor which makes an activity free (see also *GI* 49, 87, and *Cap.* i. 284).

[14] *Cap.* iii. 959. There is a second contrast between free and unfree activities which Marx uses, viz. that between activities which are ends in themselves and activities which are means to other ends (see Klagge 1986: 775). Necessary labour, according to this contrast, cannot consist of activities which are ends in themselves because ends in themselves are ends that are freely chosen and ends imposed on us by our needs are clearly not freely chosen. This contrast can therefore be understood to support my interpretation, that is, that there remains a distinction between 'freed' necessary labour and truly free activities.

Klagge (1986) has disputed the claim that necessary labour could never be free. His argument may be seen to be supported by the *Grundrisse* passage which corresponds closely to the *Capital* passage on which I base my interpretation. This earlier passage—like the import of Marx's early writings on alienated labour—is comparatively more optimistic and does seem to imply that freedom can be achieved through a transformation of the circumstances under which labour is performed, notably the imposition of conscious control (*GR* 611–12; *EPM*). It is possible, however, to understand the comparative optimism of this passage—as well as Marx's early writings—as based on his obliviousness to, but

The distributive and metaphysical theses are independent of each other. The metaphysical thesis does not have any implications about the social distribution of free activities. Indeed, it follows from it that members of the 'idle classes' in class-divided societies are free in the sense specified by it precisely because the necessary labour in these societies is performed by the oppressed classes for both their own class and that of their oppressors, the idle classes.[15] Nor does the distributive thesis specify which types of activities count as free. If, however, the two theses are conjoined, strong conclusions follow for freedom under communism. Individuals will be entirely free only if they do not have to engage in necessary labour and if such freedom is realized for each individual. Freedom which satisfies both conditions is therefore realized only if nobody has to engage in necessary labour, that is, if necessary labour is abolished. Only complete abundance allows such freedom, since only complete abundance will free everybody of necessary labour by providing external circumstances which require no further work by humans for their needs to be met. Alternatively, short of complete abundance, freedom is realized to the extent that necessary labour is minimized.

It follows from the conjunction of the two theses, then, that necessary labour ought to be reduced or even abolished altogether. The question, however, is, to what extent this is possible. This question raises the necessary labour problem. Following this presentation of the problem, the communist utopia can then

later realization of, the other respect in which necessary labour will always remain unfree, that is, the constraints imposed by human nature. It is this respect that Marx stresses in the passage in *Capital* vol. iii: 'Just as the savage must wrestle with nature to satisfy his needs . . . so must civilized man . . . in all forms of society and under all possible modes of production' (p. 95). I cannot discuss this question in detail here (but see n. 50 below), but two further points in support of my interpretation are the following: first, the only reason why Marx would be interested in minimizing necessary labour under communism would be that he thinks that 'truly free' activities are incompatible with it and that free development takes place outside production, not during it (see his further condition on supposedly free necessary labour that it be 'accomplish[ed] . . . with the least expenditure of energy' (*Cap.* iii. 959) and his assertion of the necessity to reduce the working day). Secondly, why should he insist that, even if necessary labour becomes 'free' in the sense given above, it nevertheless 'always remains a realm of necessity', if not because he thought there was indeed a significant distinction between activities in the two realms (ibid.)?

[15] See e.g. *GR* 708; *TSV* iii. 256; *Cap.* i. 667; *Cap.* iii. 958.

be understood as Marx's attempt to provide an answer to it, in that this utopia represents a situation of comparative if not complete abundance which Marx thought would develop in the long run out of capitalism once the productive forces—promoted but later fettered by the capitalist mode of production—were unleashed by the socialization of production and once various types of superfluous labour which were necessary only under capitalism were abolished.[16]

In conclusion, then, whilst the metaphysical thesis makes the reduction or even abolition of necessary labour desirable, the distributive thesis requires a universal and equal distribution of this reduction. Marx was certainly exercised by this problem about necessary labour even if, in more optimistic moments, he may also have thought it was not a real problem because necessary labour could be transformed into free activity. What interests me about this problem is not so much whether it is spurious or not and whether it has a solution if it is not spurious, but, on the one hand, the basic idea underlying it, namely the recognition of the fact that there are certain kinds of activities human beings as a collective will always have to engage in, regardless of what else they may want to do or how they perform and distribute activities among themselves.[17] On the other hand, and more specifically with regard to a conception of women's work, I am interested in two more specific points: first, what Marx's treatment of the necessary labour problem indicates about the kinds of activities he thought were necessary labour, and, secondly,

[16] For Marx's confidence in the development of the productive forces see *GR* 701, 704–6; for a statement on superfluous labour see *Cap.* i. 667.

[17] This recognition is crucially important for any feminist discussion of women's work and will be made explicit in my discussion of women's work as care. Unlike Marx (when he pursues the distinction between the two realms of freedom and necessity), however, I do not think that the fact that we have to engage in certain activities because we have to meet certain basic human needs implies that we cannot also develop our human faculties whilst engaging in them, nor do I think the sense in which we are unfree when thus engaged is in any way significant *metaphysically*, that is, in terms of human freedom. It is significant *politically*, though, that is, in terms of social justice first because the existence of such activities constrains people's time and secondly because they can be distributed unevenly, thus constraining some more than others. But I shall not argue with Marx about these points because the purpose of this chapter is to elucidate the logic of (some of) his own thoughts about work and premature critique may cloud the respects in which a close reading of his work can nevertheless be fruitful for feminists.

the distributive considerations that the problem led him into. I shall deal with these two points in the next two sections.

(ii) *Abundance and women's work*

If, and to the extent that, Marx believed in the possibility of relative if not complete abundance and therefore in abundance as a solution to the necessary labour problem,[18] it was certainly because he was very impressed by the rapid development of machinery in the nineteenth century and by the ever increasing automation of production which, in their turn, made ever increasing productivity a real prospect and abundance seem feasible. Thus note his discussion of machines in *Grundrisse*, which may also serve as an illustration of how closely linked are his thought on the automation of production and his treatment of the necessary labour problem:

But to the degree that large industry develops, the creation of real wealth comes to depend less on labour time and on the amount of labour employed than on the power of the agencies set in motion during labour time, whose 'powerful effectiveness' . . . depends rather on the general state of science and on the progress of technology, or the application of this science to production. . . . Labour no longer appears so much to be included within the production process; rather, the human being comes to relate more as watchman and regulator to the production process itself. . . . As soon as labour in the direct form has ceased to be the great well-spring of wealth, labour time ceases and must cease to be its measure . . . With that, production based on exchange value breaks down, and the direct, material production process is stripped of the form of penury and antithesis. The free development of individualities, and hence not the reduction of necessary labour time so as to posit surplus labour, but rather the general reduction of the necessary labour of society to a minimum, which then corresponds to the artistic, scientific etc. development of the individuals in the time set free, and with the means created, for all of them.[19]

Despite its incompleteness, the last sentence of the quote provides a clear indication of the link Marx saw between the

[18] As and when he was exercised by it, see my comments in the preceding section.
[19] GR 704–6; see also Marx's discussion of increasing productivity in *Cap.* i. 666–7.

reduction of necessary labour time to a minimum through automation and the increasing possibility for the free development of all. Thus Marx sums up his long paragraph on 'machines etc.' by quoting approvingly (and correcting) an anonymous author on the real wealth of a society:

'Truly wealthy a nation, when the working day is 6 rather than 12 hours. *Wealth* is not command over surplus labour time' (real wealth), 'but rather, *disposable time* outside that needed in direct production, for *every individual* and the whole society.'[20]

Increased productivity through automation, then, presented for Marx not only a desirable state of affairs, but also clearly the solution to the necessary labour problem. Although it could not abolish the constraints imposed on humans by our needs, it could reduce or even abolish the time we have to spend working toward the satisfaction of those needs, thus freeing us for other, truly free activities.

Now whether such increased productivity would indeed create complete or even relative abundance—given that, as Marx stated himself, needs would expand with increasing productivity and that necessary labour would increase with increasing needs[21]—can be questioned on various grounds, not least that of ultimately restricted resources.[22] I shall not discuss this question any further, however, but instead look at a part of necessary labour that Marx obviously overlooked completely because it certainly does not lend itself to being mechanized or automated: I mean (a part of) that part of necessary labour that is overwhelmingly performed by women—women's work.[23]

In order to focus our minds on women's work and clarify what it is that I am arguing about, I shall start off with a rough common-sense characterization and typification of it. Women's work can, roughly, be divided into three types—housework,

[20] *GR* 706. See also his renewed discussion of this anonymous author in *TSV* iii. 252–7, esp. pp. 256–7.
[21] *Cap.* i. 667; but see also *TSV* iii. 256, for a relatively optimistic evaluation of the possibility of abundance.   [22] See Ward and Dubos 1972.
[23] I use the term 'women's work' descriptively and as a useful shorthand for the particular kinds of work that, traditionally and in most if not all societies, women have been responsible for and taken on more or less as a matter of course. As will become obvious in the course of the book, I do not mean to imply that this kind of work is necessarily done by women.

child care, and caring work—and typically consists of the following kinds of activities:[24]

1. *Housework*. Housework involves the following activities:[25] the cleaning and tidying of the household unit; the fabrication, mending, washing, and ironing of clothes and linen (the fabrication being less important in industrialized societies); the provision of goods consumed in the house such as household appliances, furniture, clothes, food (now mostly through shopping rather than production); the preparation of meals and the work related to it such as washing and cleaning up.

2. *Child care*. Child care consists basically in looking after children and attending to their needs whenever required. This work changes substantially with the age of children: most time is required for infants, a more or less twenty-four-hour job involving continuous availability for feeding, nursing, and playing. As children grow up, decreasing amounts of time have to be spent with them and the nature of the attention and activities changes: playing, talking, and sharing activities with them increases. In industrialized societies, children have to be brought to school, to various social and medical services, various leisure and educational activities.

3. *Caring work*. Caring work involves looking after members of the household or the (extended) family if required by sickness, physical or mental disability, or frailty. It is often restricted to limited periods of time but can be time-consuming and require constant availability. It also involves looking after elderly relatives, which can be a twenty-four-hour job depending on their needs and their infirmity, and the meeting of the emotional needs of all members of the family.

---

[24] I shall use this rough characterization via an exemplary list of three types of activities until I revise this way of conceptualizing women's work in my own theory of care in Ch. 4. For the purposes of the discussion in this and the following two chapters, this rough characterization will do, since the reader only requires a general idea of the kind of work I have in mind. Also, my own definition and theory—which are a result of the argument in the preceding chapters —would have prejudged too many issues.

[25] This list is illustrative of the main types of work that fall under that category; it is not meant to be exhaustive.

Now while there is no doubt that these three types of work are traditionally women's work,[26] am I right in saying they are necessary labour? I think I am, although this can certainly be disputed. First, it might be said that there is so much variation across societies and time with regard to what is seen to 'need doing' that such activities, arbitrary as they are, could not possibly count as necessary labour. But whilst the amount of such work may be historically variable and whilst it may be disputed whether, say, a house has to be cleaned every day or a clearly disabled infant should be cared for,[27] it seems nevertheless clear that some amount of this work has to be done. In fact, none of us would have survived had we not been cared for as children. In so far, then, as our nature is such that we need livable surroundings, food that needs preparing and clothes that need washing, that we need to be looked after as children, and that we need others to care for us if we are sick, frail, or disabled, women's work is certainly part of that work which is intended by the notion of necessary labour even if it was not intended by Marx.[28] Furthermore, historical and cultural variations in the amount and kind of necessary labour performed are, of course, part of the development of productive forces over time and space, and as such very much part of Marx's own thought about work, whether necessary or not.

Secondly, it might be said that necessary labour is labour that allows us to 'maintain and reproduce' *ourselves*, i.e. meet our own needs, whilst women's work is typically and to a large extent geared towards meeting other people's needs. Now it is true that a lot of women's work is work that we could not do ourselves if we were in need of its benefits—children could not bring themselves up, nor would somebody who is bedridden be able to care for herself—but it is nevertheless work that needs to be done. Moreover it is work that needs to be done because human nature makes us thus dependent at various points in our lives. The fact, therefore, that not all necessary labour can be performed by ourselves to meet our own needs does not introduce a serious problem with regard to the conception of neces-

---

[26] See also Ch. 4 sect. v.
[27] See the ancient Greek practice of infanticide.
[28] See Ch. 2 sect. iv, and this section below.

sary labour.[29] It merely illustrates the fact that human nature forces not only us, but also others, to engage in certain activities that need doing because our needs have to be met. The important point about necessary labour, it seems to me, is not that it will meet the needs of the person who performs it, but that it is performed because human nature requires it to be performed (even if the perception of what is required itself varies historically and culturally).

Assuming then, that women's work is part of necessary labour, is it amenable to the abundance solution, too? The answer is: some of it is, but a lot of it is not. More specifically, housework may be, but child care and caring work are not. Remember that abundance was to be possible through increases in productivity through automation—but only housework is the kind of work where automation of some or even all of its component activities is possible. Thus in Western industrialized countries, in contrast with less developed countries, a lot of the work which used to be done by women in the home has been taken over by industrial and hence increasingly automated production. These industrially produced goods are sold as commodities on the market and arrive in the household ready made rather than as raw materials which require further work before they can be consumed. The production of household goods such as clothes and linen, and increasingly of food, now takes place in the sphere of production and thus relieves modern housewives in the industrialized countries of considerable amounts of work. Taken together with the increasing number of household machines, the necessary labour time to be spent in housework has been reduced already, and there is no reason in principle why it would not be amenable to even further reductions.[30]

The solution to the necessary labour of child care and caring

[29] Marx, in fact, did at least sometimes remember that the 'reproduction of labour power' included generational reproduction, hence that necessary labour did not exclusively benefit the worker himself: see Ch. 2 sect. iv.

[30] Bebel's classic work on the emancipation of women through the 'socialization' of housework is a very good example of a writer who was impressed by the progress of technology and the consequent savings in labour time for women (Bebel 1971). Note, however, that historical experience indicates that although a lot of labour is saved through machines and industrial production, more labour has been added as standards have risen (see Cowan 1983 on the effect of industrial and household technology on women's housework).

work, by contrast, cannot possibly lie in increasing automation. Thus imagine a society in which sick, old-aged, and disabled people are put into fully automated hospitals and asylums, and where children are brought up by robots. While such a society can be imagined, it would certainly strike most of us as a society not worth living in. In fact, a society in which caring and childrearing is done by machines or robots is a nightmare vision, a dystopia to avoid rather than a utopia to aim for. If the reduction of necessary labour by way of automation is to be the key to the solution of the necessary labour problem, however, this vision has to be part of the communist utopia.

Before I discuss this point further, I would like to explore why the prospect of automation strikes us as possible with regard to housework, but as fundamentally wrong with regard to child care and caring work. Unlike care, housework is very similar to the type of work that Marx has in mind when he discusses the reduction of necessary labour. Mostly, it is work that produces material goods, but it may also produce use-values by transforming goods: examples are a warm room or a clean and ironed shirt. The production of material goods as well as other such use-values, however, is not a goal in itself: it is instrumental toward the meeting of people's needs. The way these use-values are produced, in other words, does not matter as long as they fulfil the intended purpose of production. Hence, given equal quality of goods or other use-values, that is, equal potential for satisfaction of needs, the more efficiently produced use-value is the more desirable one since less time was spent in its production. Completely automated production—the goal of the abundance solution to the necessary labour problem—is therefore the most desirable form of production in virtue of the metaphysical thesis since it achieves the complete abolition of necessary labour without diminishing the satisfaction of needs.[31]

---

[31] This claim needs some clarification, although not qualification, given that we do value individually made things more than mass produced things. The higher enjoyment derived from an individually produced thing, however, is not intrinsically related to the need it meets, but to our preference for variety and uniqueness: mass produced bread fills the stomach as much as home produced bread does, even though it may leave our taste buds bored. Individually produced bread may also taste better because somebody has baked it specifically for us, as a token of friendship or love—but such considerations take us beyond the material level at which Marx's as well as my current argument is pitched.

These characterizations of housework, however, that is, the instrumentality of the work and the desirability of efficiency with regard to labour input, do not apply to child care and caring work. Care consists of interactive kinds of activities which essentially involve social contact between people.[32] This does not imply that considerations of efficiency cannot be applied to those activities. Time can certainly be wasted in those activities that constitute caring and the raising of children. There is, nevertheless, an intrinsic relation between the time spent and the 'good' which is produced which does not apply to the other kinds of necessary labour. The time spent in child care or caring activities cannot be reduced to zero without these activities losing their character and without our giving up the whole purpose served by our engaging in them. Completely automated 'care' for the needy is an abandonment of people to machines. It ceases to be care. Furthermore, children who grow up without any human contact (or animal contact, for that matter, remembering the few 'wolf children' we have evidence of) do not survive infancy: in bringing up children, we cannot be replaced. The only way to reduce time spent with children to zero, then, is to stop bringing up children altogether. If that reduction of time spent on child care were realized universally, however, society would die out with the current generations.

Care, then, is the kind of work that not only needs to be done, but that people need to do. It involves human beings, carers and those cared for as human beings, communicating and interacting with each other, and it requires the exercise of our most distinctive capacities: language and thought and a complex emotional life which allows us to empathize with and understand others and meet their very individual needs.

Now it might be objected to my argument that, of course, nobody would want to abolish care, not only because humankind would actually lose out if care were abolished, but also because people would want to continue doing this kind of work because it is intrinsically rewarding. This in itself, the objection might continue, shows that I have misinterpreted the notion of necessary labour by applying it to care. The objection, however, is mistaken. First of all, any work that produces things that meet

[32] See my theory of care in Ch. 4.

needs is valuable and should only be abolished if needs can nevertheless continue to be met. The case for automation was only possible because needs could continue to be met whilst the time spent on necessary labour could be reduced. Care, unlike other necessary work, just happens to be the kind of work that cannot be automated so that humankind would lose out if it were reduced or abolished altogether. Far from proving that care is not necessary labour, however, this point proves that not all necessary labour can be automated.

Secondly, the reason for reducing necessary labour was not that nobody liked doing it,[33] but the fact that it was unfree because imposed on us by our own, or others', needs. People may like baking bread as much as they like caring for children, and nobody may ever like cleaning toilets or collecting rubbish. The point is that all of these activities are necessary labour, and *qua* necessary labour, according to Marx, they take up our time which we could otherwise use for activities that further our free development. This, and not its lacking attractiveness, is the reason why, following the metaphysical thesis, it is desirable that necessary labour be reduced or abolished. Again, it seems to me, this point does not show that care is not part of necessary labour. Rather, if it shows anything, it shows that the conclusion Marx drew from the metaphysical thesis, that is, that necessary labour ought to be reduced as much as possible, is highly questionable. I am not concerned, however, with a critique of Marx's interpretation of the metaphysical thesis or the necessary labour problem, but with an exploration of how women's work can be understood through it.

In conclusion, then, that part of women's work which is care points up the limited scope (or even the complete wrongheadedness) of the abundance solution to the necessary labour problem. If care is necessary labour, then certain parts of necessary

[33] See e.g. Cohen's interpretation of Marx on necessary labour: 'His idea is . . . that, being a means of life, it cannot be wanted' (Cohen 1974: 261). Cohen may be right in so far as Marx was inclined also to want to reduce necessary labour on the grounds that, precisely because it was imposed on us because our needs imposed certain ends on us, it was demeaning to have to do it and therefore nobody would want to do it if they could choose their ends freely (see n. 14 above). Even if this is true, however, the crucial point remains the *unfreedom* of necessary labour—from which follows its lack of attractiveness—not its attractiveness itself.

labour cannot be abolished without letting society die out and abandoning people in need, nor can they necessarily be reduced because machines and robots cannot replace people's efforts in care. The automation of care presents us instead with the dystopic nightmare vision of robotized 'care' and 'parenting'. Abundance achieved through automation, therefore, could only seem to Marx to be a solution to the necessary labour problem because he failed to notice—because he failed to think about women's work— the different nature of a lot of the necessary labour that women perform.

(iii) *The distribution of necessary labour*

If the abundance solution to the necessary labour problem relied mostly on one of the conditions that Marx thought would make necessary labour as free as it could possibly be, that is, the conscious mastery of nature through the application of science and technology to the process of production, the alternative solution to be discussed in this section focuses on the other condition: the conscious social regulation of necessary labour.[34] The *distributive* solution to the necessary labour problem is based on the acknowledgement that it is likely—or, as we should insist after having discussed women's work, inevitable—that there will always be some necessary labour left to do. Hence individuals will never be entirely free in the sense intended by the metaphysical thesis. The best possible solution to the remaining amount of necessary labour is therefore the attempt to minimize it. More specifically, the distributive solution focuses on minimization through social distribution.

There are several ways in which necessary labour can be minimized. As discussed in section ii, it can be minimized in its aggregate amount through increasing automation, but only with regard to material production including housework, excluding care. Marx also thought that it could be further reduced through the abolition of waste in production and the abolition of work that was necessary in the capitalist mode of production but would

---

[34] See sect. i above.

be superfluous once production was controlled by the producers. Apart from these strategies, labour can be minimized for
individuals or groups through its social distribution.[35] Two types
of such minimization through distribution are possible in principle: distributions that minimize necessary labour for certain
groups (group-specific solutions) and distributions that minimize
necessary labour for all individuals (universal solutions).

Group-specific solutions are those with which humankind has
been familiar throughout history: necessary labour can be reduced
to zero for one or more particular social groups while being done
by the rest of society. Forms of such group-specific minimization are realized by all class-divided societies where necessary
labour is minimized for the ruling classes while being performed
entirely and exclusively by the oppressed classes. Minimization
of necessary labour for one or more social groups thus implies
exploitative relations of production: those who are exploited
(slaves, serfs, and wage workers) perform not only the labour
which will 'maintain and reproduce' their own lives, but also
that labour which will maintain and reproduce the lives of, and
create the luxuries for, their exploiters in the form of surplus
labour.

While Marx took minimization based on class into account,
he did not consider other possible forms of group-specific minimization. There are, however, at least three other forms worth
mentioning: minimization based on country, race or ethnicity,
and biological sex, which I shall mention only in passing at this
point. First, minimization based on country is usually known as
'unequal exchange'.[36] Typically, industrialized countries exchange
high-technology goods which are highly capital intensive but
not labour intensive in their production with goods from developing countries which are highly labour intensive but involve
comparatively small capital investment, such as primary and
manufactured goods. Industrialized countries thus engage in a

[35] The abundance and distributive solutions are not mutually exclusive and
can be held and pursued jointly. In fact, this was probably Marx's intention, and
it is further recommended by my argument in the last section, given that some
necessary labour will always remain to be done. I discuss the two solutions sep-
arately because they are distinct solutions which are differently motivated and
have very different implications, not because they are mutually exclusive.

[36] See e.g. Roemer 1983.

form of minimization of necessary labour. Secondly, minimization based on race or ethnicity usually means that menial or particularly hazardous types of necessary labour are performed almost entirely and exclusively by members of racial or ethnic minorities in a society and thus minimized for the majority.[37] Thirdly, minimization based on biological sex is structurally very similar to that based on race or ethnicity in that a particular part of aggregate necessary labour, in this case what I have called women's work, is almost entirely and exclusively performed by women whilst it is minimized for men. Now although the exclusivity of performance of particular types of necessary labour by racial or ethnic minorities or women does not by itself imply that these groups are exploited, given that the work they do is only a part and not the whole of necessary labour, the fact that it is 'dumped on' certain groups in society should nevertheless arouse our suspicion. Whether and how women are exploited will occupy me in most of the following chapters, but only incidentally in the rest of this chapter.

Now it is obvious that any of the group-specific minimization strategies are excluded as valid solutions to the necessary labour problem by the social thesis. If, under communism, free development is to be realized equally for all it follows that necessary labour will have to be minimized for *each individual*. Group-specific solutions, therefore, are not acceptable as realizations of the marxist utopia because they minimize necessary labour for some at the expense of others. Notice that this implication of the social thesis tallies with Marx's claim that communist society would be the first society in which exploitation has ceased to exist.[38]

Universal solutions, then, are those which minimize necessary labour for each individual. Such minimization in fact implies the universal and equal distribution of necessary labour. This solution is mentioned by Marx in his discussion of productivity in relation to the working day in *Capital* i:

The intensity and productivity of labour being given, the part of the social working day necessary for material production is the shorter, and hence the amount of time gained for the free, intellectual and social activity of individuals the greater, the more evenly the work is divided

[37] See Young 1990: 52.   [38] CM 125–7, and Preface 504.

among all the able-bodied members of the society, and the less a particular stratum is able to shift the burden of necessary labour from its own shoulders to those of another social stratum. The absolute minimum limit to the shortening of the working day is, from this point of view, the universality of labour. In capitalist society, free time is produced for one class by converting the whole lifetime of the masses into labour time.[39]

In this passage, Marx contrasts universal minimization, which results from the universal and equal distribution of necessary labour, with group-specific minimization under capitalism, which is exploitative and obviously unacceptable.[40] The 'universality of labour' or universal minimization is thus a very central part of Marx's thought about communism.[41]

Two points about this universal and equal distribution are worth mentioning, given my discussion of women's work in the last section. First, and *contra* Marx, women's work is part of the aggregate necessary labour which is to be distributed. Secondly, as able-bodied members of society, women are to be included in the scope of 'universal' distribution. While the second point was probably intended by Marx and marxists after him,[42] the first point raises a further question: if women's work is part of the necessary labour that is to be 'consciously regulated', can anything more be said about its distribution? Unfortunately, the distribution solution by itself does not provide any further answers since it stays on a relatively abstract level. All that is required by it is that both men and women do equal shares of necessary labour.

Thus note that, if we continue to distinguish between women's work and the rest of necessary labour (which I shall call 'material production' in order to contrast it with women's work),[43]

---

[39] *Cap.* i. 667.

[40] It is unacceptable even if it is historically necessary according to Marx, see GR 701, 831–2. See Introduction, n. 13.   [41] See e.g. CM 127.

[42] See Ch. 2, sect. i.

[43] This contrast is misleading in at least one respect: as argued in sect. ii above, housework has in some respects similar features to that work which Marx refers to as material production, and arguably even care could be subsumed under this term given that it is part of the 'production and reproduction of immediate life' as understood by Marx and Engels (see Engels's description of materialist theory in his Preface to the *Origin of the Family* (Engels 1972: 71); also GI 41, where 'production of life' refers to both). The contrast is useful, however, in so far as that part of women's work which is care is different in nature and logic from that work that Marx had in mind as 'material production' (see sect.

this requirement can be realized by a number of different arrangements. Some of these arrangements may realize an equal distribution of necessary labour, but may be unacceptable for different reasons. Assuming, for example, roughly equal numbers of able-bodied men and women in a given society and roughly equal aggregate amounts of material production and women's work, a possible equal distribution could be realized by the 'separate but equal spheres of work' model in which women would do equal shares of women's work and men equal shares in material production. Such a strict sexual division of labour, however, may not be desirable and, as I shall argue below, in fact renders women vulnerable to exploitation.[44] Given the abstract requirement of equal shares in necessary labour, however, this arrangement seems at least on the face of it perfectly acceptable. Another possible arrangement could be, of course, that both men and women share in both kinds of work equally, doing half of their share of necessary labour in material production and half in the caring 'sector'. Alternatively, any combination of different amounts of both kinds of work adding up to the individual minimum share would qualify as a realisation of the universal minimization solution.

In conclusion, then, the universal minimization solution or the 'universality of labour' stays at a relatively abstract level. Only those arrangements can be excluded that are clearly exploitative in that they burden one part of society with all the necessary labour whilst leaving the rest free of it. As I have pointed out above, however, there may be other forms of exploitative arrangements which are not as obvious because they concern only particular parts of necessary labour such as women's work or particularly unpleasant or hazardous work. The minimization solution to the necessary labour problem is, therefore, not sufficiently fine an instrument to weed out all objectionable distributions of necessary labour although the reason why Marx favours universal minimization is precisely because it minimizes necessary labour for everybody and thus supposedly abolishes exploitation.

ii above and Chs. 4 and 6). The contrast is, therefore, both misleading and meaningful: it is misleading because the *extensions* of the two terms may overlap, but it is nevertheless meaningful because their *intensions* are distinct. Since their intensions represent a contrast crucial to my argument, however, I shall use the contrast in this sense.　　　　　　　　　　　　　　[44] See Chs. 4 and 6.

(iv) *Marx's dialectic of labour*

In this last section I shall look at a different strand of Marx's thought: his conception of the 'dialectic of labour'.[45] This conception is in tension with his conception of the necessary labour problem which I have discussed in the preceding sections, but I shall not be concerned with a discussion of this tension as this would lead me too far away from the topic of women's work.[46] Instead, I shall discuss whether and how the dialectic of labour applies to women's work and point out the conclusions that can be derived from the dialectic of labour with regard to the place of women's work in the communist utopia.

Marx's conception of the dialectic of labour deals with the development of the relationship between individuals and their work. In the first phase of this dialectic, the phase of 'undifferentiated unity' which is illustrated by the artisan or craftsman, the individual is 'engulfed in' his work. His life is his work, and his work marks him as the individual he is. No clear-cut distinction is possible between the individual as an individual and the work he does. He stands in a 'slavish relationship' to his work, or, as Marx often says, his work is 'naturwüchsig', that is, naturally his.[47] Trades or crafts are passed on from father to son and change little in the process, and the social conditions of the work seem as natural as the work itself.[48]

The second phase, that of 'differentiated disunity', is brought about historically by capitalism. The 'slavish' and 'naturwüchsige' relationship of individuals with their work is severed once they start selling their labour power. Labour under capitalism is not performed for its own sake, but for survival as far as the

[45] The summary and discussion of the dialectic of labour in this section draws heavily on Cohen's presentation of it in Cohen 1974. I shall not give references to Marx's work in my presentation except at crucial points. Detailed references can be found in Cohen 1974.

[46] Note, however, my comments in n. 50 below.

[47] 'Naturwüchsig', literally translated, means 'grown and/or growing out of (a thing's) nature'. Marx uses either 'naturwüchsig' or 'natürlich' to refer to properties or conditions that are (not yet) shaped by human beings, that seem to have developed 'naturally'—and are therefore often taken to be natural (see *GI*, *passim*; *GR*, *passim*; but also later works; see n. 55 below for references to women's 'natural' work). Marx, of course, does not believe that anything that seems 'natural' or has developed 'naturally' has to remain so, although his beliefs about women's work are a notable exception—see my discussion later in this section.

[48] See Cohen 1974: 241–5.

worker is concerned and for profits as far as the capitalist is concerned. Labour and the goods it produces thus become subject
to instrumental considerations. Given these instrumental considerations, the particular labour engaged in for a wage ceases
to matter to the individual worker, and he might change his
work any time, either because he loses his work, or because he
finds better paid work. At the same time, work itself is con-
stantly revolutionized as a result of the capitalist's drive to profits.
None of the old ways of producing are sacrosanct because the
form of production is now determined by the aim of producing
better goods in ever more efficient ways so that sales and profits
can be maximized, that is, by the drive for profits. The original
close relationship between the individuals, their work, and the
products of their work is thereby severed. This allows the individual for the first time in history to become truly individual,
to conceive of himself as separate and different from the work
he does. His self-conception stops being dependent on any particular work precisely because work has become instrumental.
Thus while work is alienating and alienated in capitalism, it also
frees the individual from his 'natural' relationship with his work
and hence opposes the individual clearly to the work he does.[49]

This phase of differentiated disunity is historically necessary,
according to Marx, before people are able to relate freely and
consciously to their work. It is only in the phase of 'differentiated unity', realized under communism, that the relationship
between the individual and his work can become one of conscious and self-conscious choice rather than being 'naturwüchsig' and 'slavish'. What work individuals now engage in is
dependent on the way they conceive of themselves and of their
abilities and skills. Work has become the prime means for individuals to realize themselves.[50]

---

[49] Ibid. 242–6.

[50] This is the point at which the tension between Marx's conception of the
dialectic of labour and his discussion of the necessary labour problem is most
obvious. My own view of the tension is that the dialectic of labour with its cor-
respondent view on the transformation of labour under communism is characteristic of early Marxian thought, that is, Marx's thought up to the *Grundrisse*.
It is the early Marx of the *German Ideology* who celebrates the abolition of 'labour'
under communism (*GI* 85) or the 'transformation of labour into self-activity'
because at this stage 'self-activity coincide[s] with material life, which corresponds to the development of individuals into complete individuals and the
casting-off of all natural limitations' (ibid. 84—this latter passage also invokes
the dialectic of labour), whilst it is the later Marx who discusses the necessary

As Cohen has concluded from this dialectic of labour, the resulting picture of communism is that of a society in which the constraints of social roles are abolished, in which everybody is free to choose whatever activity or work they want to do or conceive of as part of their development. Nobody is bound to the activity he engaged in the day before should he choose to engage in something else today.[51] This vision is supported by Marx's opposition of the pre-communist division of labour to free activity under communism in the *German Ideology*:

... the division of labour offers us the first example of how, as long as man remains in natural ('naturwüchsige') society ... as long, therefore, as activity is not voluntarily, but naturally ('naturwüchsig') divided, man's own deed becomes an alien power opposed to him, which enslaves him instead of being controlled by him. For as soon as the division of labour comes into being, each man has a particular, exclusive sphere of activity, which is forced upon him and from which he cannot escape. He is a hunter, a fisherman, a shepherd, or a critical critic, and must remain so if he does not want to lose his means of livelihood; while in communist society, where nobody has one exclusive sphere of activity but each can become accomplished in any branch he wishes, society regulates the general production and thus makes it possible for me to do one thing today and another tomorrow, to hunt in the morning, fish in the afternoon, rear cattle in the evening, criticise after dinner, just as I have a mind, without ever becoming hunter, fisherman, shepherd, or critic.[52]

labour problem (see sects. i and ii). The most plausible interpretation of the tension, it seems to me, therefore, is that there is a turning-point in Marx's thought which arises with Marx's immersion into political economy. This introduces for him the distinction between necessary and surplus labour and, more importantly, the consequent opposition between necessary labour time and time for free, all-round development. According to this interpretation, the later Marx thought indeed that individuals were only free to realize themselves *beyond* the 'sphere of necessity', but not for the reasons that Cohen gives (Cohen 1974: 260–1 and my argument in sect. ii above). Many commentators have glossed over this tension in Marx's thought or tried to reconcile it (see e.g. Avineri 1968: 231–5; McLellan 1980: 160; Singer 1980: 64–5). It may be more instructive, however, to acknowledge the fact that the tension is indeed there and that it may be irreconcilable. See also Lukes 1985: 96 ff., for a discussion of what he thinks is a 'contradiction, or at least a tension, between the individualistic and the communitarian impulses in Marx's thought' (p. 96). The tension he intends is not the tension I have referred to, but there is some overlap between their implications with regard to the communist utopia.   [51] Cohen 1974: 258–9.

[52] *GI* 44–5, see also pp. 431–2.

This picture is compatible, however, with individuals deciding to become artisans, as Cohen points out, since under communism, their decision is an expression of true choice.[53] What distinguishes the artisan under communism from his pre-capitalist brother is the fact that he has chosen to be one and that he can reverse his decision at any time, hence he has not been slotted into a rigid social structure without having much choice. The vision of the communist utopia resulting from the dialectic of labour is thus voluntaristic and libertarian, a pastoral idyll quite removed from the sterner and *dirigiste* vision answering to the necessary labour problem. The freedom individuals have in this utopia is that of a free choice of activities which, in turn, is the necessary condition for individuals to be able to develop and realize themselves.[54] These two visions may or may not be reconcilable: whilst social distribution of necessary labour is irreconcilable with completely free choice, it is nevertheless true of both visions that individuals will spend most of their time in freely chosen, self-expressive activities which are conducive to their self-development. I shall leave this question aside, however, and ask instead how women fit into the 'pastoral idyll' and whether and how the dialectic of labour can be applied to women's work.

Note, to start with, that the dialectic of labour is conceived with a focus on what is typically men's work. The first stage of the dialectic focuses on the artisan and his work, the second stage on the industrial process of production, typically 'manned' by male workers,[55] and the hunters, fishermen, shepherds, and

[53] Cohen 1974: 255–6.

[54] Of course, not all activities are worth choosing, according to Marx, since the quality of the activities matters crucially with regard to whether they are conducive to self-realization, but since I am concerned here with the change in the relationship between individuals and their work, the quality of the work is irrelevant to the argument.

[55] That Marx thinks of workers in industrialized production as men is evident not only from his discussion of the value of labour power (see Ch. 2, sect. iv), but also from his discussion of its particular effects on women wage workers (*Cap.* i, ch. 15 sect. 3a, entitled 'Appropriation of Supplementary [*sic*!] Labour-Power by Capital: The Employment of Women and Children'): women's morals are especially and specifically corrupted by such work (p. 522), and there is an 'unnatural estrangement between mother and child' (p. 521). More generally, according to Marx, women are prevented by wage labour from engaging in their tasks at home, and these tasks, he thinks, are naturally women's (see later in this section).

'critical critics' of the pastoral idyll are obviously male, too. Not only is the conception of the dialectic of labour male focused, however, what is even more remarkable is Marx's own very consistent usage of the very notion of 'Naturwüchsigkeit' (naturalness) when he refers to the sexual division of labour and to 'women's work'.[56] Does this imply that, according to Marx, the dialectical development of women's labour is not possible and that the sexual division of labour, unlike any other division of labour, is irredeemably natural and cannot be transcended? It is difficult not to get cynical in answering this question, but the answer is obviously either that Marx did not spend enough critical thought on this question or that he was simply yet another patriarchal thinker who assumed the naturalness of, and positively endorsed, the sexual division of labour—although Marx, if anybody in the nineteenth century, was in a unique position to realize the non-sequitur.[57]

Before looking at the question of whether there can be a dialectic of women's labour we have to start by noting that historically there has been no dialectical development in women's work. What has characterized women's work in history so far is precisely that it has always been done by women. Women were and continue to be as slavishly bound to their work as artisans used to be. Their work seems to be, and is more often than not perceived to be, natural and 'naturwüchsig' in an even stronger

[56] There are many passages throughout his work which illustrate this tendency, see *GI* 33, 42–3, 44; *GR* 612; *Cap*. i. 171. Not only is the family said to be a 'naturwüchsige' association (*GR* 612), but, more importantly, the sexual (and age) division of labour in the family is said to be 'naturwüchsig' (see all the references given in this note). Unfortunately, the notion of 'Naturwüchsigkeit' is often translated misleadingly, such as in *Cap*. i. 171, where the family is said to have a 'spontaneously developed division of labour'.

[57] See n. 47 above. Engels, although spending a good part of his *Origin of the Family* discussing women's work, never questions the sexual division of labour either (Engels 1972; see also Delmar 1976 and Leonard 1984). Gorbachev, although rethinking considerable amounts of historically accumulated dogma in his *Perestroika*, is a late example of such uncritical endorsement of the sexual division of labour: not only does he suggest that a lot of social problems are 'partially' due to the 'weakening of family ties and slack attitude to family responsibilities' which are a 'paradoxical result' of the attempt to achieve equality for women, he asks himself and his readers furthermore 'what we should do to *make it possible for women to return to their purely womanly mission*'! (Gorbachev 1988: 117, my emphasis; the only difference between Gorbachev and Marx seems to be that Gorbachev blames stalinism instead of capitalism for women giving up their 'natural' duties . . .) See also Clark and Lange 1979, pp. x–xii.

sense than that of artisans: women's work is considered appropriate and natural work for them in virtue of their sex—a characteristic which they are born with and stuck with for the whole of their lives. Women are supposedly 'naturally' caring and nurturing and therefore naturally suited to do women's work.[58] Women's work, therefore, seems to be irredeemably women's work.

Furthermore, the historical arrival of waged work does not seem to have had the same effect of severing women's slavish relationship to women's work that waged work has had with regard to material production. Although the historical picture is complex and the kind of waged work that women do and have done has changed since the beginning of the industrial revolution, certain characteristics continue to hold true even if the historical details vary:

1. The labour market is sexually segregated into typical men's jobs (which are also better paid) and typical women's jobs (which are less well paid).[59] This sexual segregation of paid work can be traced in all types of economies: developed and developing capitalist and former 'socialist'.[60]

2. Women's jobs moreover often mirror the unpaid work women are doing in the home: domestic service, child care, caring work, jobs in cleaning, catering, and clothing industries; and/or they are jobs which are supposedly ideally suited to women because of their 'female' characteristics such as their warm, caring, emotional character, 'nimble fingers' and sexy bodies.

3. Women continue to do the bulk of the necessary work located in the private sphere of family homes and the voluntary sector, i.e. unpaid housework, child care, and caring work, even if they have paid work as well.

It must be concluded from this that waged work has not had the effect of severing the 'naturwüchsige' relationship of women with 'women's' work, and this conclusion holds for women in capitalist countries as much as for their sisters in socialist and

[58] See Ch. 4 sect. v.   [59] See Hartmann 1979, Walby 1986.
[60] See e.g. McAuley 1981 and Browning 1987 for the former USSR, Einhorn 1993 for the Eastern European countries, Elson and Pearson 1981 and Brydon and Chant 1989 for Third World countries.

developing countries.[61] In fact, paid work has ultimately reproduced the sexual division of labour within the labour market
and moreover burdened women with a double workload of paid
'women's' work and unpaid 'women's' work at home. If anything, therefore, the sexual division of labour has become more
entrenched.

It is furthermore worth noting that the marxist strategy for
women's liberation—which consisted basically of women's equal
participation in socialized production and which may be seen
as an application of the dialectic of labour to women's situation[62]—has not worked, since, as I pointed out above, it has tended to burden women in the former socialist countries with a
double workload of paid and unpaid work. In fact, the sexual
division of labour is even more entrenched, and the conception
of the naturalness of women's work even stronger, in these countries than it is in Western capitalist countries.[63] Considering the
near universal participation of women in the former socialist
countries in the sphere of production in comparison to the relatively less strong labour market participation of women in
Western capitalist countries combined with some signs of the
weakening of the sexual division of labour in these latter countries, it is obvious that participation in social production has
failed to free women from their enslavement to 'their' work.

Given that the conception of the dialectic of labour has failed
with regard to women's work, it looks as if it needs to be interpreted differently if it is to be applied to women's work. If we
look at historical developments, both economic and political in
both Western capitalist and former socialist countries, it seems
clear that women's political protest in the form of the women's
movement and the social and cultural changes brought about
by it have made more difference to their relation to their work
and to the sexual division of labour than any economic change.

---

[61] For a similar argument with regard to women's increasing participation in
the labour market in the Third World see Beneria 1979; also Molyneux 1985 on
socialist countries in the Third World.   [62] See Ch. 2 sect. i below.
[63] See n. 57 above and the fact that a lot of women in these countries now
want to 'return to their homes' (see e.g. Moskalenko n.d.); note also that women
rather than men tend to be laid off in the process of restructuring these economies
with the argument that men are the breadwinners (Einhorn 1993). Of course, it
has to be borne in mind that feminism was suppressed under real existing socialism as yet another bourgeois, capitalist ideology.

This point, if true, may imply a challenge to traditional materialist explanations of social change. The issue would need a lot more discussion than I can give it here, and it is possible that other factors are equally important. I shall leave it as a suggestion, therefore, and as a pointer for further discussion of the dialectical process that will free women from their supposedly 'natural' work.[64]

I shall close my discussion of Marx's dialectic of labour by asking what the communist utopia would look like if women's work had undergone a dialectical development as well. I pointed out above that the 'differentiated unity' of individuals with their activities is realized to the extent that individuals are free to choose the activities they want to engage in and that this meant that social roles are abolished. Work is thus neither a condition in which they find themselves trapped, nor is it merely instrumental for survival. If this is applied to women, it must mean that the sexual division of labour is abolished and that women are freed from their corresponding traditional roles as wives, mothers, carers, and domestic workers. Women may choose to engage in mothering, caring, and housework, but there is no presumption that they will do so, nor is there any direct or indirect coercion:[65] the choice will be genuinely free. Furthermore, men can freely choose to engage in these formerly 'women's' activities and women can choose to engage in any of the traditionally 'male' activities. Women's work, in fact, will have ceased to be women's work.[66]

---

[64] The interesting point about women's political protest as opposed to their participation in the labour market as the factor of change is that women's political protest is a conscious opposition based on a conscious rejection of their situation, including the work that supposedly comes naturally to them. If history is made by women's protest, it does not work via economic developments behind their backs like the dialectic of labour as originally conceived by Marx, but it is consciously brought about by them. The dialectical development of labour, therefore, would have started to come about because women themselves consciously severed their 'slavish' links with women's work, not because the productive forces did it for them.   [65] See Ch. 4 sect. v.

[66] This elaboration of the meaning of differentiated unity with regard to women's work also allows us to exclude the 'separate but equal spheres of work' model for the distribution of necessary labour in the communist utopia that could not be rejected in the discussion of the social distribution of necessary labour above (sect. iii). Note, however, that the social distribution of any work is not easily reconcilable with the voluntarist picture of the communist utopia presented in this section.

In conclusion, then, Marx's thought on work has not lent itself easily to the purposes of discussing women's work. In fact, my discussion of the necessary labour problem has shown up the restricted horizon of Marx's thought on work by pointing out that the abolition or minimization of necessary labour is not a feasible option for most of women's work. Marx's consideration of possible distributions of necessary labour, however, provided an interesting way of thinking about the distribution of women's work and other necessary labour, while his conception of the dialectic of labour, without its original patriarchal bias, turned out to usher in a promising—if truly utopian?—vision of a future in which women's work would have become a genuine matter of choice. None of these trains of thought, however, have led to anything as elaborate as a conception of women's work, even if they have allowed us to highlight certain important aspects of women's work as well as to pursue certain interesting ways of thinking about the social distribution of work. They consist of initial, tentative, and very basic steps toward such a conception, based on even less than that in Marx's own work. In the next chapter, I shall turn to a genuine, although even more abortive, attempt by marxists and marxist feminists to provide a more elaborate conception of women's work.

2

The Domestic Labour Debate

The domestic labour debate arose in the late 1960s as an attempt by marxist feminists to provide an account of the oppression of women in capitalist society. This was to be achieved primarily through an analysis of women's unpaid work in their homes or domestic labour as it came to be called. This analysis was also to correct two biases in feminist and marxist theory respectively that marxist feminists were unhappy with: first, the focus by various liberal feminists on the experiential aspects of women's work at home such as its supposed repetitive, boring, mind-numbing, and alienating nature was to be corrected by a focus on the material aspects of housework,[1] and, secondly, the more or less exclusive focus of marxist theory on the sphere of production was to be complemented by a focus on the domestic sphere and the work performed within it.

The domestic labour debate is of interest for three reasons. First, it consists of a collective, very controversially discussed effort to come up with a materialist analysis of women's unpaid work, and since this is precisely what I intend to provide myself in this book, I cannot but take a close look at it. Secondly, although the debate itself may seem rather dated by now, it provides us with an interesting case-study about the general difficulty of developing a feminist analysis of any aspect of women's lives and situation within a male-biased theoretical framework. Thirdly, and related to the second point, the result of the debate was and remains scandalous and hence invites critical scrutiny: only one of the feminists that had participated in the debate dared to insist on the claim that women were exploited in performing

[1] See the liberal feminist classic *The Feminine Mystique* (Friedan 1985, originally published in 1963) and a later, but none the less typically liberal feminist argument by Richards (1980, ch. 6).

domestic work.[2] How could this happen, given not only that marxist feminists were in the best theoretical position to make such a claim, but also that there is strong evidence to support such a claim? Recall the summary of the findings of the UN Decade of Women which I presented in the introduction: women

> constitute *half* the world's population,
> perform nearly *two-thirds* of its work hours,
> receive *one-tenth* of the world's income
> and own less than *one-hundredth* of the world's property.[3]

This statistic would seem to provide ample evidence that women are exploited, given that those who are exploited typically are burdened with more work than they have benefits to enjoy.[4] Unfortunately, however, after initial bold assertions of women's exploitation by some feminists, further and more sustained enquiries were nipped in the bud by the particular dynamics of the debate.

Arguably, there were at least three reasons for this peculiar silence on the question of women's exploitation in the domestic labour debate. First, there were conceptual reasons why the claim that women were exploited proved to be a difficult one to make. These reasons—as I shall argue, spurious ones—are at the very centre of the debate and will be discussed in detail in this chapter. Secondly, there are substantial reasons related to the variability of women's material lives and to difficulties in the measurement of their work burdens and material benefits. I shall discuss these reasons in Chapter 3. Thirdly, there were political reasons: the assertion of women's exploitation raised the further question of the identity of the exploiters. The identification of men as the exploiters of women was seen as too disruptive of working-class solidarity and the anti-capitalist struggle.[5] These

---

[2] Folbre is a US marxist feminist who insisted on pursuing an (economic) theory of women's exploitation (Folbre 1982), but she did not contribute to the original debate, which was restricted mostly to the UK. See nn. 47 and 54 below.

[3] Quoted after Pahl 1988: 349. For a discussion of what exactly this quote shows, see Ch. 3 sect. iii.

[4] I cannot discuss the notion of exploitation at this point. For the general underlying idea see Introduction, sect. ii, for a preliminary exposition of Marx's notion of exploitation sect. vi below, for a more detailed discussion of theories of exploitation Ch. 3 sect. ii, and for a discussion of the claim that women are exploited Ch. 3 *passim*.

[5] It was probably also too uncomfortable for male marxists to deal with.

political reasons were not necessarily given explicitly, but were perceived by some feminists as the underlying and real agenda of the debate.[6] The politics of the domestic labour debate, however, in so far as they are not reflected in the discussion of conceptual and substantial points, are beyond the scope of my discussion.

In what follows, I shall first prepare the ground for the discussion of the domestic labour debate by looking at the history of marxist-leninist thought about women's work (section i), before I present the orthodox position within the debate and the typical form of argument used by its defenders (section ii). A more detailed analysis of two of the arguments put forth by defenders of the orthodox position allows me to criticize this position (section iii). I then introduce and evaluate the main contrasting position in the debate, the benefit position (sections iv and v), before drawing my conclusions with regard to what can be learnt from the debate, specifically with regard to the notion of exploitation (vi).

(i) *The marxist-leninist doctrine*

The domestic labour debate did not start from scratch when marxists and feminists looked at women's work in the home. In fact, women's work had already been given attention by marxists and communists before the debate set off. Before this debate, however, the account of women's work and women's oppression which had originally been proposed by Engels and subsequently been elaborated by marxist-leninists had not been contested. In this section, I shall introduce and discuss this account, which I shall call the 'marxist-leninist doctrine'.[7]

While Marx himself never addressed the oppression of women in his published works, Engels did in his *Origin of the Family, Private Property and the State*.[8] Women were seen by Engels, as

[6] See e.g. Delphy 1984, *passim*; Gail Wilson, personal communication.

[7] For further details of this doctrine which I cannot address in this section, as well as for a discussion of how it was translated into policies in socialist countries, see Molyneux 1981 and Heitlinger 1979.

[8] Engels 1972. Engels claims in the 'Preface to the First Edition' that his work is based on extensive notes by Marx on the work of the anthropologist Morgan, whom Engels discusses at length in his work, and that it is part of their materialist theory (Engels 1972: 71).

by many after him, as oppressed in the home because they were isolated in individual units of production instead of participating in socialized production. Others, such as Bebel and Lenin, added that they were furthermore oppressed because the kind of work they were performing was backward, little rationalized by machines, and stultifyingly repetitive.[9] That this was the main line of their argument can be seen most clearly in the remedy that was thought adequate to end women's oppression: women had to leave the isolation of their private homes and to start participating in socialized production. Thus Engels writes in the *Origin of the Family*:

We can . . . see . . . that to emancipate woman and make her the equal of the man is and remains an impossibility so long as the woman is shut out from social productive labour and restricted to private domestic labour. The emancipation of woman will only be possible when woman can take part in production on a large, social scale, and domestic work no longer claims anything but an insignificant amount of her time. And only now has that become possible through modern large-scale industry, which does not merely permit of the employment of female labour over a wide range, but positively demands it, while it also tends towards ending private domestic labour by changing it more and more into a public industry.[10]

Three points in this passage are noteworthy and typical of marxist-leninist doctrine. First, Engels does not envisage liberating women from their burden of domestic work altogether: he does not question that women would continue to be responsible for doing it.[11] Secondly, Engels thinks that the ultimate solution to

[9] We tend to forget that housework in the nineteenth century was physically very demanding since none of the modern conveniences such as central heating, electricity, and water supply, nor appliances such as washing machines or vacuum cleaners were available. Some of the physically hard labour in the household, however, used to be performed by men (Cowan 1983). Bebel was most fascinated by the possibility of economizing on domestic labour through appliances and through its socialization (Bebel 1971). For Lenin's views, see below.

[10] Engels 1972: 221; *Women and Communism* 1950: 12.

[11] See various critics of Engels on this point: Delmar 1976, Sayers 1987, Coole 1993. Engels shares this presumption with another famous male champion of women's liberation in the nineteenth century, J. S. Mill, in his *Subjection of Women* (Mill 1985). Lenin is more adamant in wanting to transform all of women's domestic work into 'social production', but presumes equally that women will continue to do those types of work, that is, that it will literally remain 'women's' work (Lenin 1965a, 1965b, 1965c, 1965d; Lenin 1966). Kollontai, by contrast, imagines men and women in this branch of socialized production (Kollontai 1977).

the problem of domestic labour is its gradual reduction through its integration into social production, hence he ultimately uses Marx's 'minimization through automation' solution to the problem that it continues to have to be performed.[12] Thirdly, only housework, but not any form of care, is addressed in his account.

Lenin similarly claims about the liberation of women in the October Revolution that the most important step, apart from the achievement of legal equality for women, was 'the abolition of the private ownership of land and factories. This and this alone opens up the way towards a complete and actual emancipation of woman, her liberation from "household bondage" through transition from petty individual housekeeping to large-scale socialized domestic services.'[13] Lenin's account, although substantially the same as that of Engels, is more interesting in detail. Thus he refers to women's oppression as 'domestic slavery' or even 'double slavery' (including waged as well as domestic work) and to women as 'domestic slaves', a term which suggests that women are exploited since slavery is an exploitative form of social production.[14] Mostly, however, Lenin puts the term in inverted commas. There is only a short period in 1919—Lenin's honeymoon with the women's organizations?—when Lenin omits them.[15] Now the inverted commas might in fact be thought an adequate usage of the term since women—even in the nineteenth century with its marriage laws denying full legal personhood to women—could not literally be said to be slaves. However, although the description of workers as slaves in the frequently used term 'wage slaves' was even less adequate, this did not provoke marxist-leninists to use inverted commas in this characterization of workers. The inverted commas, then, must be taken to indicate that the term 'domestic slavery' is to be taken less literally than the term 'wage slavery': women's situation is only *as if* they were slaves, but it is not really slavery. Further evidence of the 'differential treatment' of women's oppression by marxist-leninists

[12] See Ch. 1 sect. ii.
[13] Lenin 1965c: 162, and, in slightly different translation, *Women and Communism* 1950: 46.   [14] See Lenin 1963, 1965a, 1965c, 1965d; see sect. vi below.
[15] Lenin uses the inverted commas in a 1913 article on labour saving technology (Lenin 1963). He drops them in 'A Great Beginning' (Lenin 1965d), written in July 1919, and in an address to women's organizations in September 1919 (Lenin 1965a), but they reappear in his International Working Women's Day addresses in March 1920 and 1921 (Lenin 1965b, 1965c).

is the fact that women were mostly described as 'oppressed' whilst wage workers, like (real) slaves, were said to be exploited. Whilst the drudgery of women's work was criticized, no statement about their exploitation can be found in any of these early writings.[16]

The reason why women's situation should be changed, then, according to Lenin, is not because they are exploited, but because they are 'doubly oppressed': on the one hand, they are oppressed by capital, and on the other hand by the pettiness and drudgery of their work. In close parallel to Engels—and thus contributing further to the establishment of the 'marxist-leninist dogma' about women's oppression—Lenin stresses the need to emancipate women from domestic work because women 'remain in "household bondage", they continue to be "domestic slaves", for they are overburdened with the drudgery of the most squalid, backbreaking and stultifying toil in the kitchen and the family household'.[17] Lenin thus reasserts the focus on the backwardness of women's general situation and the petty form of production they are involved in as the most important specific aspect of women's oppression.

The refusal to see women as exploited rather than merely as oppressed is not explicit in these early writings and has to be inferred from the absence of any mentioning of exploitation or exploitative relations in the context of their discussion of women's oppression. It is rather surprising, however, that, although

---

[16] Lenin's treatment of the whole question is arguably quite instrumental: his explicit aim was mainly to recruit women to support the Revolution, since he believed that the Revolution was only won when women's lives had been transformed, too, and this transformation could not be achieved without the co-operation of women themselves. To recognize that women were truly slaves, then, would potentially have been counter-productive, since it would have prompted the further question of *'whose* slaves?'—and that question might have pitted women against their husbands instead of realigning them at their husbands' sides. In so far as Lenin attributed slavery (in quotation marks) to women, they were either said to be slaves to capitalism or private property (Lenin 1965a, 1965b), or they were called slaves because they were crushed by domestic work (Lenin 1965b, 1965c, 1965d). Either way men come out 'clean', free from allegations of being slave holders and able to expect women's co-operation and support (see also sect. v below). For more evidence of this basically instrumental view of women in marxist-leninist writings and policies see Molyneux 1981; for a description of bolshevik politics in the aftermath of the October Revolution see Farnsworth 1980, Porter 1980.

[17] Lenin 1965c: 161; *Women and Communism* 1950: 46.

both Engels and Lenin call for a reduction of women's work-
load through the socialization of this work, neither seem to
'notice' that women might be exploited. This is even more surprising since the domestic work-load was rather heavy at the
time and would have involved women in very long working
days. While such early marxist thought leaves one in the dark
as to why the concept of exploitation was not used to describe
women's lives, the reasons for this peculiar silence are to be
found in texts which defend what I shall call the 'orthodox position' in the domestic labour debate. I shall present this position
in the next section.

(ii) *The orthodox position*

The orthodox position within the domestic labour debate formed
itself in response to claims by feminists, in some of the very first
papers contributing to it, that women are indeed exploited. Thus
Benston, in a widely distributed and discussed paper originally
published in 1969, challenges marxist theorists of capitalist exploitation by claiming that 'there *is* a material basis for women's status; we are not merely discriminated against, we are exploited.
At present, our unpaid labour in the home is necessary if the
entire [capitalist] system is to function.'[18] The force of such claims
was immediately recognized. Morton, for example, comments in
1970 that Benston's account of women's oppression 'is significant
. . . because it challenges the view that the only *economic* basis to
the oppression of women is the super-exploitation of women in
the labour market'.[19] The preferred target of defenders of the
orthodox position in the debate, however, was Dalla Costa, who
had claimed in her essay 'Women and the Subversion of the
Community' that 'what began with capitalism was the more
intense exploitation of women *as* women'.[20] Dalla Costa used not
only 'exploitation', but also other concepts in her account of
women's work at home which had hitherto only been used in
accounts of waged work under capitalist relations of production:

---

[18] Benston 1982: 128.   [19] Morton 1982: 135.
[20] Dalla Costa 1973: 23.

Domestic work produces not merely use values, but is essential to the production of surplus value . . . [21]

. . . housework is productive in the Marxian sense, that is, is producing surplus value.[22]

It was such new and, as far as the defenders of the orthodox position were concerned, 'illegitimate' usage by feminists of marxist terms that called them into the debate. Thus in direct reference to Dalla Costa, Seccombe responds that

In maintaining that domestic labour is productive [Dalla Costa and James][23] never make the distinction between a labour's general character, and its specific relation, and so *they cannot employ a rigorous category like 'productive' at all.* . . . They use the term 'productive' primarily to emphasize the indispensable nature of domestic labour to capitalist production, and to counteract the denial of domestic labour's role by past generations of Marxists. This point is well taken, but it is surely not impossible to rectify this omission while *retaining some precision in the use of Marxist categories.*[24]

Seccombe also refuses Dalla Costa's characterization of women as exploited:

the housewife, in Marxist terms, is unexploited because surplus value is not extracted from her labour. To say this is not as James and Dalla Costa imply, to be soft on women's oppression. The housewife is intensely *oppressed* within the nuclear family under capitalism, but she is not *exploited.*[25]

The question, therefore, is what precisely was at issue between these bold feminist assertions and the insistent rejection of these assertions by defenders of the orthodox position. Note that it is not evident how the feminist claims were to be understood. First, feminists could simply have used polemically and for their own purposes terms which were very evocative and had been used for the analysis of the oppression of workers and other oppressed

---

[21] Dalla Costa 1973: 33.   [22] Ibid. 53 n. 12.

[23] James wrote a separate essay in the book which was published by Dalla Costa and James and which also contained Dalla Costa's essay 'Women and the Subversion of the Community'. The work referred to by Seccombe is the latter, not a common work by both authors (see Dalla Costa and James 1973).

[24] Seccombe 1974: 11; my emphasis.   [25] Ibid. 11.

classes in history.[26] Secondly, however, their claims could have been intended either as creative (mis)usages of terms which implied a conceptual critique of the narrow usage to which these terms had been put hitherto or as a conceptual critique by themselves. Thirdly, feminists might simply have been mistaken in their understanding of marxist political economy and hence unaware of the fact that they were transgressing accepted usage. This last alternative, however, was relatively unlikely since all the participants in the debate were well versed in marxist theory. Defenders of the orthodox position typically responded to the feminist claims either as polemics or as misunderstandings or both,[27] seeing their own task mainly in reaffirming the 'correct' understanding of marxist political economy. They thus showed no appreciation of the fact that feminists might have challenged exactly that understanding, that is, of the possibility that the feminist claims implied a conceptual critique.[28] Hence feminist polemics as well as conceptual critique were ultimately answered inadequately with a simple reassertion of what feminists had reacted against in the first place.

Accordingly, the typical form of argument in any of the defences of the orthodox position is of the following type:

A X refers to the following kinds of phenomena / entities according to Marx (or marxist theory); or: X is used in the following way; [= *the orthodox premiss*]
B Y lacks (some, or the crucial) properties of these phenomena / entities; or: does not fall within this usage;
C Therefore the claim that Y is X is wrong;

where X stands for any marxist term, and Y for domestic work or women's situation in the home. This type of argument—which I shall call the 'orthodox type of argument'—implies a straightforward reassertion of the orthodox usage of any concept since

---

[26] This is certainly true with regard to the notion of exploitation (for a late example of such polemical usage see Delphy and Leonard 1992: 42 and my discussion of it in Ch. 3 sect. iv), but probably also true with regard to the notion of productive labour (see Seccombe 1974: 11).

[27] See e.g. Smith 1978: 200; see also Seccombe 1974: 11.

[28] Unfortunately, feminist contributions to the debate were on the whole not very explicit about the exact nature of their arguments, nor very sophisticated in defending their claims. Delphy (1984) and Delphy and Leonard (1992) are notable exceptions.

this usage is what the whole argument is premissed on. Thus given the assertion of this usage (A) and a statement of the crucial difference or lack of some crucial characteristic (B), the validity of any claim which uses a particular marxist concept 'creatively' in an account of women's work and situation at home can be rejected (C). If orthodox premises were defended, they were invariably defended in direct reference to Marx's own writings, notably *Capital* and the *Theories of Surplus Value*.[29]

Note that both of Seccombe's rebuttals take exactly this form: women are not exploited at home (C1) because no surplus value can be extracted from their work (B1); their work is not productive (C2) because it is performed privately, that is, not under capitalist relations of production (B2). Only the second of the corresponding orthodox premises is spelled out by Seccombe, but both premises need to be endorsed, of course, for the conclusions to follow. The premises are:

A1   Only productive labour can be exploited, because only productive labour produces surplus value which is then appropriated by the capitalist.[30]

A2   Productive labour is that labour which is done under capitalist relations of production.[31]

These two premises, in fact, are not only central to Seccombe's argument, they capture more generally the very foundations of the orthodox position.

The orthodox position can then be described as that position which posited certain central propositions of marxist political economy as premises which, because they were taken from the 'master's own words'—that is, Marx's work—could not possibly be questioned. The most crucial of these propositions, first, is the claim that, in the capitalist mode of production, exploitation consists of the extraction of surplus value. Furthermore, and

---

[29] The writings of any of the participants in the debate contained references to Marx, but those endorsing the orthodox position contained especially many: see Adamson *et al.* 1976, Bullock 1973, Carter 1975, Himmelweit and Mohun 1977, Howell 1975, Seccombe 1974, 1975, Smith 1978.

[30] I have not seen this premiss asserted explicitly in any of the contributions to the debate—maybe because it would have been too obvious a target for rejection, although it may also have been so deeply entrenched that it was simply taken for granted by all participants in the debate—but it is a major premiss of the whole debate. For an explicit assertion in the context of an economic discussion see Glyn 1979.   [31] See Seccombe 1974: 10–11.

secondly, only a certain kind of labour—that is, productive labour—can be exploited because only that kind could produce surplus value. (Productive labour, according to Marx, is that labour which is performed under capitalist relations of production, that is, which is set to work in order to produce more than its own worth.)[32] Thirdly, only labour which forms part of either capitalist production (by working for capital) or the market (via goods produced by it and sold on the market) is also abstract, social labour which is ruled by the law of value. (The law of value is the basic law 'governing' the capitalist economy.) On the basis of these premisses, domestic work could easily be shown to fall outside the remit of the conceptual and explanatory apparatus that was thus asserted.

The difficulty, then, for feminist participants in the debate—and the ground of the seeming unassailability of orthodox arguments—was that they agreed with defenders of the orthodox position roughly on the following characteristics of women's work at home:

1. Domestic labour is *work*.
2. The content of domestic labour has changed with the development of capitalism: some of the work which used to be done at home is now *socialized*, that is, part of capitalist or state production (clothing industry, food industry, the centralized provision of water and electricity, the provision of health and education services).
3. Domestic labour *produces and reproduces labour power*.
4. Domestic labour is *unpaid* (but the wife gets her means of subsistence at least partly from her husband's wage packet).
5. Domestic labour produces *use-values*—hence is socially useful work—but it does not produce use-values for the market.
6. Domestic labour is done *privately*, that is, not directly under capitalist relations of production.

While these characteristics of domestic labour were generally agreed on by all sides in the domestic labour debate, what was hotly disputed was their theoretical analysis and interpretation. Notice, however, that once feminists had agreed particularly to

[32] See Gough 1972.

the last three characteristics which locate domestic labour socially and indicate its relation—that is, its unrelatedness—to the capitalist economy, it followed immediately from the orthodox premises that none of the concepts used to explain the capitalist economy and society could be used to explain domestic labour. More specifically, it followed that domestic labour was not exploitative.

The significance of domestic labour, as far as the orthodox position is concerned, is therefore that it takes place in a sphere which is completely separate from capitalist production. Although domestic labour is necessary for the reproduction of labour power under capitalism, it is done privately and therefore outside of capitalist production. Thus Adamson *et al.* emphasize, like Engels and Lenin had done before—that 'domestic work is privatized, individual toil. It is concrete labour which lies outside the capitalist production process and therefore cannot produce value or surplus value.'[33] It was conceded by defenders of the orthodox position that 'domestic labour remains vital for the reproduction of capital through the reproduction of labour power',[34] although it was stressed that it is 'an external necessity'.[35] It was also admitted, however, that domestic labour is 'given gratis'.[36] Now the phrase 'labour given gratis'—or 'unpaid labour'—is often used by Marx to describe that part of the working day which is not remunerated by the capitalist,[37] hence that part of the working day in which a wage worker performs surplus labour and is exploited. But far from concluding that there may be a similarity between women and workers, defenders of the orthodox position simply insisted on the basis of their premises that such notions could only be applied in the case of workers, but not in the case of women, thus spelling out their rationale for refusing even to consider women's exploitation.

(iii) *Two orthodox arguments analysed*

In this section, I shall analyse in more detail two arguments which were advanced by defenders of the orthodox position in

---

[33] Adamson *et al.* 1976: 8. Note that this is another example of the orthodox type of argument.   [34] Ibid. 11; see Himmelweit and Mohun 1977: 28.
[35] Smith 1978: 214; see also pp. 211, 212.
[36] Adamson *et al.* 1976: 11; see the same formulation by Howell 1975: 54.
[37] See Geras 1986: 15 n. 27.

order to illustrate the logic of their arguments. This will allow me to expose the problems with the orthodox position. I shall conclude that feminists found themselves in a real bind with regard to orthodox arguments, but also indicate how they could have escaped that bind.

The first argument consists of an attempt by Smith to provide more substantial support for the claim that domestic labour cannot be analysed with the marxist categories which are used for the analysis of labour within the sphere of production mainly on the grounds that domestic labour is not part of social production. Smith argues his case against contrary suggestions made by Seccombe that domestic labour can be conceived of as part of social production and hence as 'social labour' since it forms an important part in the production and reproduction of labour power which is then sold on the market. Seccombe argues that the housewife's labour 'becomes part of the congealed mass of past labour embodied in labour power. The value she creates is realized as one part of the value labour power achieves as a commodity when it is sold.'[38] While Seccombe justifies his analysis by claiming that it is consistent with marxist theory as an 'application of the labour theory of value to the reproduction of labour power itself—namely that all labour produces value when it produces any part of a commodity that achieves equivalence in the marketplace with other commodities',[39] Smith objects that his suggestions about how women's domestic labour is to be understood involve an illicit usage of central marxist concepts such as that of value and of social production.[40] As Smith swiftly points out, not *any* labour creates value, but only that labour which is 'performed within the social relations of commodity production [and] which takes the form of socially necessary, abstract and social labour'.[41] This looks again like just another example of the orthodox type of argument, especially since Smith then goes on to argue that domestic labour under capitalism does not meet these criteria. Smith is, however, aware of the objection that he is just being dogmatic and is at pains to stress

---

[38] Seccombe 1974: 9.   [39] Ibid. 9.
[40] It might be thought that Seccombe cannot himself be a defender of the orthodox position, given this lapse, but inclusion of authors in this position is a matter of degree and general structure of argument, rather than absolutely clear-cut.   [41] Smith 1978: 201.

that 'Seccombe's position is ultimately untenable—not as a consequence of Marx's definitions but as a consequence of the nature of commodity production'.[42] Smith, therefore, attempts to provide what he regards as a sustained argument to defend his orthodox claims. What is at issue between Smith and Seccombe, then, is whether domestic labour can be understood as part of social production—in marxist terminology, whether domestic labour is 'abstract and social labour'—the point being that if it could, the marxist conceptual and theoretical apparatus could then be used to analyse and explain it. Smith considers four respects in which domestic labour differs from labour which is clearly part of social production.

First, he points out that the allocation of labour under a capitalist commodity economy is regulated by the law of value— or the mechanism of the market—in that fluctuations in the price of commodities effect a reallocation of labour into different branches of production. Domestic labour, however, is not influenced by this regulating mechanism, since it is not reallocated should the price of labour power start falling. It continues to be performed even when labour power cannot be sold at all, e.g. at times of high unemployment.[43] The production of labour power is hence not affected by its 'profitability', hence not by the market mechanism.[44]

Secondly, Smith points out that, according to Marx, if labour is part of social labour under capitalism it is shaped by the fact that it produces commodities for the market: 'Abstract labour, the specific form of social labour under commodity production, develops to the extent that exchange becomes the social form of the production process, transforming the production process into commodity production.'[45] For labour to be social (= abstract)

[42] Smith 1978: 201; see also his point against Adamson *et al.*'s 'dogmatic assertions', p. 203.   [43] Smith 1978: 204.

[44] In fact, as several contributors to the domestic labour debate have emphasized, the labour women do at home is flexible, and there is an inverse correlation between what can be afforded with a wage and the amount of labour that is done at home. As real wages fall, housewives can afford to buy much less and have to start buying fewer processed goods instead and make up for the difference in value added with their own labour: see Smith 1978: 205; Gardiner 1975: 57; Molyneux 1979: 11–12. Or they have to consider taking up paid work themselves in order to supplement their husband's wage (Smith 1978: 205).

[45] Smith 1978: 205–6.

labour, therefore, it is not enough for its products to enter the market, but the products have to be *produced for exchange*, and this typically implies that the producer is indifferent to his or her products. Domestic labour, however, is not performed indifferently, and is certainly not performed with a view towards exchange of the produced commodity, i.e. labour power. (More specifically, and following on from Smith's argument, it is care which is performed for the benefit of the members of the family with a view to their welfare.) No wife and mother would see herself as producing commodities, nor could she be described as a self-interested 'producer of labour power' who would switch to producing some other commodity should she chance upon a slump in the labour market for which she produces.[46]

Thirdly, according to Smith, given that domestic labour is uninfluenced by the market mechanism, it cannot be measured at all. Not only are the boundaries between production, consumption, and leisure unclear in the home, but also domestic labour is not constrained by the competitive pressure of the market and hence does not tend toward a social average or minimum per unit of product.[47] Smith concludes, therefore, that because domestic labour takes place under such different social conditions, it is not commensurable with other labour. Hence it is not abstract labour, which is the 'substance of value':

Because domestic labour is performed in addition to labour performed in capitalist production, and so is performed independently of the regulation of labour through the value of its product, it is not equal and interchangeable with other concrete labours and so is not abstract (value creating) labour, the historical form of equal labour under commodity production.[48]

Domestic labour, therefore, is not abstract and hence cannot produce value.

Furthermore, and fourthly, since the market is the only way in which different kinds of labour can become part of social

[46] As I shall argue in Ch. 5 below, women's unpaid work is best understood as care rather than production (see also Ch. 1 sect. ii).

[47] Smith 1978: 208. Folbre (1982) argues in response to such arguments that commensurability is achieved for domestic labour on the basis of the need for households to survive which introduces a pressure towards efficiency comparable to that of competition in production for the market.

[48] Smith 1978: 207.

production, domestic labour cannot be part of social production under capitalism.

Since, under commodity production, abstract labour is the only form in which private labour becomes social labour, domestic labour, despite its being materialized in a social use value, remains private. It is not because domestic labour is private that it cannot become abstract labour; it is because it cannot become abstract labour that it remains private.[49]

Smith concedes that domestic labour could become part of social production if it was performed as part of a 'consciously regulated economy' and included into the social distribution of labour—as under socialism or communism. But under commodity production, which is the form production takes under capitalism and which is subject to the 'law of value', such an inclusion is not possible: domestic labour is performed independently of any regulation through the market and hence cannot be part of social production. Domestic labour under capitalism is therefore necessarily *external* to social production. Seccombe is therefore also mistaken, according to Smith, in thinking that the labour theory of value can be applied in an analysis of domestic labour.[50]

Rather than discuss Smith's arguments in detail, I shall make several points about them. It will emerge from these points why a discussion of his arguments would be a distraction rather than useful. Thus note, first, that whilst he makes a detailed effort to defend his rejection of Seccombe's analysis, his detailed argument involves the following: a more detailed presentation of various interrelated aspects and conceptual claims of marxist political economy (A), a more detailed description of the essentially different social conditions under which domestic labour takes place (B), and the same conclusions as those of other defenders of the orthodox position, that is, that domestic labour is not what feminists and other 'creative' users of marxist concepts say it is, hence that their analysis is mistaken (C). His argument, therefore, is another example, albeit a more elaborate one, of the already presented orthodox type of argument.

Secondly, given the structure of this type of argument, once the orthodox premisses are accepted, the conclusions seem to follow without further argument since, as I pointed out in the last section, whatever is descriptively asserted about domestic labour under (B) is generally unobjectionable, and indeed the characteristics of domestic labour expounded under (B) were usually not under dispute by the participants in the debate. The result of this particular structure of argument and, particularly, of the unobjectionable, descriptive nature of assertions under (B), is that discussion tends to focus away from domestic labour and instead on various central concepts and tenets in marxist economics, i.e. on the orthodox premisses (A). Discussion, therefore, gets very easily deflected into a discussion of marxist economics at the expense of a discussion of domestic labour. This inherent tendency of the discussion to get side-tracked no doubt was one of the sources of frustration for feminists participating in the debate and wanting to analyse and explain women's domestic work.

Note furthermore, and thirdly, that a lot of feminists found themselves in a bind because of their conception of their own attempts at analysing domestic labour as being part and parcel of marxist economic and social theory.[51] Since the orthodox premisses tended to be defended in direct reference to Marx,[52] feminists seemed to be forced into detailed discussions of marxist economic theory in virtue of the particular structure of arguments in the domestic labour debate, despite the fact that their original interests lay elsewhere. Particularly with regard to the question of whether women were exploited, most feminists were in a bind: given that it seemed impossible to use the notion of exploitation for their own purposes, should they give up their 'hunch' that women were exploited by agreeing to orthodox arguments—thereby remaining 'good marxists'—or should they insist on women's exploitation, thus becoming 'renegades'? The pressure to accept orthodox premisses was immense, given their conception of their own work as marxist. Furthermore, if they wanted to defend their 'hunch', they would have to defend it on territory that was not necessarily their own and that they were not necessarily interested in, that is, economic theory. This

---

[51] See e.g. the usage of the notion of the 'political economy' of housework in the title of two articles (Gardiner 1976, Harrison 1973b).

[52] Smith's article is a very good example of this tendency (Smith 1978).

bind may explain why many feminists in the end just gave up and moved on to other questions since the debate clearly led them away from their initial interests.[53] It also explains the pressure on participants in the debate to give up claims that seemed undeniably mistaken in the light of orthodox rejoinders, but that had initially and intuitively seemed correct.[54]

Fourthly, however, there was an alternative and a way out of the bind: feminists could have rejected some or all of the orthodox premises. Whilst this implied going against marxist political economy as it was understood by participants in the debate, as well as to some extent going against Marx himself, it did not necessarily imply the giving up of a marxist or materialist approach altogether. In particular, one of the premises of the debate was clearly wrong: whilst exploitation takes the form of the appropriation of surplus value under capitalist relations of production, the fact that domestic labour is not performed under capitalist relations of production does not establish that women are not exploited. It merely proves that women are not *capitalistically* exploited. Thus women could be exploited in other ways—not necessarily the same ways as those in which oppressed classes in other modes of production were exploited, but ways other than the extraction of surplus value.[55] Interestingly enough, only one participant in the debate took this line explicitly, also redefining herself as a 'materialist' rather than a 'marxist' feminist.[56]

---

[53] See Delphy and Leonard 1992: 70, for the observation of feminists' moving on, although they give different reasons for this.

[54] Folbre (1982) is a rare example of a feminist marxist economist who initially resisted marxist orthodoxy by suggesting a theory of women's exploitation on the basis of an argument that women's labour can be measured in value terms. (See nn. 2 and 47 above.) She seems to have given up any further work on it since then, however: in her most recent book, whilst focusing on women's unpaid work throughout, she refers to the domestic labour debate only implicitly in a footnote, ending by concluding that the labour theory of value needs to be rejected if it does not allow the usage of the concept of exploitation for women's unpaid labour in the home (Folbre 1994: 266 n. 46). In the rest of the book, she neither explicates nor defends her occasional usage of 'exploitation' in this sense. Late victory by the orthodox position?

[55] I shall argue in sect. vi below that feminists need not have rejected Marx's notion of exploitation—nor need they have given in to orthodox insistence on this point.

[56] See Delphy 1984. Delphy was predictably taken to task and accused by other marxist feminists of getting marxist theory completely or at least partly wrong (see Barrett and McIntosh 1979, Molyneux 1979). I shall discuss Delphy's theory of 'familial exploitation' in detail in Ch. 3.

Furthermore, various aspects of Marx's economic theory were under dispute at any rate, such as his distinction between productive and unproductive labour (see the second orthodox premiss)[57] and the labour theory of value which was disputed by both marxist and neo-classical economists alike.[58] It was perfectly possible for feminists to disagree with orthodox premisses, then, but such disagreement involved a rejection of part or all of marxist economics as they were interpreted by defenders of the orthodox position, either on the grounds of theoretical inadequacy, or on the grounds of irrelevance to the analysis of women's work.[59]

Lastly, Smith's argument is not only interesting because it is a good example of how orthodox arguments worked, but also because he highlights some quite important characteristics of women's work, but fails to make much of them. The claims he makes about domestic labour are not only true—as pointed out above—but actually quite interesting, except that Smith is not motivated to pursue any of them. Thus it is true that women's work is performed regardless of whether workers are needed or not in the capitalist economy and that the motivation and quality of the work is quite different from that of the usual type of waged work: this should have interested feminists much more than it did, and on the basis of understanding these differences much better, they would also have been in a better position to question the usefulness of marxist theory. If women's work has such a different logic from the work marxists discussed, why should they continue to presume marxist theory is in a position

[57] See Gough 1972, 1973, Harrison 1973a, Howell 1975.

[58] See Elson 1979 and Steedman 1981 for contributions by orthodox and neo-Ricardian marxists, Roemer 1982 for a new and more systematic presentation of the labour theory of value as well as a discussion of its limitations, and any standard economics textbook for the neo-classical critique of it.

[59] Feminists could simply have insisted that they were interested in social rather than economic analysis and that they would use marxist concepts as part of such an analysis by suitably redeploying them. Again, however, this move was difficult to make for the feminist participants in the domestic labour debate because they thought of themselves as marxist feminists and because, more importantly, such a move would have implied the rejection of a central part of marxist methodology in social theory: its economic reductionism. As marxist political economy was understood at the time, social explanations would invariably refer back to the laws by which the capitalist economy functioned, notably the 'law of value'. (See e.g. Himmelweit and Mohun 1977, Seccombe 1974, Smith 1978.)

to understand it?[60] Furthermore, Smith also points out the difficulty in measuring women's work—a difficulty which will occupy me in Chapter 3—as well as the possibility of it becoming part of a 'consciously regulated economy', i.e. part of socially distributed work, again a claim which by itself could have led to the type of questions I asked in Chapter 1. Instead, however, like all the other orthodox participants in the debate, Smith was ultimately more interested in marxist theory than in providing a satisfactory account of women's work, using a form of argument which made it close to impossible for feminists not to respond to the level of conceptual discussion at which he and others, through the orthodox form of argument, pitched the whole question.

I shall now discuss briefly a second argument put forth by holders of the orthodox position which is interesting because it illustrates the conceptual nonsense that defenders of the orthodox position were prepared to endorse. The slavery argument—as I shall call this argument—is yet another argument that domestic labour cannot be conceived of as part of social production under capitalism. The argument goes as follows. The only way domestic labour could be part of social production under capitalism would be its complete socialization. Since social production under capitalism consists of commodity production, this would imply that workers were produced as commodities and sold like any other commodity on the market by their producers. Such socialized production, however, would be a form of slavery, since workers would cease to be owners of their persons and of their labour power given that they would be sold as commodities. Capitalism, however, is a mode of production based on the workers' selling of their labour power, hence on the formal freedom of workers. Therefore, the complete socialization of domestic labour is impossible under capitalism.[61]

The argument hinges on highlighting, in reference to Marx, a central presupposition of the legal and political system under capitalism, i.e. the freedom and self-ownership of workers as members of civil society, and the further assertion that the socialization of domestic labour is incompatible with this aspect of

---

[60] As I have started to argue and shall continue to argue below, women's work is best understood as care, not as production at all.

[61] See Carter 1975: 48; Himmelweit and Mohun 1977: 25.

the capitalist system. The mistake in the argument, however, lies precisely in the assertion of the incompatibility between these legal presuppositions of capitalism and the question whether domestic labour can be socialized. I shall argue that these two issues are completely independent of each other, and that this orthodox argument in fact points up the conceptual blinkers of defenders of the orthodox position.

Thus note, first, that there already exists 'socialized' provision by both state and private industry of the kind of work that women do in their homes. The beneficiaries of such work, however, in state or private institutions such as hospitals, prisons, crèches, children's homes, boarding schools, or old people's homes do not lose their freedom or self-ownership. There is no difference between privately or state run institutions at all with respect to their 'clients'' freedom or self-ownership, and if their 'clients' do lose their freedom, they lose it on grounds other than a form of slavery instituted by them.[62] What these institutions show, therefore, is that it is possible to 'socialize' domestic labour but maintain the freedom and self-ownership of its beneficiaries at least in principle and in all legal respects. The slavery argument is therefore inconclusive.

Secondly, however, it is interesting to note the real reason why the idea of a Brave New World-like capitalist production and reproduction of human beings is repulsive and which does give a true ring to the slavery argument. What is wrong about this idea is not so much the fact that the work is organized according to capitalist principles, but rather the fact that in this image people are produced like any other commodity.[63] If the analogy with commodity production is taken literally, that is, if people are produced, reproduced, and sold by someone other than themselves, they cannot be self-owners, since they are owned by the person who produced them. The definition of a commodity as

---

[62] Patients in mental hospitals who are sectioned lose their freedom on the ground of diminished responsibility, inmates of prisons on the grounds of forfeiture of their rights, and children are not allowed all the adult freedoms on the grounds of immaturity. None of these grounds changes their underlying moral status as free, self-owning persons, they only change their legal status temporarily.

[63] We might also be disturbed by the image of mass production, but capitalistically run institutions do not necessarily—nor even usually—imply more 'mass processing' than, say, state or charity run institutions.

an object which can be owned and exchanged, bought and sold, is directly opposite to our conception of persons as subjects who can own, buy, lend, and sell, but who cannot be owned by others. Hence persons cannot be commodities according to our modern understanding of personhood.[64] This is the consideration which lends the slavery argument plausibility, but the ground of the plausibility is not the capitalist form of production, but the commodity form of production, since it is the status of a commodity as an object that can be owned which is incompatible with the status of a free person who owns herself. Note, furthermore, that if private domestic labour is conceived as petty commodity production,[65] the slavery argument applies to private domestic labour as much as to 'socialized' domestic labour.[66]

Thirdly, there is a further reason for the plausibility of the slavery argument, but one that did certainly not occur to any participant in the domestic labour debate at the time nor even to theorists very much later.[67] This reason is that the very conception of the work that women do in their homes as *production* and/or reproduction of labour power is in itself a crucially misleading representation of their work. It is, of course, true that women are in a very literal, biological sense the 'producers' of human beings, but this is not the sense which marxists usually refer to since pregnancy or giving birth is not usually counted as work.[68] The work women do in their homes to benefit others, by contrast—which is the work discussed in the domestic

[64] It has recently been argued that there are no good reasons why persons could not sell themselves into slavery (see Nozick 1974 and Philmore 1982), but such arguments are obviously highly controversial (see e.g. Pateman 1988, ch. 3). It seems to me that the subject–object dichotomy forms a central part of our conception of personhood, and it is people's instrumental relationship to objects which confirms them to themselves and others as subjects (see also GR 911).

[65] As it is by Seccombe 1974.

[66] It is interesting that none of the participants in the domestic labour debate seems to have realized this point—is this because it was difficult to imagine women as fully-fledged, self-owning subjects and producers who would sell their product, labour power (and thus their husbands and children), on the labour market rather than as servants of their husbands and children? And does this by itself not point not only to the fact that women were not taken seriously as self-owners who would own whatever they produced in private, but also to the fact that the language of production is inadequately used in a theory of women's work (see my following point)?

[67] See e.g. Walby 1990 for continued usage of the vocabulary of 'production' and 'reproduction' of labour power.

[68] I have not seen any references to women's 'biological' production of human beings in the domestic labour debate literature.

labour debate—has very different features, and follows a very different logic, from work that can reasonably be described as production, especially as the production of objects.[69] I cannot argue this point here, but merely want to point out that the very language of 'production' seems inappropriate for describing women's work.[70]

The slavery argument, then, is not only inconclusive, it also points up the inadequacy of at least some of the marxist economic concepts in a theory of women's work: any of the concepts derived from the analysis of capitalist production as commodity production are clearly misleading, but arguably also those concepts linked to the marxist analysis of work as production. Defenders of the orthodox position, however, rather than admitting to the limitations of the conceptual framework they were defending, and to the consequent possibility that women's work had to be analysed in new and 'creative' ways, used these concepts in order to come up with spurious arguments that supposedly proved that domestic labour could not possibly be what feminists said it was. The slavery argument therefore shows the absurdities that defenders of the orthodox position got into in order to defend what they thought was the correct usage of terms. In none of their arguments is the possible need for a reinterpretation of marxist concepts conceived of, let alone acknowledged or seriously discussed.

In conclusion, the orthodox position was deeply inhibitive of any new and creative usage of marxist concepts. It achieved this doubtful aim through constant reference to what it implied was the correct interpretation of Marx's texts through what I have called the 'orthodox type of argument'. Feminists were thus forced into a discussion of marxist economics instead of getting ahead with their analysis of women's work. In contrast to the orthodox position, those participants in the debate who held the 'benefit position' were more open to at least some reinterpretation of Marx's own work in order to make sense of women's unpaid work in the home. I shall present this position in the following section.

[69] As I pointed out above, Smith (1978) is more perceptive about this point than anybody else, but unfortunately only in the course of pursuing his orthodox conclusions.

[70] I shall return to this point in Ch. 4 sect. ii, where I introduce my own theory of women's work as care.

(iv) *The benefit position presented*

The 'benefit position' unites several participants in the domestic labour debate who attempted to integrate the analysis of domestic labour into the analysis of the capitalist economy by conceiving of it as labour which benefits capital indirectly. This position, unlike the orthodox position, implied a reinterpretation of at least some marxist concepts and thus a rejection of at least some of the orthodox premises that characterized the orthodox position. Defenders of this position argued that domestic labour was not completely external to the capitalist sphere of production and, more specifically, that it was linked to it through a transfer of surplus labour from the domestic sphere to the capitalist sphere. This link was mediate in that capitalists did not directly extract surplus labour from domestic workers as they did in exploiting wage workers. Domestic labour nevertheless benefited capitalists in that the latter could appropriate more surplus value than they would have been able to had domestic work not been performed in the home. This asymmetric relation between capital and domestic workers was mostly conceived of as a form of unequal exchange mediated through the wage which capitalists paid (male) workers as heads of households. As I shall elaborate below, there were differences in the interpretation of this unequal exchange via the wage. Since all interpretations focused on the wage, and therefore on the concept of the value of labour power—which, according to Marx, is expressed in value terms in the worker's wage—I shall first introduce Marx's conception of the value of labour power before discussing these interpretations.

Marx's initial answer to the question of how the value of labour power is to be determined is that it is to be determined by its 'costs of production' like that of any other commodity.[71] Similarly, he asserts in *Capital*, vol. i, where he deals with this question most systematically, that

[t]he value of labour-power is determined, as in the case of every other commodity, by the labour-time necessary for the production, and consequently also the reproduction, of this specific article. In so far as it has value, it represents no more than a definite quantity of the average

[71] WLC 158–9.

social labour objectified in it. . . . Given the existence of the individual, the production of labour-power consists in his reproduction of himself or his maintenance. For his maintenance he requires a certain quantity of the means of subsistence. Therefore the labour-time necessary for the production of labour-power is the same as that necessary for the maintenance of its owner; in other words, the value of labour-power is the value of the means of subsistence necessary for the maintenance of its owner. . . . His means of subsistence must . . . be sufficient to maintain him in his normal state as a working individual.[72]

This simple starting-point is somewhat complicated by the 'historical and moral element' that enters the calculation,[73] that is, facts about the particular historical period, the general development of the economy of the country and the political power of the working class and their corresponding 'habits and expectations'.[74] A further 'complication' arises from the fact that workers are mortal, hence that their labour power has to be reproduced not only on a daily, but also on a generational basis:

The labour-power withdrawn from the market by wear and tear, and by death, must be continually replaced by, at the very least, an equal amount of fresh labour-power. Hence the sum of means of subsistence necessary for the production of labour-power must include the means necessary for the worker's replacements [*Ersatzmänner*], i.e. his children, in order that this race of peculiar commodity-owners may perpetuate its presence on the market.[75]

Marx does not consistently refer to the value of labour power as being determined by the costs of both daily and generational reproduction,[76] but it is probably safe to assume that Marx meant to imply the costs of generational reproduction whenever he discussed the reproduction of labour without including these costs explicitly. The 'reproduction' of *wives*—as contrasted with the reproduction of future generations of workers whom Marx implies

---

[72] *Cap.* i. 274–5.   [73] Ibid. 275.   [74] Ibid.; see also p. 701.
[75] Ibid. 275.
[76] Marx proceeds in the paragraphs following this quote to demonstrate how the value of labour power is calculated, summing up his preceding discussion by saying that '[t]he value of labour-power can be resolved into the value of a definite quantity of the means of subsistence' (*Cap.* i. 276). Whose subsistence is not discussed any further. For the value of labour power said to be determined by the means of subsistence see ibid. 430; *Cap.* iii. 306, 1006. For the value of labour power said to be determined by the costs of both daily and generational reproduction, see *Cap.* i. 518 and WLC 158–9; see also *Cap.* i. 717–18.

to be male[77]—is also only implied in the few formulations where Marx mentions that the value of labour power is determined 'not only by the labour time necessary to maintain the individual adult worker, but also by that necessary to maintain his family'.[78] Although there is a certain uncertainty, then, with regard to whose maintenance and/or reproduction is included in the calculation, Marx's basic idea is relatively simple: the value of labour power is determined by whatever it takes to produce and maintain it.

There is, however, a crucial ambiguity in Marx's account of the determination of the value of labour power between two formulations:

1. The *labour time* formulation: the value of labour power is to be determined by the labour time necessary for the production and reproduction of labour power.
2. The *value* formulation: the value of labour power is to be determined by the value of a certain sum of means of subsistence.

These two formulations are equivalent only in so far as the labour time necessary for the reproduction of labour power coincides with the time necessary for the production of the means of subsistence which go into the reproduction of labour power. Marx himself seems to have assumed such a coincidence since he uses the two formulations interchangeably, or derives one from the other, as in the following passage:

Suppose that this mass of commodities required for the average [daily reproduction] contains 6 hours of social labour, then every day half a day of average social labour is objectified in labour-power, or in other words half a day of labour is required for the daily production of labour-power.[79]

Assuming there is a particular 'basket of commodities' which goes into the daily subsistence of the worker (and his family?), this basket then determines the labour time necessary for the reproduction of labour power, since it is the labour time necessary to produce these commodities which determines their value and thus, by derivation, the value of labour power.

[77] See the quote above: the German original of 'worker's replacements' is 'Ersatzmänner' (substituting men) (*Cap*. i. 275). [78] Ibid. 518.
[79] Ibid. 276.

Marx's ambiguous formulations in his discussion of the determination of the value of labour power provided a fertile ground for conflicting accounts in the domestic labour debate. Thus defenders of the orthodox position insisted on the exclusive validity of the value formulation of the value of labour power, which was usually interpreted as referring to the value of commodities needed for the consumption of the whole family rather than that of the individual worker.[80] The argument for the value formulation was, of course, that any other time spent towards the reproduction of labour power, such as domestic labour, was neither social nor abstract labour and hence could not be expressed in value terms nor, consequently, enter the determination of the value of labour power.[81]

Some holders of the benefit position used the labour time formulation and argued that domestic labour was part of the labour time necessary to reproduce labour power, hence that it did enter into the determination of the value of labour power as part of the above-mentioned 'moral and historical element' in its determination.[82] Harrison supports this move as follows:

In any real capitalist system . . . not all of the labourer's subsistence will be produced under the capitalist mode of production. . . . housework is an important element in the subsistence of the worker and his dependents. In this situation the value of labour power is clearly not just the labour time involved in the production of the part of the worker's subsistence produced within the capitalist sector. We must also take account of labour performed outside the capitalist sector which contributes to the worker's standard of living.[83]

By focusing on the labour necessary to reproduce labour power, holders of the benefit position thus argued that domestic labour was part of this labour and could be a source of surplus labour which benefited capital: 'female domestic labour within the family is a source of surplus labour for capital as well as wage

[80] See Gardiner, Himmelweit, and Mackintosh 1975: 2, 7; Smith 1978: 216 n. 4.

[81] See Smith 1978, *passim*; Himmelweit and Mohun 1977: 23, 27–8; Gardiner, Himmelweit, and Mackintosh 1975: 7; see also sect. iii above.

[82] See Harrison 1973*b*: 41. I doubt that this interpretation of the 'moral and historical element' was in line with Marx's intentions, since Marx simply never took women's domestic work seriously into account and explicitly referred to very different kinds of factors in this passage (see *Cap.* i. 275). Whilst this is a good example of a new and creative usage of marxist terminology, it is unfortunately also infelicitous.

[83] Harrison 1973*b*: 41–2; see also Gardiner 1975: 53.

labour . . . the relative contributions of the different spheres of labour to capitalist profits will depend on the conditions of capitalist accumulation ruling at a particular time'.[84] More generally, therefore, capital benefited from more than one source within the capitalist mode of production: 'profits in the capitalist sector, being the difference between value added and the wage bill, are thus not equivalent to surplus value. They include both surplus labour performed within the capitalist sector (i.e. surplus value) and surplus labour performed within the housework sector.'[85]

Holders of the benefit position disagreed, however, over the conception of the mechanism responsible for the transfer of surplus labour from the domestic sphere to capital, depending on how orthodox was their interpretation of the concept of the value of labour power. If we distinguish between the level of subsistence of workers—which is dependent on the means of subsistence available as well as on the unpaid work of the housewife —and the value of their labour power, the disagreement pertains to the question whether the two are seen to coincide or not. According to Harrison's account, they do coincide because the labour time spent by the housewife has to be counted as part of the labour time necessary to reproduce labour power. The fact that the labour of the housewife at home contributes significantly to the level of subsistence but is unpaid thus allows the capitalist to pay wages below the value of labour power. The labour done by the housewife which goes towards the reproduction of the husband's labour power thus benefits the capitalist indirectly through a reduction in the level of wages: 'the mechanism by which this transfer of surplus labour from housework to the capitalist sector takes place is the payment by the capitalist *of wages below the value of labour power*.'[86]

Gardiner, by contrast, argues that the subsistence level and the value of labour power do not coincide. The unpaid performance of domestic labour, according to her, keeps the value of labour power below the level of subsistence of workers, and thus allows the capitalist to pay wages below the actual level of subsistence:

the contribution which domestic labour makes to surplus value is one of keeping down [the value of labour power] to a level that is lower

---

[84] Gardiner 1976: 114.   [85] Harrison 1973*b*: 43–4.   [86] Ibid. 43.

than the actual subsistence level of the working class. For example it could be argued that it is cheaper for capital to pay a male worker a wage sufficient to maintain, at least partially, a wife who prepares meals for him, than to pay him a wage on which he could afford to eat regularly at restaurants.[87]

As a third version of the benefit position, Dalla Costa may be included here, although she is not concerned with the intricacies of argument about the determination of the value of labour power. Her version, as I have indicated above,[88] assumes the equivalence of surplus labour and surplus value regardless of the sphere in which surplus labour is performed. She therefore claims that capital benefits from the surplus value produced by housewives—'housework is productive in the Marxian sense, that is, is producing surplus value'[89]—and that therefore women are exploited as housewives in the domestic sphere.

According to these different versions of the benefit position, then, the domestic sphere is not completely separate from the capitalist sphere, but is linked to it through the capitalist's payment of a wage to the worker.[90] This link results in a form of unequal exchange, since it enables capitalists to accumulate more surplus value than they could have had unpaid domestic work not been performed. Domestic labour was thus seen to be similar to labour performed in the subsistence economies in the periphery of capitalist production: both forms of labour contributed to capitalist accumulation through unequal exchange.[91]

---

[87] Gardiner 1976: 54; see also Gough and Harrison 1975: 4.

[88] See sect. ii above.   [89] Dalla Costa 1973: 53 n. 12.

[90] In fact, the domestic sphere was often analysed as a different mode of production, albeit one subordinate to the dominant, capitalist mode of production (see e.g. Gardiner 1976 and Harrison 1973a, 1973b). Whilst I cannot discuss the merits and demerits of this theoretical move, one aspect of it is worth noting: by conceiving of the domestic sphere as a separate mode of production, characterized by different relations of production, these theorists could resist the imposition by defenders of the orthodox position of the conceptual apparatus used to analyse the capitalist mode of production. Thus note Gardiner's insistence that, presuming a different mode and relations of production, 'forms of surplus labour other than surplus value have to be taken into account' (Gardiner 1976: 111). Gardiner, however, does not draw the further conclusion that, therefore, women may be exploited in a form other than through wage labour—nor does Harrison—but Delphy does (see Delphy 1984, Delphy and Leonard 1992, and Ch. 3 below).

[91] See Gardiner 1976 and Bennholdt-Thomsen 1981 for explicit comparisons.

Hence the marxist concepts used in new ways in Harrison's and Gardiner's accounts were the concept of unequal exchange as well as, to some extent, that of the value of labour power. Holders of the benefit position furthermore took the beneficial effect of this unequal exchange for capitalism to be an explanation of the continued existence of unpaid domestic labour, on which the exchange was based, and, by implication, an explanation of women's oppression in their homes.[92] I shall evaluate the benefit position in the next section.

(v) *The benefit position discussed*

The benefit position, despite making some headway in so far as a detailed analysis of domestic labour is concerned, is nevertheless inherently weak and also problematic in several ways. First, and most importantly with respect to the 'dynamics' of argument in the domestic labour debate, it was inherently vulnerable to orthodox rejoinders and criticism. Thus Dalla Costa's version can easily be rejected on the grounds that domestic labour is not productive labour in the Marxian sense and hence cannot produce surplus value.[93] Harrison's version is equally vulnerable, since he reinterprets the concept of the value of labour power by claiming that domestic labour time is part of the labour time necessary for the reproduction of labour power and hence contributes to the value of labour power. Since this claim presupposes that domestic labour and the labour embodied in the means of subsistence which are bought from the wage are commensurable, it can be rejected on the grounds that domestic labour, in contrast to the labour which goes into the (social) production of the means of subsistence, is neither abstract nor social since it is not subject to the law of value.[94] Even Gardiner's version can be rejected on orthodox grounds. Although she makes more allowance for the orthodox position by taking over the orthodox account of the value of labour power as being determined by the socially necessary labour which goes into the pro-

[92] See Molyneux 1979.   [93] See sect. ii above.
[94] See Himmelweit and Mohun 1977: 24–5; Gardiner, Himmelweit, and Mackintosh 1975: 7; Smith 1978, *passim*; Coulson, Magas, and Wainwright 1975: 62–3.

duction of the means of subsistence, her account still involves an analysis of women's domestic labour as social labour: in order to determine the amount of surplus labour which women perform in the home and from which capitalists are said to benefit, domestic labour has to be quantifiable. But, of course, it is not, according to the orthodox position, since it is not abstract labour.[95]

Now these criticisms could easily have been dismissed as irrelevant at best or as an indication of the limitations of orthodox marxist theory at worst. In so far as the holders of the benefit position considered themselves marxists and endorsed the marxist analysis of capitalism, however, they were in an unstable and inherently vulnerable position. In fact, it is probably such orthodox criticism which led the two main theorists, Gardiner and Harrison, to reassess their earlier claims in favour of more orthodox claims,[96] and this indicates just how vulnerable any theorist who saw herself as a marxist was to orthodox criticism. Resistance to such criticism therefore required either a more critical attitude towards marxist orthodoxy as such or at least a more critical attitude with regard to the question of the usefulness of marxist concepts to the analysis of women's work. Harrison, a marxist economist, is an example of the first alternative, since his analysis of domestic work was part of a critical discussion of 'unproductive' work (domestic work and work in the state sector) which culminated in the rejection of the marxist distinction between productive and unproductive labour.[97] Delphy, alone in this attitude for a long time, represents the second alternative, that is, the consciously critical break with marxist orthodoxy on feminist grounds.[98] Marxist feminists in general took a

[95] See sect. iii above.

[96] Gardiner, Himmelweit, and Mackintosh 1975: 6; Gough and Harrison 1975: 4. Note that Gardiner's initial position is to be found in Gardiner 1975, 1976, although these were published either later than or at the same time as the co-authored paper reassessing this initial position.

[97] Harrison 1973a, 1973b, Gough 1972, and Gough and Harrison 1975. Harrison explicitly rejects orthodoxy when he says that '[t]o insist on retaining a concept [that of productive labour, D.B.] *solely* because it is in Marx's writings is to reduce Marxism from the status of a science to that of a dogma' (Harrison 1973a: 81). Note, however, that even Harrison revised his interpretation of the value of labour power towards a more orthodox position (see n. 96 above).

[98] See Delphy 1984, Delphy and Leonard 1992; Delphy 1984 is a collection of papers which were written mainly in the 1970s. See also the collection of papers entitled, significantly, *The Unhappy Marriage of Marxism and Feminism* (Sargent 1986), and the by now famous quote by one of its contributors that '[t]he marriage of marxism and feminism has been like the marriage of husband and wife

long time to make that break: without explicitly addressing the possibility of a systematic clash between their marxist and feminist commitments, they were an easy target for orthodox arguments and easily won over.[99]

The second problem with the benefit position is that it has to make the highly questionable assumption that capitalists invariably pay family wages. Thus the claim that capitalism benefits from the domestic labour of women is only plausible if it is assumed that the 'value of labour power' includes the costs of reproduction not only of the workers themselves, but of their families. This assumption, however—although probably in line with Marx's own position[100]—is mistaken. It would be even more profitable for capitalists if they paid individual wages which provided only for the cost of reproduction of individual workers rather than for that of whole families.[101] Moreover, such payment of individual wages would force women to find work themselves since they could not subsist on the wage of their husbands and this, in turn, would further increase potential profits for capital: given more exploitable labour, it would potentially increase the aggregate sum of profits, and it would also potentially increase the rate of exploitation and hence capitalist accumulation through increased downwards pressure on wages by an increased reserve army of labour.[102] Hence once the presumption of a family wage is revealed, the case of the benefit position collapses. The family wage, rather than hiding a benefit, in fact constitutes a cost to capital which, according to Molyneux, is the outcome of successful working-class struggle at the end of the nineteenth century.[103] The institution of the family wage, then, is not in the least in the interest and to the benefit of capital, and the substance of the claims of the benefit position is plainly wrong.

The third problem with the benefit position relates to a sec-

---

depicted in English common law: marxism and feminism are one, and that one is marxism' (Hartmann 1986: 2).

[99] North American feminists seemed, on the whole, to have made the break earlier and more successfully than European feminists, probably because they were less steeped in marxist orthodoxy, or less deferential to it, than their sisters in the Old World and the heartland of old style marxism: see Sargent 1986, which was originally published in 1981.

[100] See my presentation of Marx on the value of labour power in the previous section.   [101] See Bruegel 1978: 7.

[102] See ibid. 6; Mandel 1975: 393.   [103] Molyneux 1979: 10–12.

ond functionalist claim: that is, that women's oppression is explained by the fact that their domestic labour is beneficial to capitalism. As many critics have pointed out, even if capitalism benefited from women's unpaid domestic work, this fact would nevertheless fail to explain why it is *women* who do this work rather than any member of the family, since the benefit from unpaid domestic work would accrue to capitalists regardless of who actually does it as long as it is unpaid.[104] Moreover, as Molyneux argues, there is nothing in this analysis to suggest that a more egalitarian distribution of domestic tasks between husbands and wives would be impossible or less 'beneficial' to capital. Hence the benefit position has certainly not shown that women's oppression is a necessary feature of capitalism.[105]

Fourthly, by focusing on the value of labour power as the link between women's domestic work and capital, the analysis of the benefit position tended to focus on that part of the domestic work which goes into the reproduction of the husband's labour power and thus excluded discussion of all other work that women do unpaid—not only child care,[106] but more generally any kind of care of members of the family or extended family that women provide. Given the approach of the benefit position, this is hardly surprising. While it may be argued that it is to the benefit of capital—although certainly not of individual capitalists who pay family wages—that women do all the unpaid work of child care and caring for the sick at home, since they thereby produce future generations of exploitable workers or render the sick fit for further exploitation by capital, the functional argument fails completely with regard to other forms of care. Thus it is hard to imagine how capital would benefit from women's care for their elderly parents or parents-in-law, or for other long-term dependants such as disabled or terminally ill members of the family, since such care will not even potentially result in exploitable labour power. Once the range of work, especially caring work, that women do is taken into account, therefore, the benefit position looks not only weak, but also beside the point: as in the

[104] Bruegel 1978: 5; Barrett 1980.   [105] See Molyneux 1979: 21.
[106] See Molyneux 1979: 21. One of Harrison's papers is a typical, but at least explicit, case in point: whilst he admits at an early point of his analysis that he is 'in effect abstracting from the problem of reproduction *at this stage* by assuming the family has no children', the topic of childcare remains unaddressed throughout the rest of his long paper (Harrison 1973b: 43, my emphasis).

slavery argument discussed above, the theorization of women's work is simply not adequate.

Finally, and most importantly, the benefit position shares with the orthodox position a preoccupation with relating the analysis of women's domestic work to the analysis of the capitalist mode of production, and thus more generally a rather uncritical endorsement of marxist theory. This uncritical attitude turned out to be deeply disabling to the feminist quest. Whilst holders of the benefit position made more creative usage of at least some marxist concepts than the defenders of the orthodox position, and thus were able to provide a more elaborate analysis of domestic labour instead of simply distracting from it,[107] they were nevertheless preoccupied with fitting their analysis into an already existing theory by looking at the link between domestic labour and capitalist accumulation. This focus obscured from view, and purged from the analysis, a discussion of the benefits that *men* might derive from women's unpaid labour,[108] and more generally an analysis of women's oppression by men.[109] It is worth reminding oneself, however, of the ironical fact that the domestic labour debate started off as the attempt to provide a marxist account not only of women's domestic labour, but also of women's oppression by men.

In conclusion, then, whilst the benefit position as compared to the orthodox position seemed at least to have made progress in providing a substantive analysis of women's work and its relation to the capitalist economy, its functionalist mode of argument was based on a false assumption, it failed to explain certain features of women's domestic work such as the fact that it was women who did it in the first place, and it obscured from view not only a lot of the work women do in the home, but also the point that capital might not be the sole beneficiary—if at all—of their work. In the last section, I shall draw more general conclusions for feminist theory and argument as well as rescue the concept of exploitation from the grip of marxist orthodoxy.

[107] See my criticism of the orthodox position in sect. iii above.

[108] Remarks about the benefit of women's work to men can be found in some contributions to the debate, but these remarks seem to have no weight in any of these writings (see e.g. Harrison 1973b, *passim*; Gardiner, Himmelweit, and Mackintosh 1975: 7). See also Molyneux (1979: 21–2) on this point.

[109] Again, the notable exception among all contributors to the debate is Delphy (see Delphy 1984, Delphy and Leonard 1992, and Ch. 3 below).

(vi) *Conclusion and outlook: the concept of exploitation reclaimed*

The two main positions in the domestic labour debate that I have discussed in this chapter proved ultimately to be weak and a dead weight which positively obstructed real progress in the feminist analysis of women's unpaid work. If anything can be learnt from the domestic labour debate at all, it is how not to get paralysed, side-tracked, and bogged down by attempting to solve the wrong problems.[110] As I have argued throughout this chapter, the main problem for the feminists who participated in this debate was their own allegiance to marxist theory and their on the whole uncritical acceptance of this theoretical framework. Looking through the marxist lens darkly, what feminists saw were the wrong connections and theoretical economic problems which had nothing to do with women's domestic work, instead of women's work more clearly. What they needed, but on the whole failed, to do was to take a more irreverent and discerning look at marxist theory and marxist concepts themselves: to take what seemed useful and leave what seemed irrelevant or obstructive. Growing up and out from underneath marxist patriarchal wings turned out to be hard work itself.

What, then, can be learnt from the domestic labour debate? First and foremost, it seems to me, what can be learnt by feminists is a healthy dose of scepticism toward any theoretical and conceptual framework which is not explicitly developed with a view to describing and explaining women's social position. While marxist theory in particular may have seemed a better starting-point for feminists than other theories—given its focus on the analysis of various forms of exploitation and oppression—it turned out not only to be fiercely guarded by those to whom any reinterpretation was anathema, but also to distract from questions that feminists needed to ask even if the theory was reinterpreted to some extent. Feminists thus needed to be discerning about what they could take over and use for their own

---

[110] I do not mean to underestimate the gain in terms of learning progress that can be had from such utter failures, but the actual discouragement engendered by such attempts should not be underestimated either—as I know from my own painful immersion into the domestic labour debate and marxist economics.

theoretical purposes. They needed to reject orthodoxy for orthodoxy's sake, and, more specifically, as I argued in the last sections, the use and/or interpretation of specific marxist concepts
such as that of commodity production or even production as a
model for women's work, the functionalist link of women's work
to capitalist accumulation and the interpretation of exploitation
as the extraction of surplus value. This, however, does not imply
that other parts of marxist theory would not have been of use.
I shall argue in the rest of this section that Marx's notion of
exploitation is a case in point.

Interestingly enough, Marx's theory of exploitation lends itself
much more easily to feminist purposes than the arguments of
the domestic labour debate would make one believe. Thus note,
to begin with, that Marx's concept of exploitation is necessarily
general because it is applied to several modes of production in
his historical materialism. Hence when Marx claims that all class-
divided societies are based on the exploitation of the immediate producers he has to use this general concept of exploitation.
In Marx's own words: 'What distinguishes the various economic formations of society—the distinction between for example a
society based on slave-labour and a society based on wage-
labour—is the form in which . . . surplus labour is in each case
extorted from the immediate producer, the worker.'[111] The implication of this claim is that exploitation occurs whenever surplus
labour is extracted (or 'extorted') from that class which produces
whatever needs to be produced.[112] The general concept of exploitation, according to this quote—which is representative of most if
not all of Marx's writing on exploitation—is therefore that of the
extraction of surplus labour, whilst it is also asserted that the extraction of surplus labour can occur in various forms. More specifically,
then, while exploitation takes the form of the extraction of surplus value from the workers in the capitalist mode of production, exploitation takes other forms in other modes of production.

Furthermore, Marx also thought that exploitation can occur in
more than one form in a given society even if one mode of production—and therefore the one form of exploitation which corresponds to it—is clearly predominant. Marx was in no doubt
that slavery in the Southern states of the USA implied the exploita-

[111] *Cap.* i. 325; cf. p. 680.
[112] Marx's use of 'the worker' is generic in this quote, not singular.

tion of slaves,[113] which consisted of the extraction of surplus labour from them.[114] There is, therefore, no reason to think, even on the basis of Marx's own writings, that exploitation cannot take several forms under the capitalist mode of production. Now, as I pointed out in section i, Marx himself never claimed that women were exploited nor did any marxist after him and before the domestic labour debate. The case of slavery under the capitalist mode of production sets an interesting example, however, that feminists could and should have taken as their starting-point. It also contradicts directly one of the unstated premisses of the orthodox position, namely that all exploitation in a capitalist society takes place under capitalist relations of production and consists of the extraction of surplus value through wage labour[115] and the consequent claim that women's work is not exploited because it does not take place under capitalist relations of production. It could be replied, of course—and no doubt would have been replied by holders of the orthodox position had this point been made—that slaves, unlike women, take part in social production since they produce commodities for the market.[116] The point, however, is that Marx's treatment of the case of slavery could have been read as allowing for various forms of exploitation even in societies in which a particular mode of production with its particular form of exploitation was predominant. Or, even more simply, his concept of exploitation could have been used in an analysis of women's work. How much of marxist orthodoxy in addition to this claim, or in addition to Marx's notion of exploitation, feminists should have taken on board is a separate question and should be answered according to how useful such orthodoxy is for their own purposes. If it helps them articulate their 'hunch' that women are exploited in doing all the unpaid work they do, it is useful and can be taken on board. If it is obstructive, however, and prevents them from making any headway, as the imagined orthodox rejoinder clearly does, it should simply be ignored.

In conclusion, then, feminists could have used (some of) Marx's thought for their own purposes, and they could certainly have used the general concept of exploitation that can be found in his

---

[113] *Cap*. iii. 509, 940.   [114] *Cap*. iii. 940.   [115] See sect. ii above.
[116] Strictly speaking, according to orthodox interpretation, only slaves working on the fields do, domestic slaves do not. Marx never made the distinction.

work. It is thanks to the fierceness and relentlessness of orthodox rejoinders as well as to the generally uncritical marxist alle-
giances of the feminist participants in the domestic labour debate
that only one of the participants—Delphy—ended up taking such
an instrumental stance toward marxist theory.[117] I shall discuss her theory of women's exploitation as wives in the next
chapter.

[117] It is interesting to note that holders of the benefit position, despite arguing that capital benefits from women's surplus labour in the home, never claimed
that women were exploited in performing it, even though, by definition (of the
general concept of exploitation), anybody who performs surplus labour is exploited! (See also n. 85 above.)

3

Delphy and Leonard:
The Exploitation of Women as Wives

Unlike the marxist and marxist feminist participants in the domestic labour debate, Christine Delphy set out in the early 1970s to discuss women's work on her own materialist terms rather than on the dogmatic marxist terms that hindered so many feminist accounts from focusing on women's oppression by men fairly and squarely.[1] This shift introduces a different focus of enquiry as well as different conceptions of women's work and exploitation. In the terms of my discussion of the domestic labour debate in the last chapter, what Delphy did was to develop a *specific* conception of exploitation, based on Marx's general concept of exploitation, but aimed specifically at elucidating women's exploitation by men. Subsequent to Delphy's initial work, Delphy and Leonard recently published a much more elaborate version of Delphy's early arguments. I shall base my discussion on this most recent work by Delphy and Leonard.[2] After introducing the main aspects of their theory of women's exploitation (section i), I discuss the function of theories of exploitation in general in order to prepare the ground for a discussion of Delphy and Leonard's theory (section ii). I then discuss the two main difficulties that Delphy and Leonard, like any theorist of women's exploitation, face (section iii). Delphy and Leonard can then be understood as responding to these difficulties by reinterpreting the notion of exploitation, but with the effect that their new notion of exploitation is not recognizably about exploitation any

---

[1] Apart from her first, widely circulated and widely discussed pamphlet, *The Main Enemy*, a collection of her writings (including 'The Main Enemy') was published in Delphy 1984.

[2] Delphy and Leonard 1992. This latest version of Delphy's theory, whilst being more elaborate and complemented by an extensive section reporting empirical support for the theory, can nevertheless be seen as a systematization and elaboration of her early claims rather than as a substantially new theory.

more (section iv). Their theory of exploitation has further problems, however, mainly based on the outdated model of family
relations and family obligations that they have to presuppose
(section v). I therefore conclude that their theory does not provide us with an appropriate understanding of women's exploitation (section vi).

(i) *Delphy and Leonard's theory of women's exploitation*

Delphy and Leonard conceive of their theory of women's exploitation in explicit contradistinction to the narrowly orthodox marxist claims and arguments of the domestic labour debate:[3]

many accounts of women's oppression which call themselves marxist
or marxist feminist are not in fact true to the spirit of marxism. Instead
they have taken over a series of dogmas developed since Marx's death
which have become marxist orthodoxy (or orthodox marxism), and tried
to develop these in various ways to explain women's oppression by
connecting it to capitalism.[4]

Delphy and Leonard claim to be developing an analysis which
is 'true to the spirit of marxism' in that it focuses on social
inequality and the causal mechanisms which produce and reproduce it.[5] This approach, according to them, 'shows yet again, in
a new field, how productive marxist methodology can be. But
neither we nor anyone else can stick to the letter of Marx's own
writings if we want to understand the oppression of women,
since this did not concern him'.[6] They thus call their theory
'marxist' and 'materialist' while making it clear, however, that
the marxist concepts they use have to be understood and interpreted in new ways in order to account for women's oppression.

Their main claim is, then, that it is men—rather than capitalists—who oppress women in the family and who exploit women
by benefiting from women's unpaid work in the home: 'Within
the family in our society, women are dominated in order that

---

[3] I shall use the terms 'orthodox marxist' or 'dogmatic marxist' interchangeably throughout this chapter specifically to refer to what I termed the 'orthodox
position' in the domestic labour debate in the preceding chapter, since it is this
position that Delphy and Leonard oppose.
[4] Delphy and Leonard 1992: 29; see Delphy 1984: 160–1.
[5] Delphy and Leonard 1992: 36–7.   [6] Ibid. 3.

their work may be exploited and because their work is exploited. . . . although capitalism may benefit indirectly, it is men who are the major, direct beneficiaries of the familial oppression of women.'[7] The family, moreover, represents a specific mode of production with its own characteristic relations of production. Women are located in this mode of production either as daughters, sisters, or mothers of the (male) head of the household, i.e. via kinship relations, or they enter it as wives through marriage.[8] Whilst kinship relations may still be relevant in some families, however, the main way in which, in the age of the nuclear family, women do unpaid work for men is undoubtedly as wives. I shall focus on this case in the following discussion.[9]

The relations of production in family households consist of the dominant position of the male head of the household, who has an obligation to provide maintenance to all members of the household, and of the subordinate position of all other members whose labour is appropriated by the head, that is, who work for the head without being paid: 'family relationships are essentially hierarchical and comprise an exploitative system—but a system with a structure and a process very different from that of the (also but differently exploitative) market system'.[10] The main

---

[7] Ibid. 18.

[8] Delphy and Leonard include less formal, quasi-marital relationships such as those of cohabiting heterosexual couples in their analysis since, according to them, the social constraints for such couples are more or less the same as those for married couples: 'Individuals can make choices about which partner to marry [or to set up a household with, D.B.], and they choose as a couple how to organize their lives within marriage (to an extent) . . . But they do not choose the nature of marriage, kinship, age divisions or heterosexual relations. These, like the language of their country, they are born into and have to "speak". The family as a system in space and in time is a social institution which pre-exists them and sets parameters to their choices.' (Ibid. 265–6; see also pp. 14, 18, 116–18.) I should therefore be taken to imply reference to cohabitees as well as wives whenever I refer to wives for reasons of economy.

[9] Delphy and Leonard's theory covers exploitation in the family, hence the exploitation not only of women as wives, but also of all other family members, by the head of the household. Their theory therefore covers not only the exploitation of women (*qua* wives, mothers, unmarried sisters), but also the exploitation of men *qua* younger brothers as well as the exploitation of children. The exploitation of women as wives is a special case which has some additional features that the other forms lack, according to Delphy and Leonard: wives' sexual servicing of husbands, their taking on the main burden of child care. The exploitation of women as wives is, however, the main focus both of their and of my own discussion, and I shall therefore not discuss their theory with regard to other family members. [10] Ibid. 110.

difference between exploitation through the wage labour system and exploitation in the family, according to Delphy and Leonard, is that exploitation in the market is mediated by an exchange relationship between employer and worker, whilst exploitation in the family is based on the members' economic dependency on the head of the household as well as the distinctly and independently defined respective obligations of family heads and members. Unlike in an exchange relationship, there is therefore no link between the work family members do and the benefits they receive:

Dependants' maintenance (and inheritance) is not handed out in exchange for the work they do . . . It is rather a duty of their family head. He is obliged to provide for their basic needs. But he may give them a good deal more than this if he is able to and if he chooses to. On the other hand, he is obliged to support them even if they are sick or disabled and unable to work, or if they refuse to work.

The level of maintenance dependants receive is, in turn, also independent of the work they do. They must work for their household head and respect him whether he is generous or mean and whether he earns a huge salary or a pittance. . . . whatever the maintenance provided, wives are always obliged to do family work.[11]

Wives, then, unlike workers, cannot *demand* anything in return for the work they do for their husbands: their relation to their husbands is one of personal dependence.

Women may gain a measure of material independence by also engaging in waged work, but, even in this case, Delphy and Leonard point out that they

are still obliged to perform unpaid family work to the extent that it is needed. They must either do family work on top of their job, or replace their family services from their earnings. Their conditions of employment are therefore conditioned by their family obligations, and family obligations are used as a pretext by employers to exploit those with the status of family dependant.[12]

Hence wives have a price to pay for wanting to earn their own money: either a double burden of paid and unpaid work, or they lose most of their earnings through having to pay others to do the child care and/or housework they would otherwise have had to do themselves.

[11] Delphy and Leonard 1992: 111–12.　　　　[12] Ibid. 112–13.

The family, according to Delphy and Leonard, is thus the major site of women's oppression which determines their overall material position as an oppressed and exploited class. Within the family, they have to perform unpaid work and often consume (and inherit) substantially less than men. Furthermore, their disadvantaged position in the family also determines women's material position and options outside the family in the labour market so that they lose twice from being oppressed and exploited in their homes.

Delphy and Leonard illustrate and support their theory by reference to several studies covering different social sectors, such as French farming households—the original subject of Delphy's research—several studies of English working-class life, as well as a study of wives of men in very diverse, but mostly middle- and upper middle-class occupational brackets, such as doctors, academics, architects, writers, lawyers, diplomats, politicians, managers, businessmen, shopkeepers, police.[13] It is clear from all these studies that wives do work for their husbands, and that the work they do is unpaid. Their work is also extremely varied because it mainly answers to the specific requirements of a particular husband's occupation or business. Moreover, it is the requirements of their husbands and children (and other family members who may need their care) for unpaid work which determine whether and how much wives can take up paid work themselves. The pattern of women's work is thus determined not on the basis of their own material needs and security, but on the basis of the needs of the rest of the family. This fact illustrates the subordinate, subservient, and dependent position that women enter upon marriage. It also explains why women's work at home is so invisible: 'The work which wives do for their husbands' occupations, for men's leisure activities, and for their emotional and sexual well-being, gets completely lost sight of because it is so varied, so personalized and so intimate.'[14] Whilst women's performance of unpaid work in their homes is thus not easily 'seen', it is nevertheless a fact that Delphy and Leonard are well capable of illustrating by pointing to a wealth of research material as well as common-sense knowledge.

With respect more narrowly to a conception of women's

[13] Ibid. part III.   [14] Ibid. 226.

exploitation, Delphy and Leonard argue against orthodox marxists that exploitation via the wage labour system and the appropriation of surplus value, that is, exploitation as it is conceived of under capitalism by both Marx and marxists after him, is not the only form in which it can exist.[15] They point out correctly that

[i]n non-capitalist systems ... the extortion of surplus labour does not necessarily go through an initial monetary transaction (that is, the sale of products incorporating surplus labour). Labour may be used directly by whoever extorts it. For example, a slave owner can directly consume the labour of a slave to give him a massage or build a house. Nor are labourers necessarily given a wage with which to pay for their upkeep. They may be given 'protection' and land on which to grow their own food (as in serfdom), or food, housing and clothing directly and with little or no choice in what they consume (as in slavery and, though it is less apparent, in the family).[16]

They thus make the right move against orthodox marxists in insisting that exploitation can and does take more than one form. They also assert correctly that

Appropriating the products of other people's work via owning the means of production is a subterfuge to steal indirectly (part of) the labour owned by its purveyor. But this labour can be, has been in past economic systems, and is still in various existing systems, 'stolen' directly. Owning the means of production is unnecessary if you own slaves or serfs or wives and children.[17]

Exploitation, then, is the extraction of (unpaid or otherwise unremunerated) labour from those who are exploited to the benefit of the exploiter. In the specific case of interest here, it is the extraction of unpaid labour from women by and to the benefit of men.[18]

More specifically, according to Delphy and Leonard, this exploitation takes place in the family mode of production, and

---

[15] Delphy and Leonard 1992, ch. 2. Recall that it was one of the main claims of the orthodox position in the domestic labour debate that exploitation under capitalism takes the form of extraction of surplus value. [16] Ibid. 41.

[17] Ibid. 43.

[18] I discuss Delphy and Leonard's notion of exploitation in more detail in sect. iv.

it is men *qua* husbands who extract labour from women *qua* wives. Furthermore, men extract labour from women in the home because they own their wives' labour power. Thus Delphy and Leonard summarize their conception of familial exploitation as follows:

The specific exploitation of family workers is not based on the extortion of surplus value but rather on the fact that their labour is not 'free'.... Family subordinates do not own their labour power in the same way as heads of households, and so cannot sell it, or can sell only some of it—and then they do not fully own the money received. *The specificity of family work is that the worker's whole work capacity is appropriated;* that it is appropriated by a particular individual from whom it is difficult or impossible to separate; and that the worker is not paid but maintained.[19]

Delphy and Leonard's theory of women's exploitation thus consists of two key claims. They claim that

1. Men *qua* husbands exploit women *qua* wives.[20]
2. It is the specific relations of production women enter—the husband's appropriation of his wife's labour power—which determine their exploitation.

Now compare claim (1) to the following more general claim:

3. Men (as a social group) exploit women (as a social group).

It is worth noting that even if claim (1) is false—as I shall argue below it is—claim (3) may still be true since it is possible to point to social institutions (or arrangements) other than that of marriage which would render claim (3) true.[21] Thus it may be the case that all men are capitalists and all women are wage workers. In this case, claim (3) is true although claim (1) is not. Similarly, we might imagine a society in which only women can have the status of slaves and only men that of slave owners: thus men as slave owners would exploit women as slaves, rendering claim (3) true, but claim (1) false. There are, in other words, several possible social orders, arrangements, or institutions which can make the general claim that men exploit women

---

[19] Ibid. 159 (my emphasis).
[20] 'Men *qua* husbands' includes reference to men cohabiting with women (see n. 8 above).
[21] I use 'social institutions' here in a wide sense which is inclusive of economic institutions as a subclass of social institutions.

true. Claim (1) specifies only one of these, and its falsity does not imply that men do not exploit women.

Claim (2) asserts the crucial role of the relations of production in the household in women's exploitation. I have chosen the vague formulation of relations of production 'determining' women's exploitation because quite what their role is will be a subject of further discussion below.[22] All I want to do here is to note that claim (2) has an important place in Delphy and Leonard's theory of women's exploitation. Before I can discuss Delphy and Leonard's theory, however, I have to take a step back and look at theories of exploitation more generally.

(ii) *Exploitation stories*

In this section I shall analyse the function of theories or 'stories' of exploitation, when such stories become necessary and which aspects are particularly important. This general analysis will, in the following sections, serve to illuminate the specific issue at hand, that is, women's exploitation.

To begin with, I would like to take a quick look at already existing claims and theories of exploitation, notably Marx's own claims about the exploitation of various classes in the course of history. When Marx claimed that exploitation takes place in all class-divided societies he had to be able to show that in all class-divided societies there is a particular form of exploitation of one class by another. Hence, given that, as I argued above,[23] Marx's general concept of exploitation was that of the extraction of surplus labour from the oppressed class by the ruling class, he had to show, for each mode of production, that there is a particular mechanism based on particular social institutions which brings it about that the ruling class can appropriate the surplus labour of the oppressed class.

Now there is only one mode of production in which the social institutions are such that exploitation is easily recognizable. In the feudal mode of production, the performance of surplus labour is spatially and temporally distinct and can easily be pointed out: serfs work for their lords, and the products of their labour are appropriated by their lords, whenever they do corvée, that

---

[22] See sect. v.   [23] Ch. 2 sect. viii.

is, work on the lord's demesne for the lord's benefit. The rest of
the time they work for themselves and enjoy the fruits of this
labour. There is thus a clear distinction between the labour they
do for their own benefit and the labour they do for their lord
because the latter takes place on different plots of land. There
is a corresponding clear distinction between serfs' labour and
their surplus labour, and it is obvious, therefore, that serfs are
exploited when they do corvée.[24] As long as lords manage to
enforce the serfs' performance of corvée, then, it is also obvious
that they exploit their serfs. I shall call this particular form of
exploitation the 'paradigm case' of exploitation because the fact
of exploitation itself is obvious.

Exploitation is not as obvious, however, in the capitalist mode
of production. As Marx stresses, under capitalist relations of production, it looks as if the workers are remunerated for all their
work, that is, as if they did not perform any surplus labour,
whereas in reality some of their labour is appropriated by the
capitalists in the form of surplus value.[25] This, in fact, is Marx's
great discovery: capitalism, according to him, is a system which
is based on the exploitation of workers although it disguises this
very fact at the same time. Now since exploitation is not obvious under capitalism Marx is forced to tell what I shall call an
'exploitation story' which will make plausible the fact that, despite
appearances to the contrary, wage workers are exploited by capitalists. The 'story' he tells—that is, his theory of exploitation
under capitalism—points to the fact that capitalism as an economic system is based on the generation of surplus value which
is appropriated and reinvested by capitalists. However, the story
continues, this surplus value is in fact produced by the workers
and constituted by the surplus labour that workers perform not
to their own benefit, but to the benefit of the capitalist. The capitalist mode of production, the story concludes, is therefore based
on the systematic exploitation of wage workers.[26]

[24] If the surplus labour is extracted in the form of 'rent in kind' or 'money
rent', the performance of surplus labour is not distinct anymore, but it is still
obvious that the lord appropriates some of the serfs' labour by appropriating
some of the products of their labour or some of the money that they earned by
selling the products of their labour. See Marx, *Cap*. iii, ch. 47; *Cap*. i. 680; also
Cohen 1978: 332–4.   [25] *Cap*. i. 680.
[26] I do not mean to downplay Marx's theoretical achievements: of course, the
'story' is much more intricate and takes up most of *Capital* vol. i. The point I

More generally, exploitation stories are required whenever a claim of exploitation is not obviously true. Not every case of exploitation has to be obvious, then, but if it is not, an exploitation story has to be provided to make the claim of exploitation plausible. Now there are at least two factors which necessitate exploitation stories because they obstruct an appropriate understanding of the material reality of various social classes or groups. First, the mechanism by which surplus labour is extracted may not be obvious, and therefore it is not obvious that exploitation takes place: material inequality can have causes other than exploitation. Secondly, the material status of an exploited group or class (and that of the exploiters) may not be clear because of too much variability among them.[27] Of the two factors, the second one is less important because if the mechanism by which surplus labour is extracted is either clear (as in the case of slavery) or can be reconstructed in an exploitation story (as in the case of capitalism) it is clear that the material status of those from whom the surplus labour is extracted is that of being exploited while the material status of those who appropriate or benefit from the surplus labour is that of exploiters. If, however, the mechanism by which surplus labour is extracted cannot be reconstructed, any exploitation claim which is not obvious fails. The

want to make here is that Marx's theory of capitalist accumulation can be understood as just such an exploitation story.

[27] By 'material status' I refer to the position somebody or a social group or class have with regard to the labour burdens they incur and the material benefits they enjoy. Thus, by definition, if a person or a social group or class are exploited their labour burdens exceed their benefits, and conversely, if a person or social group or class are exploiters their benefits exceed their labour burdens. The concept of 'material status' can only be a very tentative and rough and ready measure, however, since it assumes the comparability of labour burdens and material benefits. (I shall address this question in section iii below.) Furthermore, it is reliable only in the special case in which people have only one exploitation status, that is, are either exploited or exploiters, but cannot be both. It thus precludes the existence of more than one system of exploitation in regard to which people can occupy different places. This last point is not a problem for orthodox marxists since they deny just that possibility, but it is for anybody who wants to keep an open mind. (Correspondingly, marxist feminists have been distinguished from socialist feminists in reference to their (theoretical) unwillingness to consider several independent systems of exploitation: see Jaggar 1983.) See also my discussion of the systematic variation introduced in women's material status by their location with respect to various social divisions (class, ethnicity, sexual orientation) in sect. iii below. If material status is thus unmeasurable, the exploitation story bears the whole burden of proof in an exploitation claim: see this and the following paragraph.

reconstruction of the mechanism of exploitation is, therefore, the most crucial part of the exploitation story, although the existence of material inequality—that is, obviously distinct and opposed material statuses—certainly plays a role in confirming that exploitation does take place.

Correspondingly, there are two main ways in which exploitation can be obvious, but one is more conclusive than the other. First, if there is an obvious transfer of unremunerated labour or of the products of that labour from the labourer to somebody else—or from one class to another class—that is, if there is an obvious mechanism by which labour is extracted, it is obvious that exploitation takes place, and the material status of exploiter and exploited follows from the places people occupy with regard to that mechanism. Thus in the feudal 'paradigm case', the mechanism of exploitation is obvious and the corresponding material statuses can easily be inferred. In fact, the feudal case is a paradigm case precisely because the exploitative mechanism is obvious. Secondly, if the material status of a person or class is obviously skewed towards heavy burdens of labour or obviously skewed towards massive benefits, exploitation is likely to be the cause. Thus compare, for example, the material situation of the industrial proletariat with that of their employers in the nineteenth century. Obviously skewed material statuses, however, have to be confirmed by an exploitation story if the claim of exploitation is to be conclusive.[28] Thus while obvious material inequality makes the occurrence of exploitation likely and plausible, the pointing out of the mechanism of exploitation confirms that the material inequality exists *because* of exploitation. Both factors, then, play an important role in exploitation stories, although the reference to the exploitative mechanism is ultimately decisive.

(iii) *Two problems with claims about women's exploitation*

The difficulty with claims about women's exploitation, following the general analysis of exploitation stories in the last section,

---

[28] The starkness of material inequality, i.e. of the difference between material statuses, and the subsequent dawning upon workers that there might be a systematic relation between the wealth of the capitalist and their own poverty, is beautifully captured in Sergej Eisenstein's early caricature of class struggle in pre-revolutionary Russia, his film *Strike*.

is not only that the mechanism by which women are exploited is not obvious, but also that women's material status is unclear for two reasons. The first reason is that there are difficulties with quantifying and making commensurable women's burdens and benefits. The second reason is that women's work burdens and enjoyment of benefits vary immensely. I shall discuss these two problems with assessing women's material status in this section before moving on to discuss Delphy and Leonard's response to these problems in the following section.

The first problem is that, given that most of women's unpaid work is not in any way part of the market economy, it is not clear how it can be measured.[29] Whilst some women work unpaid in their husbands' businesses, whether farms or other small businesses, and thus produce for the market, most unpaid work is not even indirectly part of the market nexus. The advantage of a market economy is that it puts a price on any labour, service, or product that is offered and bought in it. Participation in the market thus guarantees the quantifiability and commensurability of benefits and burdens of particular people or classes, even if the process by which prices are determined is skewed in various ways. Bad quantification, it would seem, however, given the problem at hand, is better than none, and in so far as exploitation is not visible, quantification and comparison of benefits and burdens seem indispensable to any claim of exploitation. But the problem with women's unpaid work is that it is difficult to see how it could be quantified as a burden, as much as it is difficult to see how the benefits deriving from it for others could be quantified as long as these benefits are distributed within the household. So how can women be shown to be exploited at all?

There are in principle two possible ways to measure women's benefits and burdens, both, however, saddled with difficulties. The first way is to price both women's labour and the benefits they enjoy (in so far as they are produced within the household) at market rates. Thus the burden of women's unpaid work at home might be priced in terms of opportunity costs (income

---

[29] This problem affects the measurement of the (male) serf's, slave's, or wage worker's material position, too, in so far as their material position benefits from women's unpaid work. Marx and most if not all marxists after him have overlooked this problem because of their male-biased focus on 'material production' and/or the economy at the exclusion of women's unpaid work.

from paid work forgone),[30] or it might be priced according to the price this kind of work could command in the labour market.[31] Both these methods, however, are problematic. The actual paid work forgone may be a typical low-paid women's job—if, however, women had real equal opportunities, it might well have been the career job that the woman in question decided not to pursue because she was planning on having children and she knew she had to choose between one or the other. This measure is therefore systematically distorted precisely because most women are either barred from pursuing the best-paid types of jobs or they do not choose such jobs in the first place because of their incompatibility with 'family responsibilities'. Similarly, as far as the second alternative is concerned, the kind of work women do unpaid in their homes is usually deemed low skilled and badly paid compared to 'men's' work precisely because it is 'women's' work. Hence market prices may not reflect 'real' value, but depressed value because of the gendered nature of the work, the comparatively low bargaining power of women workers, and because of discriminatory trade union strategies in the past.[32] Both measures are therefore problematic. However, pricing both labour and benefits makes them at least commensurable.

The second way of measuring women's benefits and burdens is the Marxian alternative of measuring both in terms of labour values, that is, to compare the time women work in the home (and outside) with the time embodied in the goods they have access to or consume. This is feasible in principle, as a rough and ready kind of comparison, but a reliable quantification is only possible with the concept of a market equilibrium which determines labour values.[33] Women's work in their homes, however, does not necessarily and not even usually produce goods or consist of services which ever reach the market. Both methods of quantifying and comparing women's benefits and burdens are therefore riddled with difficulties.

[30] See e.g. Joshi's work on the 'cost of caring' (Joshi 1992).
[31] See e.g. Chadeau 1985 and Waring 1989: 277 ff.
[32] See Phillips and Taylor 1980; Walby 1986.
[33] See Roemer's theory of exploitation where the expression of exploitation in terms of labour values is a special, but market equilibrium dependent case of his more general theory of exploitation (Roemer 1982, 1988).

The second problem, however, is even more intractable. The problem is that there is so much variation in women's burdens and benefits that any generalization is at least problematic.

Note, to start with, that women's work-loads vary enormously. They depend on a number of factors:

1. On the *number and age of children* who have to be cared for. The younger the children are, the more care and attention they need. Also, their needs add substantial amounts of housework (washing, preparation of meals, cleaning and tidying up) to the child care itself and the usual amount of domestic work needed by a childless couple. The work-load related to children tends to decrease with increasing age of the children. Once they have entered state institutions such as kindergartens (if available), pre-school education, and school, the burden of the carer gets reduced from a twenty-four-hour job to one of hours per day. New needs arise, however, at that age, since children may have to be transported to various places and events, their homework has to be attended to, and their very experience with institutions and the public may require occasional interventions, and certainly also understanding and a caring response.

2. On whether the household includes other *members of the family who have to be cared for*, such as elderly parents and long-term sick or disabled members of the family. Again the work burden can be a matter of a few hours per week, or it can be a twenty-four-hour job, as it is with confused or very frail elderly people.

3. On the *occupation and source of income of the husband*. As Delphy and Leonard have pointed out, some households which are at the same time units of production, such as farm households and small businesses located in households, require the unpaid work of the wife to function and produce sufficient income. Alternatively, men may have occupations which require the occasional or regular co-operation and services of wives to be well executed and/or to allow them to rise in the career ladder.[34]

4. On the *willingness of the husband to 'help out'* with some of the work. Some 'new men' may be willing to take on an

---

[34] Delphy and Leonard 1992, ch. 9, and Finch 1983.

equal share of the work-load in the home, but time budget studies suggest that men's share in housework and care is still significantly lower than that of their wives, even if their wives hold down full-time paid jobs, too.[35] Furthermore, most men's jobs are not flexible enough to allow them to accommodate a substantial share in child care or other care if needed.[36]

5. On whether women have *access to either paid or unpaid work of others* to relieve or replace them. Access to the paid work of others obviously depends on the availability of material resources or on the availability of publicly provided care, while access to unpaid work depends usually on whether close relatives (mothers, sisters, daughters) are nearby or members of the household.

6. On whether women engage in *paid work* in addition to the unpaid work they perform at home. It is a consistent finding of domestic work studies that women who have paid work outside their home reduce their domestic work burden to some extent.[37] However, it is significant that the work-load of 'working' wives (i.e. women who perform both unpaid and paid work) is the absolutely highest work-load of all women. It should also be noted that women's engagement in paid work is constrained by the requirements for unpaid work (care and servicing their husbands) they face. Lastly, it is significant that only paid work not only burdens women but also provides them with a source of material benefits which is (to some extent) under their control.[38]

7. On women's *ethnic identity*. Membership in ethnic minority groups can mediate women's work burdens in many ways

[35] See Pleck 1985: employed wives have an 'overload' (compared to men) of 1.3 to 2.4 hours per day (seven days a week). These data are from studies of the late 1960s and early 1970s (p. 33). Later studies confirm the pattern, but find slightly higher contributions by husbands (p. 40). See also Hartmann 1987 and Meissner *et al.* 1988.

[36] This fact has been called the 'breadwinner trap' by Pleck 1985: 54.

[37] See Hartmann 1987; Meissner *et al.* 1988.

[38] See Delphy and Leonard on this point: they argue that women's income is often not completely under women's control since part of it may have to be spent on 'buying themselves out' of existing unpaid work-loads such as child care or housework which they would have had to take on had they not been able to pay somebody else (usually another woman) to do it (Delphy and Leonard 1992: 144 and *passim*).

and both directions: such groups are on the whole materially less well off and have less access to well-paid jobs,
hence women would have less occasion to 'buy themselves
out'. They may also tend to have more children and more
work obligations to members of the extended families. On
the other hand, they may have more access to unpaid work
by other women through their extended families or neigh-
bourhood networks. There is also much variation between
different ethnic minority groups.

8. On women's *sexual orientation*. Lesbian couples tend to share
   their unpaid work burdens more evenly than heterosexual
   couples, hence their work-load would tend to be less than
   that of heterosexual women.[39] They are also less likely to
   have children and tend to have fewer children than heterosexual couples, hence fewer care obligations.[40]

Women have some control over some of these factors, hence
have some control over their work burden, but their control may
also be significantly restricted. Thus without access to birth control, the number of children is out of women's control. Without
access to respite care or more extensive forms of socially provided care, women may be stuck with being the main carers of
family members dependent on their care.[41] Some husbands are
more open to negotiation and argument about work-loads than
others. Access to the unpaid work of others may depend on
women insisting on staying close to their family of origin, which
in turn may depend on women's bargaining power in their marriage, while access to the paid work of others depends on the
level of income women can achieve by taking up paid work
themselves, on the willingness and ability of the husband to pay
for the services of others, or on state provision. Further systematic variation in work burdens is introduced by women's differential location with respect to social divisions such as class,

[39] See Blumstein and Schwartz 1983.

[40] Women's sexual orientation does not introduce any difficulty for Delphy
and Leonard's theory since they restrict their theory to women as wives or cohabitees of men, but it is obviously a factor introducing variation in women's work-
loads.

[41] With regard to all forms of care, it is worth noting that it is in fact mostly
women who adjust to increased burdens of care in a household (see Berk 1985,
Delphy and Leonard 1992: 251–2).

ethnicity, and sexual orientation. These social locations have direct and indirect, but variable effects on women's work-loads. They represent differential structural constraints within which women may have some room to manœuvre, but are also confronted with real limits.

Women's work-loads, then, are highly variable, and are to a varying but ultimately only limited degree under their control. Given such variability, generalizations about women's work-loads are difficult to make, since *de facto* women's work-loads can vary from the zero work burden of a 'conspicuously leisured' wife of a husband who is rich enough and willing to buy all the services that his wife would have had to perform otherwise[42] to anything up to a quadruple work-load of two paid jobs, housework, and child care.[43]

Women's enjoyment of benefits is equally variable. Again their actual benefits depend on various factors:

1. On the *husband's income*, that is, on his class position. Obviously, the wife of a successful businessman can command and spend more money than the wife of a blue-collar worker. Thus it is generally in women's material interest to get married to as wealthy a man as possible.[44] However, a husband's income is under his control, and how much of it he shares with his wife and family is basically up to him. Therefore, women's access to benefits also depends—

2. On the *goodwill of the husband*. There are various practices of family budgeting. As Delphy and Leonard point out, the tighter a family budget, the more likely women are to take on the ungrateful task of handling it, as in the working-class practice of men handing over their whole wage to their wives, while otherwise the allowance system is common, where husbands give a monthly allowance to their wives. In some households, a shared bank account system, to which both husband and wife have access, is adopted.

[42] Excluding, possibly, sexual relations and emotional support, which, according to Delphy and Leonard, would count as services too.
[43] Note the recent trend in the USA for single mothers to have to hold down more than one job in order to provide for themselves and their children.
[44] The equivalent of the (gendered) 'American dream' for women can thus be seen to be the dream of Marilyn Monroe in *How to Marry a Millionaire*. The female version is, of course, as elusive and as ideological as the male version.

This is most common in dual earning households.[45] In all three systems, however, it is the husbands who ultimately decide to make (some of) their income accessible to their wives: as Delphy and Leonard point out, women may have delegated control, but they never have absolute control, nor any entitlement to control.[46]

3. On whether a woman has her *own sources of income*: either from property or, more likely from her own paid work. Note, however, that in the latter case the income may be reduced substantially by the costs she incurs through having to pay others to provide the services she would have provided for free as a housewife and mother. The benefit of a personal income for women, if it has to be earned through paid work, thus may exact quite a high price.

4. On existing *practices and ideologies with regard to distribution of goods within families*. It is a consistent finding of research into family consumption both in developed and developing countries that women tend to put the needs of their husbands first, those of children second, and their own needs last. This applies in situations of scarcity as well as relatively well-to-do circumstances: differential consumption is an expression and outcome of various ideologies about the respective needs of men and women and about the self-sacrificing mother and wife. Moreover, differences are reproduced from one generation to the next through differential inheritance, which tends to favour men's economic independence and women's dependence.[47]

5. On women's *ethnic identity*. Again, women's benefits in ethnic minority groups will tend to be less because they and their husbands tend to have access only to less well-paid work. It may not be culturally acceptable for them to work in the public sphere, hence they will only be able to engage in minimally paid homeworking,[48] or, on the other hand,

---

[45] See Pahl 1990.

[46] An exception to this rule are the few households in which women are the higher earners, but such households are very rare and even in these households, couples have varying strategies of dealing with this unusual situation (see McRae 1986).

[47] See Whitehead 1981, Delphy, 'Sharing the Same Table: Consumption and the Family', in Delphy 1984, Delphy and Leonard 1992, chs. 7 and 8.

[48] e.g. Pakistani and Bangladeshi women in the UK.

they may be more likely to be single parents and hence be
more likely to be poor.[49]

6. On women's *sexual orientation*. Since lesbians do not have
access to men's incomes and women's incomes are lower
than men's, lesbians do not even indirectly share in men's
comparative wealth, hence will tend to be less well off.[50]

As can be seen from these factors, it is only an independent
source of income which provides women with a reliable source
of material benefits, and even in this case some of these resources
may get lost because they have to be used to replace women's
unpaid work (see 3). Women's enjoyment of all other material
benefits is only mediately under their control and again varies
enormously: they may manage to marry a rich husband, but
they may not be able to keep him. They may find a husband
who discloses all his income to them and who gives them an
equal say in its expenditure, but they may not. Women are also
brought up to be self-denying and to put their own needs last,
but of course this socialization produces worse effects in some
than in others, and whether women are able to negotiate household expenditure with their husbands or not, and how much
they are able to let their own needs and wants figure in these
negotiations, again depends on many more factors. Lastly, again,
class, ethnic, and sexual divisions produce systematic variations
in women's enjoyment of benefits (although these, in turn, are
mediated by economic dependency).

In conclusion, women's enjoyment of benefits is as variable as
women's work burdens. Women's economic dependency on men
expresses itself mostly in the fact that they have only indirect
and very variable control over the benefits they enjoy, although
they may actually enjoy a lot of benefits. Women's varying social
locations introduce further variation. Thus, women may live in
luxury as well as in squalor, as they may live without having
to raise a finger as well as with a triple work-load of paid work,
housework, and child care: generalizations about 'women's' material position seem problematic if not impossible if we look at their

[49] e.g. Afro-Caribbean women in the UK, compared with Asian and white
women.
[50] Again, these points are not relevant for Delphy and Leonard's account: see
n. 40 above.

actual lives.[51] If there is so much variation, however, how can we tell whether women's work burdens are greater than their benefits and whether they are materially less well off than men? Furthermore, if this is already so difficult to assess, how could we possibly claim that women are exploited by men?

My scepticism about generalizations about women's material position and exploitation status could be resisted, however. Could one not insist, first, on the UN statistic I quoted before—and in favour of my argument—that women

constitute *half* the world's population,
perform nearly *two-thirds* of its work hours,
receive *one-tenth* of the world's income
and own less than *one-hundredth* of the world's property?[52]

Does it not show that women are exploited? Not clearly, I think, although it captures and seemingly confirms a persistent feminist suspicion. First, one major problem with this statistic is that it does not give us any idea about women's actual enjoyment of benefits—as contrasted with their control of benefits—since their enjoyment of benefits is mediated by their economic dependency. Thus the mere fact that women receive only one-tenth of the world's income and own less than one-hundredth of the world's property does not imply that they do not enjoy any of the benefits of the income and property of men. The estimation of women's material status, however, has to take into account women's actual enjoyment of benefits rather than their control of benefits. (Note that if the control of benefits were taken as the measure of material status, slaves would count as not having any benefits, which is clearly wrong.) A second problem with this statistic is that it generalizes over all countries, developed as well as developing. It thus glosses over the fact that women's material situ-

---

[51] Spelman (1988) has argued on more principled philosophical grounds that the very existence of 'other' social divisions which locate women differentially implies that no generalizations can be made about women as a category, social group, or class. I find her argument interesting, but ultimately not compelling, mainly because I think that the validity and truth of generalizations is an empirical question, to be answered by reference to the world, not to abstract arguments. (Some generalizations about women may be true, some may turn out to be true only of a subclass of women, but not all women, and thus reveal a bias in the theory in question.) The difference between her argument and mine, then, is that mine is empirical, not categorical.

[52] Quote taken from Pahl 1988: 349.

ation in any of the developed countries is much better in virtue of their access to labour-saving devices, pre-processed goods, and to goods produced cheaply often by women's labour in developing countries as well as in virtue of their relatively high levels of income-generating activities than is the material situation of women in developing countries. Women in developed countries have also benefited more from changes resulting from second wave feminism both in terms of (some) women's higher income and in terms of (some) men's performance of unpaid work in the home so that, arguably, patriarchal structures in these countries are less well entrenched and there is more material equality between men and women than in developing countries. The difficulty of the variability of women's material position, therefore, particularly with regard to women in developed countries, remains unresolved and cannot be glossed over by reference to statistics which exacerbate the inequalities on the basis of aggregation over vastly different situations.[53]

But could it not be replied, secondly, that even in Western developed countries it is clear that women's material situation is much worse than that of men, given, for example, the by now well-established trend of the 'feminization of poverty'?[54] This reply is both valid and beside the point. On the one hand, this 'trend' indicates that households without a (male) breadwinner wage are at or below the poverty line, in other words, that women do not have the same earning power as men. Single mothers are most certainly less well off than single fathers, and they have a high care burden, hence single mothers are the most likely candidates for being exploited. On the other hand, the poverty of single mothers does not make the life of the conspicuously leisured wife disappear.[55] The variability *between* women remains, and that was one of the respects that rendered generalizations about the material status of women problematic.

[53] Note also that Delphy and Leonard explicitly restrict the scope of their discussion to Western developed countries.

[54] See Scott 1984, Goldberg and Krenen 1990, Glendinning and Millar 1992. Lewis and Piachaud (1992) stress that, contrary to the implication of this term, 'throughout the last century women have always been much poorer than men' (p. 27).

[55] It highlights how vulnerable to exploitation women are. See my argument below in this section and in Chs. 4 and 6. See also Okin's much more comprehensive and detailed discussion of women's 'vulnerability by marriage' in Okin 1989, ch. 7.

Thirdly, it might be said that I am simply asking for too much: generalizations in the social sciences simply are not as hard and fast as they are in the natural sciences. There will always be exceptions to the rule, but this does not imply that the rule does not exist, or the generalization cannot be made. More specifically, despite the variability in women's material status, it might still be true that women are materially worse off than men (whose material status will similarly vary) because they are exploited by men. But how would we know that this claim is true, if not because we can detect a pattern within the myriad of differences? And how do we detect such a pattern? I cannot pursue these questions any further here, nor do I have any definite answers to them. Let me point out instead—and then clarify my position—that the assessment of women's material status poses a difficulty to which one could react in two very different ways: first, one could simply shrug the difficulty off as an obvious characteristic of social life which consequently informs the nature of claims in the social sciences and social theory, but does not vitiate such claims; or, secondly, one could take it to be a substantial difficulty which renders certain general claims wrong.[56] First, if women's material position is so variable because it is a composite of various exploitation statuses determined by their class, ethnicity, and sexual orientation, their overall material position will indicate nothing about their exploitation *qua* women.[57] Secondly, I do not think that those women whose class, sexuality, and/or ethnicity (combined with various other factors) allows them to live a life of comparative wealth and leisure are exploited. I shall not argue these points any further, however.[58] What I nevertheless hope to have made the reader see is that the establishment of women's material status is difficult because of both the measurement and the variability of their burdens and their benefits.

Assuming, then, there is a problem with women's material status, several responses are possible. The first response is to deny that women are exploited. Note that it is no doubt the difficulty of establishing women's material status that allows those

---

[56] Thanks to Sabina Lovibond for pressing me on the point discussed in this paragraph, and to Rodney Barker for the cheerful social theorist's response.

[57] See n. 27. I do not argue this point here, but it seems to me to be a strong one.   [58] For more argument see sect. v.

who want to deny that women are exploited to insist either on the claim that, in fact, all the income that men work hard to earn is then spent on their wives and children and is not to their own benefit at all, or on the claim that benefits and burdens are shared equally between men and women. This response is undercut by the fourth response. The further claims that are made to illustrate the falsity of the claim that women are exploited are also contradicted by my argument in Chapters 4 and 6 below. I shall therefore not deal with this response any further at this point. The second response is to conclude that the real problem with women's situation is not women's exploitation—given that it seems doubtful at any rate whether it exists or not—but women's economic dependency on men, which is obvious and undeniable and which is responsible for a lot of variation in women's material situations. The problem, in other words, is not so much the quantity of benefits they have access to and the weight of their work burdens, but the fact that they have very little *as of right*, not even their own time, their own bodies, souls, and minds.[59] This response seems valid to me—and the point about the wrong of dependency is well taken and important—but it gives up too quickly on the quest for a story of women's exploitation.

The third and fourth responses both persevere in this quest. The third response withdraws to the claim that whilst women's material status might be too variable to provide evidence for the general claim that men exploit women, it certainly goes a long way to confirming the claim that women are highly vulnerable to exploitation. Thus whilst it might not be true of all women at all times that they are in fact exploited, it is certainly true of all women at all times that they have little to no control over whether a situation will become exploitative for them. Thus note in particular that it is mainly women who adjust to increased labour demands in a household (such as, most typically, any care that has to be provided for dependants in the family, but also work for the head of household)[60] by either giving up paid

---

[59] Such an argument might lead to very interesting conclusions with regard to the question of women as second-class citizens. I am not aware of any such argument in recent second wave feminist thought, although such arguments were very common before women's legal and political emancipation, most famously in Wollstonecraft's *Vindication of the Rights of Woman* (Wollstonecraft 1985).

[60] See Delphy and Leonard 1992, ch. 9.

work or switching to part time work. In so far as women do this, they find themselves in a situation with a high labour burden but no guaranteed benefits. Men, on the other hand, in virtue of their socially sanctioned 'breadwinner role' are protected from such situations. Not only does their work reliably and predictably produce material benefits which are under their control, it is also typically better paid and less flexible than women's work so that there is little incentive for them—and they are excused from—taking on unpaid work in the home instead. Hence men's material situation is relatively stable, reliably productive of material benefits, and protects them from high unpaid labour burdens,[61] whilst women's situation is highly unstable with regard to both burdens and benefits in virtue of their tendency to shoulder any burden of unpaid work that may have to be provided in the home. This response is, in prototype, the response I shall give in Part II below and I shall therefore not discuss it here. Two points, however, are worth noting about it now. First, it withdraws to a weaker version of the claim that men exploit women, but it does not give it up altogether. Giving up an implausibly strong claim, however, may in fact improve the overall account. Secondly, even the weaker claim still hinges on an exploitation story which indicates the mechanism which makes women thus vulnerable to exploitation and men the beneficiaries of it. I shall return to these points in the following chapter.

The fourth response is the insistence on the original claim of women's exploitation by men and is, in fact, given by Delphy and Leonard. This is not necessarily a bad response, but it is the most onerous one. As I pointed out in the last section, it is possible to claim a social group's exploitation even if their material status is not obvious. The plausibility of such a claim, however, then hangs exclusively on the plausibility of the exploitation story a theorist comes up with, and more specifically, on whether the story can point out the mechanism responsible for the exploitation that is claimed to occur despite rather varying appearances.[62]

[61] Unless they are unemployed. Men's unemployment combined with their wives' employment does not produce a reverse situation, however, since the effects are mediated by gender norms and other social and economic constraints: see Morris 1990.

[62] It will also depend on whether its reader takes the cheerful social scientist's perspective on generalizations or is more demanding. See my discussion of generalizations about women's material position above.

Note that the third and fourth responses are successful to the extent that they circumnavigate the two problems discussed in this section with regard to the establishment of women's material status. Given that the indication of the exploitative mechanism is the conclusive part of the whole exploitation story, the problems with the measurement of women's material status do not matter to the same extent, nor does women's material status have to be established conclusively. Thus note that the exact measurement of the serf's labour burden and the lord's benefit in the feudal paradigm case of exploitation may raise problems of measurement and variability as well,[63] but that these do not matter since the serf's exploitation is obvious in any case. With regard to women's exploitation, then, the burden of proof lies with the indication of the exploitative mechanism.

In the following section I shall discuss Delphy and Leonard's notion of exploitation in order then to be able to assess their success with their version of the fourth response—that is, the plausibility of their exploitation story—in the last two sections.

(iv) *Delphy and Leonard's notion of exploitation*

Unfortunately, the discussion of Delphy and Leonard's exploitation story is complicated by the fact that they reinterpret the notion of exploitation in the course of their argument. There are two main senses in which they end up using the term: one sense is indistinguishable from that of oppression, while the other, more narrow and more technical, sense is that of the appropriation of women's labour. I shall introduce both in the following.

Whilst, on the one hand, Delphy and Leonard start off in their book discussing and explicitly wanting to endorse Marx's materialist approach and his notion of exploitation, on the other hand, they redefine the notion of exploitation so extensively that it ceases to have the meaning that they started off with. Thus on the one hand, Delphy and Leonard clearly mean to tell an exploitation story which parallels that of Marx's story of the mechanism by which wage workers are exploited[64] when they refer, for

---

[63] See n. 29 above.
[64] See their reference to Marx's aim as being that of finding 'the cause, ... the mechanism of the exploitation' (Delphy and Leonard 1992: 37; see also p. 89).

example, to the 'processes which ensure the continued appropriation of [women's] (productive, emotional, sexual and reproductive) labour'.[65] On the other hand, however, they end up,
arguably, not with a theory of women's *exploitation*, but with a
theory about the many ways in which women are oppressed
and the many wrongs that women suffer.

It seems that one reason why Delphy and Leonard call their
theory a theory of women's exploitation rather than oppression
is that they want to stress against the orthodox left that it is a
materialist theory and that women's oppression is at least as
serious as the oppression of the working class. 'Exploitation', in
the orthodox left's political jargon, according to Delphy and
Leonard, refers to more serious wrongs than 'oppression':

> Exploitation connotes greater political urgency, something which should
> be of primary concern to everyone, whereas oppression, what women
> (and especially middle class women) suffer, is less pressing and less
> onerous. . . . To say that women are oppressed but not exploited is there-
> fore generally not to say anything precise, but merely that their situa-
> tion is less serious than that of the proletariat. It is just a refined
> putdown.[66]

Whilst I agree with their analysis of the orthodox left, I suspect
it has not helped Delphy and Leonard's theoretical enterprise to
insist on using such a central term more for its 'emotive and
political' connotations[67] than for its actual reference. This suspicion is borne out by the fact that Delphy and Leonard end up
changing the meaning of 'exploitation' so that it is no longer
recognizably about what it was supposed to be about. Thus note
the extremely wide interpretation of 'exploitation' Delphy and
Leonard use in summing up their theory in their conclusion:

> The exploitation of wives thus consists not in getting less than we might
> for the hours we work . . . but in the appropriation of potentially all our
> labour and in our dependence and subordination. . . . our exploitation
> consists in all the aspects of society which push and pressure women
> into marriage, femininity and heterosexuality in order that we continue
> to accept relationships with men.[68]

---

[65] Delphy and Leonard 1992: 45.   [66] Ibid. 35–6.   [67] Ibid. 42.
[68] Ibid. 260. It is worth noting that the two sentences of the quote occur at
the beginning and the end of the paragraph which sums up their theory, and
in which they seem to use 'oppression' and 'exploitation' more or less interchangeably: Delphy and Leonard start off by saying, 'The exploitation of wives

Not only is 'exploitation' here used indistinguishably from 'oppression', but it has also lost the meaning that Delphy and Leonard started off with—that is, the extraction of surplus labour—when arguing for the possibility of a theory of women's exploitation.[69]

Now what may be seen to happen between Delphy and Leonard's endorsement of the 'original', Marxian meaning of exploitation at the beginning of the book and the completely loose usage of exploitation at the end of the book is a process of progressive reinterpretation of 'exploitation'. This process, however, is never explicitly marked as a real departure from their initial narrow usage, nor do we find an explicit definition or redefinition of exploitation anywhere in the book. Delphy and Leonard start on this departure by making several points about the concept of exploitation which are significant for a theory of women's exploitation and which they think have been overlooked or not understood in previous discussion.

The first point is that not all benefits from exploitation are '"material" in the narrow sense',[70] that is, the benefits may consist of 'non-tangible goods and services, and . . . things used for display or pleasure rather than instrumentally'.[71] More specifically, with regard to men's benefits from women's work, they give the following examples: the husband having 'someone to look interested while he tells his stories over and over again, or to make sure the food he gets on holiday does not upset his stomach, or

---

thus consists . . . in . . .', then continue (after two more sentences elaborating on this point) with the following sentences, 'Wives' oppression also consists in . . . . And in . . . . Women's oppression also consists in . . .', to end with the second sentence of the quote 'Finally, our exploitation consists in . . .'. Both the seemingly interchangeable usage of 'oppression' and 'exploitation' in this enumeration of points and the completely non-distinct usage of 'exploitation' indicate the change of meaning the concept of exploitation has undergone in the course of the book.

[69] See their claim that 'the extortion of surplus labour does not necessarily go through an initial monetary transaction (that is, the sale of products incorporating surplus labour)' (ibid. 41) and that 'Appropriating the products of other people's work via owning the means of production is a subterfuge to steal indirectly (part of) the labour owned by its purveyor. But this labour can be, has been in past economic systems, and is still in various existing systems, "stolen" directly. Owning the means of production is unnecessary if you own slaves or serfs or wives and children' (p. 43). Both claims seem to indicate that Delphy and Leonard mean to use exploitation in the sense of 'extraction of surplus labour' in analysing women's exploitation, too.   [70] Ibid. 41.

[71] Ibid.

to keep the children quiet when he wants to catch up on his sleep, or to make sure all the trousers bought for him have back pockets for his golf tees.'[72] Now this is a point worth making, but not necessarily a new point, nor a point marxists would necessarily disagree with, since all these 'goods' can be understood in marxist terminology as use-values produced by services.[73]

Delphy and Leonard point out, secondly, that there is more than one mode of exploitation, hence that exploitation can take forms other than the extraction of surplus value. This point has been discussed at length and hence does not need any further attention.[74] They argue thirdly, and again correctly, that the explanatory monism of orthodox marxism makes it impossible to understand women's oppression by men as a social system which is independent of—though interlinked with—capitalism, but nevertheless a system of exploitation.[75] Now these three points, it seems to me, are perfectly valid and need to be made in order to rescue a theory of women's exploitation from the orthodox marxist lion's den. It is with their fourth and last point that Delphy and Leonard move away entirely from a theory of exploitation which is recognizably about exploitation in the sense of the extraction of surplus labour.

Thus Delphy and Leonard argue, lastly, that 'the gains and losses of exploiter and exploited are not identical, not commensurable . . . and are not even comparable'.[76] In order to support this claim they point out, first, that workers under capitalism lose 'far more than the equivalent of a few hours of labour a day': they have to fear for their jobs, their jobs are alienating, and they are dominated by their bosses. Secondly and similarly,

---

[72] Delphy and Leonard 1992: 42; see also ch. 9 for a more elaborate account of the many ways in which men benefit from women's work.

[73] Even Marx thought that service work could be exploited: whether it was exploited or not depended for him on the relations of production under which it was performed (hence on whether these services were 'productive', i.e. contributing to the accumulation of capital): see Marx, 'Results', 1044 and *TSV* i. 157, 164–73.

[74] Delphy and Leonard 1992: 42–4. Note that this section is headed 'The means of exploitation: the *variety of mechanisms* and the social rules involved' (my emphasis), and that Delphy and Leonard still refer to exploitation as the extraction of surplus labour in this section.

[75] Ibid. 46–8. I have formulated the first half of this point in my own words, but I think I would probably have Delphy and Leonard's agreement on this formulation.   [76] Ibid. 45.

they stress with regard to familial relations that '[t]he gains and losses of exploiter and exploited are not zero-sum. Women/wives lose and suffer far more and in various ways from the processes which ensure the continued appropriation of their (productive, emotional, sexual and reproductive) labour than just the benefits men/husbands gain.'[77] Women are not only economically dependent, they are also not in control of their sexuality and may be subjected to violence.[78] Now this point, it seems to me, leads Delphy and Leonard to give up completely the meaning of exploitation as the extraction of surplus labour. Instead, they start using the notion of exploitation, first, to refer to 'the appropriation of women's labour', as in the above quote,[79] and even, secondly, to refer to all the various wrongs that are part and parcel of the oppressive system that produces and reproduces women's exploitation (in the narrow sense).[80] On the whole, the interpretation of exploitation as the appropriation of women's work seems to reflect their intention and usage throughout most of the book, but the even wider interpretation of exploitation that is interchangeable with oppression does seem to be used and intended by them as well.

Before I look at Delphy and Leonard's rationale for these reinterpretations more closely, let me stress that I am in agreement with them about all the wrongs they argue women incur in marriage or cohabitation with men, most of all those of economic and personal dependency and of physical and sexual violence. I do not think, however, that it is a good idea to include these wrongs in a conception of women's *exploitation* since such a move undermines the whole point of the concept, which is to capture the systematic transfer of material benefits from one person or class of persons to another. Furthermore, while the other wrongs may be intimately connected to the fact that women are exploited

[77] Ibid. 45. Note also the following formulation in their final summary: 'What men get from marriage is different . . . from what it costs women. Putting it crudely, what men get from marriage is 57 varieties of unpaid service, whereas the institution of marriage and the family restricts and (ab)uses (married and unmarried) women in all areas of their lives.' (p. 260)   [78] Ibid. 45.

[79] See also ibid. 130, 159, 260 and the suggestion at many places that the family structure is such that all or part of women's work is appropriated by the head of household, and see my discussion of this claim in sects. v and vi.

[80] See Delphy and Leonard's summary of their theory on p. 260 (quoted in this section above, p. 108), and n. 68 in this chapter.

(in the narrow sense), or even necessary for it to happen, exploitation itself is a distinct and different wrong. Thus it may be true that women cannot be exploited in their homes unless their sexual pleasure is controlled by men, but the control of women's sexuality is not constitutive of, nor even part of, their exploitation, although it may be strictly correlated with it.[81] It seems appropriate, therefore, to use 'exploitation' narrowly and thus to be able to distinguish it from other wrongs, even if other wrongs are correlated with the occurrence of exploitation.

Delphy and Leonard could be seen to provide an argument in defence of their adoption of a wider conception of exploitation. Thus they claim that, in the case of the exploitation of wage labourers, '[t]o identify the gains and losses in terms of surplus value alone is to take the point of view of the exploiter'.[82] They similarly assert in their summary of their theory that '[t]he exploitation of wives . . . consists not in getting less than we might for the hours we work (*which is to apply an inappropriate, capitalist measure to family labour*), but in the appropriation of potentially all our labour and in our dependence and subordination'.[83] To restrict the usage of 'exploitation' to the extraction of surplus labour,[84] in other words, is, first, to endorse the perspective of the exploiter (and thereby presumably deny that other wrongs are involved, too) and, secondly, to want to apply an inappropriate measure. I have responded to the first point already, although it might be worth pointing out that the *real* issue is not whether or not one endorses the perspective of the exploiter, but whether one acknowledges the reality of oppression, which may consist of many wrongs, one of which is that of exploitation. The second point, it seems to me, either reduces to the first point—in so far as it is inappropriate to want to measure a complex and multifaceted situation with a simple unidimensional

---

[81] If the control of women's sexuality were part of the mechanism by which surplus labour is extracted from women, it would, of course, figure in the corresponding theory or story of exploitation which indicates this mechanism, but it would be a necessary condition, not a part of women's exploitation. What women's exploitation *consists in*, in other words, is the extraction of surplus labour from women. [82] Delphy and Leonard 1992: 45.

[83] Ibid. 260, my emphasis.

[84] Or surplus value, as in the first quote which refers to the exploitation of workers by capitalists. To focus on surplus value, however, also implies a focus on surplus labour.

measure[85]—or it amounts in fact to a capitulation to the problems of measurement and variation in women's material status that I discussed in the preceding section under the guise of a politically and theoretically correct move. Thus note that the formulation of what women's exploitation consists of that is rejected in the quote is a formulation implied by the narrow interpretation of exploitation as the extraction of surplus labour, and it is exactly that claim that it seemed so difficult to establish in the preceding section. Note, furthermore, that Delphy and Leonard consistently avoid the formulation of 'extraction of surplus labour' after their argument that women lose more by being exploited than their husbands gain and that they start using instead the formulation of 'appropriation of women's labour'. This usage allows them not to face up to the difficulties related to establishing women's material status that I discussed in the last section, since these difficulties relate precisely to the attempt systematically to compare women's material burdens and benefits in order to establish the fact that their burdens are higher than their benefits and thereby the fact that surplus labour is extracted from them.

What seems to have happened, then, under the guise of a correct theoretical and political move, is a complete but unacknowledged, and furthermore badly supported, reinterpretation of the notion of 'exploitation' in two distinct senses: first, that of the 'appropriation of women's labour', and, secondly, that of 'women's oppression'. With regard to the latter, wider meaning, Delphy and Leonard seem to be making the same mistake as their orthodox marxist opponents in wanting to have one neat and powerful 'emotive and political word' to use in order to describe what is wrong about women's position in society.[86] There does not have to be one overarching wrong that we call 'exploitation' in order to make the point, however, and in fact to imply that there is may be a misrepresentation of a situation which is factually and morally far more complex than could be captured in one 'neat' word. Furthermore, as I argued above, there are good reasons for distinguishing the material wrong of exploitation

---

[85] This interpretation is suggested by the parallel rationale for the reinterpretation of the exploitation of workers and women (Delphy and Leonard 1992: 45) and by the rest of the paragraph whose beginning I quoted (p. 260).
[86] Ibid. 42.

(narrowly understood) from other moral and political wrongs such as women's economic dependence and enforced subservience to men and physical and sexual violence used against them. Lastly, however, and with regard to the more technical meaning of 'the appropriation of women's labour', this reinterpretation renders Delphy and Leonard's exploitation story—if it can still be called thus—quite shaky. I shall discuss the ramifications of this central theoretical move in the final two sections.

(v) *Delphy and Leonard's story of women's exploitation*

Presuming, then, that Delphy and Leonard's theory is mostly about women's exploitation in the sense of the appropriation of women's labour by men, what exactly is the story they tell and what difference does the reinterpretation of 'exploitation' make?

The story that Delphy and Leonard tell can be summarized as follows: women are exploited in the family because of its asymmetrical, hierarchical structure. Women as wives (but also as cohabitees or daughters) find themselves in a subordinate position within this structure, while men as the heads of households have, in virtue of their position, the power to control the activities of all members of the household. They also benefit from this position in various ways. Women's subordinate position implies that their time is not theirs and their labour is not 'free', that is, they are not free to dispose of it as they choose. Women are exploited, then, because of this asymmetrical structure of the family.

I have told this story without using any materialist terminology. Delphy and Leonard tell it partly with, partly without it. Here is how Delphy and Leonard apply materialist terms when they do use them: women are exploited because of the relations of production in the family mode of production. The relations of production consist in the head of household's ownership of the labour power of all other members of the household. The head of the household, in virtue of this ownership of other people's labour power, is therefore able to set their labour power to use as he sees fit and to benefit from that labour. It is his duty in turn to maintain the subordinate members of the family (his dependants). The subordinate members of the family thus have to do unpaid work for the head of household 'in return for' being maintained by him (although this is not a relationship of exchange).[87]

In these two versions of Delphy and Leonard's story, I have omitted one crucial term, however, which they use very extensively and which leads us to the very heart of their story. This term is the notion of 'appropriation'. Thus Delphy and Leonard claim, as I have indicated above, that women's exploitation consists in the appropriation of their labour by their husbands. How does this claim relate to the rest of the story? The best way to understand it, I think, is by understanding the appropriation claim as a claim about the causal effect of the familial relations of production: husbands appropriate women's labour *because* they have the power to do so in virtue of their position within the familial relations of production. If this understanding is correct, Delphy and Leonard do tell a causal story, and ostensibly one which points to the causal mechanism that is responsible for women's exploitation. Note, moreover, that their causal story parallels the original exploitation stories by Marx in so far as it points to the crucial role of the relations of production in systematically producing and reproducing exploitation. It is the social institution of the family, then, which provides the mechanism responsible for women's exploitation, and it is men as husbands and heads of households who benefit from women's exploitation.

There are, however, at least three problems with this story. The first and most important problem is that it is not a story of women's exploitation anymore because of Delphy and Leonard's reinterpretation of the notion of exploitation. In other words, it is not a story about how surplus labour is systematically extracted from women, although it remains a very impressive story about how material inequality between (some) men and women is systematically produced and maintained through the structure of the family, relating to women's and men's performance of work, their consumption, and the passing on of inheritance.[88] The case

[87] See their summary on pp. 111–13, which is relatively free of materialist 'jargon', but also the remainder of this chapter, especially pp. 116–26, and *passim*.

[88] Delphy and Leonard's theory is impressive because of their acute observation and the wealth of the empirical research they discuss. It is their theoretical stringency which is less than impressive.

of the conspicuously leisured wife may serve to illustrate this point.

According to Delphy and Leonard's reinterpretation of exploitation, even the conspicuously leisured wife is exploited. This is because her labour is appropriated by her husband, in virtue of his ownership of her labour power, as much as is that of any other wife, except that the rich husband chooses not to set his wife's labour power to work. The husband

controls who does what within the home: he regulates the responsibilities of members and their hours of work . . . He decides what human resources to put into the particular tasks he thinks need doing, and he allots different tasks to different people—*including sometimes requiring wives and children to do no 'work' but rather to be conspicuously leisured*: to play, or to engage in philanthropy. He has to negotiate these decisions with his dependants, but providing he makes decisions which are over-all to the family's good, he will get their support, because the well-being of the household is the best guarantee of each member's individual well-being.[89]

Given their redefinition of 'exploitation', then, Delphy and Leonard are in the lucky position of being able to claim that all wives are exploited in virtue of the relations of production they find themselves in.[90] They are only able to do so, however, at the cost of having emptied the notion of 'exploitation' of any content. If women can be exploited by being leisured, i.e. by not working at all, exploitation has ceased to imply the burdening of those exploited with labour for which they get no returns: the leisured wife is by definition not burdened with work. What, according to Delphy and Leonard, is wrong with her situation is that 'her labour power is appropriated' like that of all other wives:[91] in an important sense she is not free to decide whether to work or not because these decisions are not hers as of right, because as a wife, her time is not hers to dispose of. The crucial characteristic of her situation, therefore—and one that she shares with all other wives—is that of dependency, not that of exploitation. Now

---

[89] Delphy and Leonard 1992: 142, my emphasis; see also p. 236: 'Husbands may want their wives to . . . be conspicuously leisured'.

[90] They thus 'solve' the variability problem (see sect. iii) by focusing on an aspect of women's situation (as wives) that they do share in common: their position in the familial relations of production.   [91] Ibid. 117, 119, 120, 159.

dependency may and often does lead to exploitation in the original sense, but it may not, as the case of the conspicuously leisured wife shows. As a result of Delphy and Leonard's redefinition of exploitation, then, their theory has turned into a theory focusing on women's dependency.[92] It has certainly ceased to be a theory of women's exploitation (in the original sense). It also fails, therefore, to tell the exploitation story which was required to save their claim that women as wives are exploited by men as husbands.

The following rationale may illuminate in more general terms why their theory cannot be both a theory of women's dependency and a theory of women's exploitation. A theory of dependency focuses on relations of production, or power relations, while a theory of exploitation focuses on the production and reproduction of certain unequal outcomes. Only if the relations of production can be shown systematically to produce such outcomes—that is, different material statuses—can the two theories complement each other. The variability problem that I have presented in section iii above, however, implies that there is no such systematic outcome in the case of women as wives. By insisting that the leisured wife's labour power is owned by her husband, although not put to work, Delphy and Leonard focus on the relations of production that all wives have in common—thereby 'solving' the variability problem at the level of relations of production—at the expense of being able to link them to a specific outcome. They therefore preclude the possibility of coming up with a theory of exploitation as the systematic extraction of surplus labour. Alternatively, instead of focusing on the relations of production, they could have attempted to find a mechanism that ensures that unpaid labour is extracted from (some, if not all) women. This is the alternative that I think is more promising and that I have pursued in my theory of women's exploitation as carers.[93] The drawback of this alternative, of course, is that it will not apply to all women, and that it is debatable whether it is systematically linked to specific relations of production.

Before I can address the other points of criticism of Delphy

---

[92] See ibid. 262, where they identify women's oppression in marriage as an oppression of 'allegiance—of personal dependency', together with domestic service, slavery, and serfdom.   [93] See Ch. 4.

and Leonard's theory, I have to clarify the notion of 'appropriation' which they use to define their reinterpreted notion of exploitation and which is therefore crucial in their story. The following passage renders their own elucidation of the meaning of 'appropriation':

By appropriation we mean that the labour is owned by/belongs to someone other than the worker, that someone else has a monopoly on it. Hence the worker is not free to decide what shall be done with it, nor to sell it to whomever she/he wishes.[94]

Now they cannot mean that men literally own women's labour, since women are not slaves. Nor do men own women's labour for certain spans of time as capitalists own the labour of workers for the time that workers work for them. The following quote, then, may come closer to their intended meaning:

The marital obligations do not involve a discrete workload (that is, particular responsibilities which are limited in nature and in the time taken to do them), which when they are completed leave women free to work elsewhere. Rather, wives' familial duties involve an obligation to devote whatever of their time and energy is needed to whatever their husbands require.[95]

Ownership of women's labour here implies, rather, that women, in virtue of their status as wives, have certain duties, and that these duties restrict women's freedom to choose what they want to do, notably their freedom to engage in paid work, but also their leisure time and other activities.[96] Husbands then 'own' women's labour in that they have rights to their wives' performance of work for them that correspond to the wives' duties:

The rights husbands are given through the marriage contract, though no longer as extensive as in the mid nineteenth century when wives had the legal standing of property, still include husbands' rights to their wives' work and unlimited sexual access to their bodies.[97]

The sense in which husbands appropriate their wives' labour, then, is best seen as the sense in which the institution of marriage imposes certain work obligations on women to the benefit of their husbands. Now this interpretation in itself is not objec-

---

[94] Delphy and Leonard 1992: 96.   [95] Ibid. 118.
[96] See e.g. ibid. 159, 247, 250.   [97] Ibid. 119.

tionable. What makes it problematic, however, is Delphy and Leonard's interpretation of both the strength and scope of these obligations. I shall deal with these two points in turn.

The second problem, then, with Delphy and Leonard's 'exploitation' (aka appropriation) story, is that they stress too much the directly compulsive nature of the familial relations of production as they describe them and thus underestimate the extent to which they may be changing and/or being replaced by other structures. Thus whilst Delphy and Leonard are keen to stress that women are not simply victims of these structures and do make choices, they insist, in typically structuralist vein, that while 'women certainly contribute to the making of their own worlds', they do so 'in conditions not of their own choosing'.[98] Now the family structure they do assert implies that a husband has extensive control over his wife's working life[99] including the control over, for example, whether she can take up paid work: 'all these decisions ultimately rest with him. In the end a wife has either to accept her husband's decisions—or leave.'[100] The question, however, is whether husbands still have as much power as Delphy and Leonard say they have.[101] Thus, in particular, it seems questionable that in all or most rather than some and increasingly fewer cases '[i]t is [the husband] who has the final say on whether he will "let his wife work"'.[102] It seems to me, then, that Delphy and Leonard overemphasize the compulsive nature of

---

[98] Ibid. 261, see also pp. 139, 265.   [99] See ibid. 142.   [100] Ibid. 144.

[101] Note that more and more women do take the option of leaving even if this implies a sharp drop in living standards for them (and this fact by itself would seem to strengthen Delphy and Leonard's case that women have a stronger interest in getting and staying married than men and therefore less power within a marriage). If leaving is an option that more and more women take, however, every husband's power within marriage is reduced because of the plausibility of every woman's threat to leave.

[102] Ibid. 143. Note that in the particular case Delphy and Leonard are discussing in this passage, they do have the evidence in front of their eyes: they quote one of the studies on working-class life as reporting 'considerable explicit disagreement' between husbands and wives in otherwise 'non-conflictual' marriages about the issue of wives' employment (Porter 1983, cited in Delphy and Leonard 1992: 179). Wives seem to have put their foot down, however, since 'in the end most men grudgingly accepted their wives' insistence that they be allowed to submit themselves to further exploitation, to the couple's mutual benefit' (pp. 179–80). Furthermore, again in Delphy and Leonard's own words, at what point do wives who are 'talking back and arguing' start being seen to be their husbands' equals rather than to be 'mak[ing] their choices from a subordinate position' (p. 180, see also p. 236)?

familial relations and therefore often sound as if they are describing familial relations pre- rather than post-World War II.[103]

Now this might not matter so much if one of the questions that arise from their account were not what difference social change toward more equality between men and women would make to their theory and whether they could take such change into account. My suspicion is that they could not, precisely because they do not see familial relations as having changed that much at all.[104] Note also that the family structures they postulate do already seem outdated at points and hence involve them in rather implausible redescriptions of the interaction between family members, and more specifically husbands and wives. The challenge to be put to them, then, is the following: granted that women do do some work for the benefit of their husbands, is it still true that their husbands have the final say over what work they do and, furthermore, is it true that whatever work they do in the household they do for their husbands? The answer to the last two questions, it seems to me, is closer to 'no' than to 'yes', and to the extent that it is closer to 'no' their theory is describing a family structure that is on its historical way out.[105] I have dealt with the answer to the first question in the last paragraph. I shall deal with the answer to the other question in the following.

The third problem with Delphy and Leonard's story about men's appropriation of women's labour, then, is that they vastly

---

[103] This date is somewhat arbitrary, but somewhat less so with regard to the specific question of women's performance of paid labour, given the massive changes in this respect since the Second World War, and given that these changes must have contributed their share to eroding a husband's power to have the 'final say' over whether he will 'let his wife work'.

[104] See e.g. Delphy and Leonard 1992: 223.

[105] It is difficult if not impossible to make such historical evaluations because of the generality of the judgement involved. This is why I choose such tentative formulations. I do not mean to imply that we could not understand some phenomena in contemporary family life and structures as a kind of historical residue of the age-old patriarchal family structure that Delphy and Leonard describe. But the question is how much of current family reality is determined by the old structures, and how much is determined by new and changing structures. This in itself seems an impossible question to answer. The easier question, therefore, it seems to me, is what account makes more sense of a historically developing and changing situation. Delphy and Leonard, in my view, focus too exclusively on the old structures and hence miss too much of the more dynamic aspects of a no doubt very complex and evolving reality.

overshoot on the range of work that women supposedly perform for men. I need to introduce a further aspect of their appropriation claim in order to make this point. Consider what Delphy and Leonard have to say about work that women do in the household, but which does not ostensibly benefit the head of household, notably care for other dependants: 'it is the head of the family who appropriates the labour incorporated in the service. It is work for the maintenance of *his* household ... and he would have to perform such work himself if his wife (or sister or daughter) did not do it. It is delegated work/care.'[106] It is the obligation of the head of household to provide, for example, child care, according to Delphy and Leonard, since he is obliged to do whatever is required for the maintenance of his household (including that of its members) and child care is work which 'maintains' dependent members of his household.[107] Child care, therefore, is yet another service that women perform for their husbands, and they perform it because it is part and parcel of the work they owe to their husbands:

wives' familial duties involve an obligation to devote whatever of their time and energy is needed to whatever their husbands require. It is still quite possible for wifely obligations to be so extensive that the possibility of a woman's working outside the home is excluded, for instance, when there are young children ...[108]

Now this seems plainly wrong: why should the obligation to care for offspring lie exclusively on the husband? It is interesting to note Delphy and Leonard's admission that Delphy, in her earlier work, 'suggested that perhaps childcare is analytically (though not empirically) different from the rest of domestic work' in that '[t]he obligation on women to provide unpaid childcare may perhaps not stem from marriage and family relations'.[109] Delphy and Leonard override this qualm, however, by announcing that '[i]n this book we shall ... treat sex, procreation and childrearing as being among the various forms of labour women perform for men specifically within the family.'[110] And this is precisely what they do. But why?

---

[106] Delphy and Leonard 1992: 125.   [107] See ibid. 111.   [108] Ibid. 118.
[109] Ibid. 23. See esp. Delphy, 'Continuities and Discontinuities in Marriage and Divorce' in Delphy 1984.
[110] Delphy and Leonard 1992: 23; see also p. 260.

The only reason I can suggest is that it gives their appropriation claim more support. Note that the only model on which this construction of care obligations for dependants makes sense is the arguably even more outdated model in which the paterfamilias owns his family and has exclusive responsibility for its maintenance and welfare because nobody else in it could be responsible: persons who are owned can be made to do things, but cannot be held responsible for what they do; it is their owner who bears that responsibility. On the basis of this model, they can assert that all work that women do, even if it does not benefit their husband directly, benefits him indirectly because it was his duty to do it in the first place. Hence he benefits because he is able to make his wife do what he would have had to do. Now while this would imply that husbands do indeed appropriate all of women's unpaid work in the home, the truth of this claim is won mostly on the basis of stipulations about work responsibilities stemming from an even more outdated model of family relations than the one presumed in Delphy and Leonard's claims about the husband's power to command his wife's labour. Note that this is even more obvious when we look at women's performance of care for their own elderly parents. Clearly, such care is not work that is owed to their husbands (although, by the same token, care women perform for their in-laws clearly is work that would have been the husband's obligation had he not been able to delegate it to his wife). Once one realizes, then, that no small part of the work that women are claimed by Delphy and Leonard to perform for their husbands is work the responsibility for which is only the husband's on an even more outdated model of family responsibilities, one is much less inclined to agree with their claim that husbands appropriate and benefit from 'potentially all [of women's] labour'.[111] In fact, this part of Delphy and Leonard's story is revealed to rely on a model of family relations which is historically not just on its way out, but arguably long gone.

In conclusion, then, Delphy and Leonard's 'exploitation' story is not really a story of exploitation in the original sense of exploitation as the extraction of surplus labour, but of women's personal dependency on men. As such, it fails to support Delphy and Leonard's original claim that men *qua* husbands exploit women

---

[111] Delphy and Leonard 1992: 260.

qua wives, and it therefore also fails to show that men exploit women. Furthermore, it is based on assumptions about family obligations and power structures within the family which raise questions—to say the least—about the historical adequacy of Delphy and Leonard's theory. Their theory is certainly not able to capture any of the historical dynamics in family relations over the last century and, more specifically, over the last thirty years or so.

(vi) *Conclusion*

In this conclusion, I would like to draw out a few more points about Delphy and Leonard's theory which will also allow me to introduce the problems that I tried to respond to in my own theory of women's exploitation as carers.

In arguing the last point of criticism in the last section, I introduced a distinction between women's work that directly benefits husbands and work that does not, notably care of other dependent members of the family. By introducing that distinction I was able to point out the rather outdated model of family obligations that underlies Delphy and Leonard's story. The question then arises, however, what model reflects current family obligations best, and how this model can be evaluated. Now the main rival to the old-fashioned patriarchal model—and that model which is generally believed to describe the structure of contemporary family obligations—is what I shall call the 'egalitarian model'. According to this model, husbands and wives share their obligations equally. This might be taken to imply that husbands and wives share their obligations to provide for their family and to do the caring and housework within it equally, hence should do equal shares of both paid and unpaid work. I shall call this the 'equal shares' version. According to the more usual interpretation of the model, however—the 'equal but separate spheres' version—it is taken to mean that husbands fulfil their share of the obligations by providing for the family while women fulfil theirs by doing all the caring and housework. Now there is no doubt, it seems to me, that it is the latter version rather than the former that is the social norm, hence the model which structures the work that both men and women do inside and outside their homes. The challenge arising from this model of the 'egalitarian' modern family, then, is to show that even on the basis of this model, men nevertheless exploit women.

I think it can be shown, but showing that men do exploit women requires a different conception of women's work: it requires a conception of women's work as care and the specific features and logic of care, instead of Delphy and Leonard's focus on generally any kind of work that women do for their husbands. By focusing on care, furthermore, and the mechanism of exploitation that is specific to it, I am also able to side-step the question that is so problematic in Delphy and Leonard, that is, the question of how much power men have over women in the family. Note that this question plays such an important role in Delphy and Leonard because they focus on familial relations of production and therefore on women's dependency on men. The focus of a theory of women's exploitation as carers, instead, lies on the following question: what is it that makes women (continue to) take on unpaid care for others even if this is not in their material interest and even if they are supposedly free to do what they like? While Delphy and Leonard have to answer, implausibly, that it is ultimately their husbands who make them do what they do, my answer is more complex and more structural: it refers to the peculiar activity that care is, to women's identity and morality, as well as to gendered norms and material inequality.

Lastly, then, I believe that my theory of women's exploitation as carers will remain valid historically for much longer than Delphy and Leonard's theory of women's 'exploitation' as wives precisely because it does not prescribe a model of unequal power structures in the family which is too static and too backward-looking to do justice to a historically dynamic situation. Thus at some point in the future, women may be as powerful as their husbands and may long since have refused to service their husbands, but they may still be more vulnerable to taking on care and thus be vulnerable to being exploited as carers. The challenge for any post-second wave feminist theorist, it seems to me, lies in coming up with a theory that can accommodate the changes towards equality that have taken place in the last thirty years, but can nevertheless also explain how it is that women continue to be exploited. I shall expand on these points in the following chapter.

PART II

4

Women's Work as Care

In this chapter, I shall develop my own conception of women's exploitation as carers, based on an account of women's work as care. This account looks at four aspects of care which I shall introduce after defining care (section i): the properties of care as an activity (section ii), the psychology of care (section iii), the ethic of care (section iv), and the gendered nature of care (section v). These four aspects together make up what I call the 'circle of care' which is women's part in the sexual division of labour (section vi), reference to which is also the central part of my own 'exploitation story' (sections vii and viii). Understanding women's work as care, however, also introduces new topics and problems which have not been discussed adequately in the literature. I argue that the practice of care, based on a certain understanding of the ethic of care, raises questions of justice both about the distribution of the benefits of care to those in need and about the distribution of the burden of care to carers. Yet in so far as women endorse a contextualized ethic of care such as that proposed by Noddings, they are not only vulnerable to a specific form of exploitation, i.e. exploitation *as carers*, but also rendered incapable of addressing themselves to this problem. I conclude, therefore, that a theory of care needs to incorporate considerations of justice, especially a conception of women's exploitation as carers (section vii). Finally, I draw the argument of this chapter and part as well as that of Part I to a close by elaborating on some aspects of my exploitation story in the light of the discussion in Parts I and II (section viii).

(i) *The definition of care as an activity*

'Caring' can refer to an emotional state or to an activity or to a combination of the two.[1] This dual reference of 'care' is reflected

---

[1] This dual reference could in principle be distinguished by using 'caring about' to refer to the emotional state and 'caring for' to refer to the activity, but

in the literature on care. Thus Noddings has argued that it is the emotional-cum-moral state of 'engrossment' in another person's reality that is basic to care,[2] while Parker on the other hand has discussed caring as an activity comprising the tasks of 'tending'.[3] Graham, by contrast, refuses to settle for either aspect by discussing caring as indivisibly both activity and emotion, when she analyses it as a 'labour of love'.[4]

Caring can also be defined very broadly and inclusively or rather narrowly. Fisher and Tronto provide an example of an extremely inclusive definition by referring to care as a 'species activity that includes everything that we do to maintain, continue, and repair our "world" so that we can live in it as well as possible'.[5] This world 'includes our bodies, our selves, and our environment' and the caring includes 'healing' as much as 'house-building'.[6] In contrast to this very broad definition, the *Oxford English Dictionary* defines 'caring for' as 'providing for' and 'looking after'. Presumably, this definition excludes inanimate entities as recipients of care, but it is still rather wide in that it includes under the description of 'providing for' activities such as earning money in order to pay for one's parents' stay in a sheltered home for the frail elderly or in order to pay alimony for the children living with the divorced mother. A son could thus 'care for' his parents and a father for his children without ever interacting with them, or without ever even seeing those he cares for.[7] More typically, however, under the

there is no agreement in the literature about the usage of these terms. Thus the distinction between 'caring about' and 'caring for' has been used to make various and very different conceptual distinctions: it has also been used to distinguish between different types of objects of caring (Tronto 1989) as well as between different components of care (Fisher and Tronto 1990). I shall therefore not use the two terms to make any of these distinctions.

[2] Noddings 1984; see also Mayeroff 1971.

[3] Parker 1981: 17. Noddings (1984) suggests at some point that the activity of caring 'might properly be called care-taking', hence seemingly brackets out caring as an activity from her discussion of caring altogether on the grounds that it is caring as an attitude or emotion that 'gives meaning to the caretaking' (p. 22). For a detailed discussion of Noddings see section iv.

[4] Graham 1983, *passim*; see also Tronto 1993: 105.

[5] Fisher and Tronto 1990: 40; see also Tronto 1993: 104.

[6] Fisher and Tronto 1990: 40. Tronto retains this wide interpretation (Tronto 1993, *passim*).

[7] These examples are deliberately chosen: see sect. v below on the gendered nature of care and the question whether and in what sense men can typically be said to care.

description of 'looking after', caring involves some interaction between the carer and the cared for, such as in child care where those caring for children spend a lot of time with them, partly because children's safety has to be guaranteed, but more importantly because children need interaction with others and help in various ways. Caring may also involve various forms of physical 'tending', whether that is the washing of a frail elderly person, the dressing of a child, or the relaxing massage given by a practitioner.[8] Caring may, however, just be the listening and talking to a distressed friend who needs the company and sympathy of another person in this situation.

In contrast to these rather wide definitions, I would like to offer my own, more restrictive definition of care as an activity. I shall use 'caring' in the following sense in my discussion:

> Caring for is the meeting of the needs of one person by another person where face-to-face interaction between carer and cared for is a crucial element of the overall activity and where the need is of such a nature that it cannot possibly be met by the person in need herself.[9]

I shall elucidate this definition before pointing out its merits.

First, the concepts of 'carer' and 'cared for' refer to the two positions or roles that the activity of care establishes, that is, that

---

[8] See Parker's definition of caring as 'tending' in the context of a discussion of care for elderly people (Parker 1981). It is worth mentioning that tending is not an activity and form of care restricted to the care of elderly people as Parker's list of tending activities seems to imply.

[9] This definition takes up some elements from Parker's definition of care as tending which specifies that 'care describes the actual work of looking after those who, temporarily or permanently, cannot do so for themselves. It comprises such things as feeding, washing, lifting, cleaning up for the incontinent, protecting and comforting. It is the more active and face-to-face manifestation of care' (Parker 1981: 17). Parker's definition has subsequently been widely adopted in social policy literature. There is no further discussion of the definition and its merits in Parker's article, however, nor has the concept of care been discussed in the social policy field until very recently, presumably because what care consists of (a certain list of tasks, as the one given by Parker) and its delineation against other types of activity was not taken as controversial in the social policy discussion (recent exceptions are Thomas 1993 and Ungerson 1990*b*). For an acknowledgment of the centrality of the meeting of needs in care see Tronto: 'What is definitive about care . . . seems to be a perspective of taking the other's needs as the starting point for what must be done' (Tronto 1993: 105). Tronto, however, does not seem to *define* care as the meeting of needs in others.

of the person who does the caring and that of the person who
is the recipient of the other person's care, respectively. These
may be temporary roles that are interchangeable, as between
friends, or relatively fixed roles, as between caring professional
and client. Even the roles of caring professional and client, however, are only relatively fixed because it is possible that a client
cares for the caring professional in certain situations. Some roles
are not interchangeable at all, as for example the roles of parent and infant or young child, although, of course, a grown-up
child can become a long-term carer for her frail elderly parent,
and these roles in turn may be relatively fixed. Also, in some
forms of care that have to be provided over extended periods
of time, such as child care or the care of disabled or elderly people, the permanently required role or position of the 'carer' can
be filled by more than one person: both parents, other members
of their family, as well as paid carers may share in the care of
children. It is worth stressing, then, that as such, the concepts
of 'carer' and 'cared for' can refer to both fixed and flexible,
momentary and long-term, shared and 'singly occupied' roles
or positions and should not be taken to refer to relatively long-
term, socially fixed roles or positions only.

Secondly, the definition makes interaction between carer and
cared for a central element. Consider that a lot of activities, notably all services and, even more widely, all activities productive
of use-values—and this could include most paid work in the
various sectors of the economy—could be described as at least
mediately 'meeting needs':[10] unless there were need in a wide
sense, translated into market demand, most of these activities
would not be performed, and their performance leads, via a market transaction and the consumption of the use-value, to the
meeting of such need. But presumably nobody would think it
adequate to describe the production of a car as 'caring', so obviously the 'meeting of needs' has to be qualified appropriately.
Now the most typical cases of care, as illustrated above, seem
to involve interaction between carer and cared for, although the
interaction may not cover the whole activity or set of activities
that is or are described as caring. Take the following examples:
cooking her favourite dish for a sick child, arranging an appoint-

[10] See my discussion of 'material production' in Ch. 1 sects. ii and iii.

ment with a physiotherapist for an elderly person who is hard of hearing, enquiring into possibilities of help for one's partner who is depressed. None of these activities involves interaction with the cared for except at the time where they are asked what they want or informed of or presented with the result of these activities, but I would still want to count them as care. There are other activities which are even more questionably described as 'caring', such as washing one's children's clothes, putting the rubbish in the bin (for one's frail neighbour), cleaning one's sick father's flat. Now in so far as these activities could not be performed by the persons for whom they are done, hence in so far as they meet a need that could not be met by the cared for themselves, they would still qualify as care. There would then be a further question, however, as to whether, for example, the baker cannot be said to care for the frail elderly person, too, since he produces what meets her need and she could not have done so herself. The only way to exclude such counter-examples, it seems to me, is to make face-to-face interaction a crucial element of the activity.[11] This may leave some cases undecided or questionable,[12] but I do not think this matters as long as the central idea and the typical cases are clear, and the most typical cases do involve face-to-face interaction in various ways.

[11] I understand 'face-to-face interaction' to include, in an extended sense, cases of 'ear-to-ear' telephone conversations, 'eye-to-eye' letter writing and reading, and similar cases based on more modern forms of telecommunication. The important point is that certain kinds of communication in themselves constitute care, such as e.g. counselling, comforting, or even merely actively listening and constructively responding to somebody's problems, worries, anger, or despair—whether such communication is immediate or mediate.

[12] If, for example, a baker baked an especially soft bread for a frail elderly man because she knows from previous conversations that he would not be able to eat it otherwise, this might well be counted as care. (Care does not have to be unpaid to be care—see my argument in Ch. 5, sects. iv–vi.) I do not have a problem with this, because her baking of this particular loaf of bread is functionally different from the baking of all other loaves which are not produced for specific people and which may or may not meet needs which cannot be met by the persons who will then eat the bread. Hence a baker's activity, on the whole, is not care, although some aspects of it may arguably be. Kissing may be care, too, according to this definition, but only in so far as it meets a concurrent need to be shown affection and love—if it is merely an expression of love without meeting such a need (the person kissed may not want to be loved by that particular person, or may not need to feel loved in this particular moment) it is obviously not care. See my distinction later in the section between care and acts expressive of love, friendship, and consideration.

Thirdly, the second qualification of the definition—that care meets a need that cannot possibly be met by the person in need herself—is meant to capture another important element of care as well as to distinguish care from other types of activities. This qualification restricts what counts as care quite considerably: only those activities may be counted as care which the cared for could not possibly engage in herself. By 'not possibly' I mean to exclude activities satisfying two types of need. The first type consists of basic human needs which a healthy, able-bodied adult is nevertheless capable of meeting herself at least in principle. If others meet those needs for her, they provide a service, but do not care for her. Thus the housewife cooking a meal for her husband is providing a service, whilst her cooking the same meal for an infant would be care.[13] The second type consists of what we might call socially caused needs (and also wants, desires, and interests) where the person in need could do whatever she has to do to satisfy the need (want, desire, interest) herself if she had learnt how to do so or if she made up her mind to do them or if she had chosen a different occupation. In our modern societies there are various things we need that we cannot produce or provide ourselves, not because in principle we are not capable of doing so, but because of the very advanced social division of labour or specialization. The interdependency produced by such diversification of occupations, skills, and knowledge is socially caused, but not strictly, that is, humanly necessary. Caring, by contrast, meets needs which neither derive from the social division of labour nor are satisfiable by the person in need, but which are absolute in that they make those in need necessarily depend on others. Thus a child cannot bring herself up, nor can a bedridden person provide food for herself, nor can somebody in need of talking a problem over with somebody talk to herself.

The idea underlying this second qualification is that throughout the lives of all human beings there are times when we do need others to care for us in various ways, especially at the beginning and the end of our lives, but also whenever we are faced with needs that we cannot possibly meet ourselves. It would take a theory of human nature to elaborate on the various needs

---

[13] See my distinction between care and services below.

we have that we cannot meet ourselves, be they physical or emotional, temporary or permanent, arising from disabilities or illness or from general human conditions shared by all such as life-cycle conditions (childhood and old age) or certain physical (pain) or emotional conditions (shock, loss, grief, fear, despair, confusion). All I can do here is to point out that there is a distinction between, on the one hand, needs that are socially caused based on the social division of labour and basic needs that can, however, be met by the person in need and, on the other hand, needs that are absolute in the sense of being part of human life regardless of the society one happens to live in and particularly urgent in that they cannot be met by the person in need herself. Care, then, is a response to a particular subset of basic human needs, i.e. those which make us dependent on others.

This distinction between types of needs also captures the distinction between care and services. Services are given, paid or unpaid, in response to a broad range of needs, wants, or interests, but any of these could be satisfied by ourselves at least in principle. The repair of one's washing machine, the dinner provided for the husband by his wife, or the setting up of a computer, are all activities that answer to needs, wants, or interests, but unlike care, services do not answer to needs that could not possibly be met by the beneficiaries of those services themselves: the husband could cook his dinner himself (or buy one), and one could, at least in principle, acquaint oneself with the mechanics of washing machines or computers and do the job oneself, transport one's rubbish to the dump, or fetch the water from the local fountain. Again this distinction is not without its problems since a lot of the services we rely on cannot be provided without a division of labour. Take the provision of news from all over the world: a single person could not possibly get the news from all over the world since she could not be all over the world at the same time. So it might be said that the provision of news from all over the world is an activity that could not possibly be done by an individual herself. But, first, the 'need' to have news from all over the world—if it is a need—is socially created on the basis of a social division of labour and the appropriate technology, and secondly, this need is relative to technologically advanced societies. It is thus certainly not a universal need and therefore does not fall into the core of basic human needs that

I mean to focus on in my definition. Ultimately, it may be difficult or even impossible in certain cases to say whether or not they would count as care. There remains a core of typical activities, however, that everybody recognizes as care, and the activities in this core characteristically have the properties specified by my definition, most importantly the property of meeting a certain type of need. As long as this core is recognizable, the definition works, even if the boundaries of what is to count as care and what is not are not as neat as one might have wished for.

Fourthly, there is another distinction which may further elucidate my definition of care: the distinction between care and activities or acts which are expressions of love, friendship, or consideration. Such activities—e.g. making a cup of tea for one's partner who has just returned from a long day's work, cooking a friend's favourite dish, doing various kinds of favours—may be thought to be care, and they may or may not meet a need (doing somebody a favour does usually not imply meeting a need). They are only care, however, if they do meet a need which the person in need could not meet herself. They can be both, expressions of love as well as care, since care can be done very lovingly if it is done between partners, friends, or parents and children. It is furthermore true, especially in the private sphere of the home, that activities are often both care and activities expressive of love. This may lead one to think that care has to be an expression of love, i.e. that my definition lacks this element and is the worse for it. I think, however, that there are good reasons for keeping the two aspects—the meeting of a particular type of need and the expression of love—distinct, whilst acknowledging that they may often coincide (especially in the private sphere). First, as I shall argue in the next chapter when looking at care in the public sphere, care does not require the existence of an emotional bond between carer and cared for.[14] Secondly, activities and acts expressive of an emotional bond are not necessarily care according to my definition: they may be and often are services, that is, satisfy needs, wants, or interests that the person could have satisfied herself. This is especially the case with activities that women engage in for the benefit of men in the private sphere. They may be done out of love, friendship,

---

[14] See Ch. 5, sects. iv–vi, esp. sect. v.

or consideration, but this does not imply they are care, nor do they share with care some of the properties that make care so distinct, particularly its urgency and compellingness.[15] What confuses the distinction quite considerably, unfortunately, is the fact that women themselves often think of those they provide care and services for as more helpless and needy than they in fact are, especially if they are male: 'My husband/son (who is 25!) doesn't even know how to boil an egg, so how could I not be there to cook breakfast for him?' Such an 'infantilization' of the beneficiaries of actual services (often under the cloak of love, but also happening in professional care) implies that women mistakenly think of what are in fact services as care.[16] Since care has been mystified in so many ways—and this mystification is part and parcel of the exploitative 'circle of care'[17]—it is all the more important to be clear about what exactly care is and what it is that women do and why they do it. Both distinctions, that between care and activities expressive of love, and that between care and services, will hopefully contribute to more clarity.

Fifthly, the difficulty in delineating care from other types of activities derives from the fact that the definition of care I have given is a *functional* definition. Hence whether a particular activity counts as care or as a service is not dependent on the activity itself, but on the function it has, that is, on whether it meets a certain type of need. This is why lists of activities cannot delineate care from other activities: cooking a meal may be caring for someone (if it is done for an infant, for example), but it may also be a service (if it is done for one's perfectly capable partner, friend, or parent or for customers of a restaurant).[18] Furthermore, whether such activities are expressive of emotional bonds is also immaterial for definitional purposes—although it is, of course, important in real life—since it is the function of

[15] See sect. ii and Ch. 6 sect. i.

[16] It also makes the service provider (who mistakes herself for a carer) feel more needed, hence more important. Since women are socialized into deriving their own sense of self-worth from how important they are for others through caring for/servicing them, they have an (apparent) emotional interest in mystifying their own activities to themselves: see sect. iii below.

[17] See the discussion in this chapter, especially sects. vi and vii.

[18] Hence the definition cross-cuts the common-sense distinction between housework and care that I started off with in Chapter 1. This does not mean the distinction has become meaningless, it simply means that caring can involve activities usually described as housework.

the activity that qualifies it as care. The definition thus hinges crucially on the concept of a 'need [that] cannot possibly be met by the person in need herself', and it is this focus on the meeting of needs through certain activities that anchors care firmly in the material world of burdens and benefits.[19] I cannot develop a fully-fledged theory of need in this context and hence can only refer the reader to a common-sense understanding of our shared human condition, that is, of the fact that human beings have needs at various points in our lives, both physical and emotional, which we cannot meet ourselves. The needs of children and frail elderly, sick, or disabled persons and of persons in need of emotional support are obvious instances and responses to these needs form the core of activities that are care as I have defined it.

Last but not least, let me add some of the strengths of my definition. First, it is immediately obvious from this definition why care cannot be 'rationalized away' like other kinds of work in Marx's utopia of abundance:[20] if care is the meeting of the needs of one person by another person and involves face-to-face interaction, it follows that carers could not be *replaced* by machines, or that they would be replaceable only to the extent that some of the activities they engage in as part of their caring can also be carried out by machines (washing machines, dish washer, vacuum cleaner) or can be 'socialized' (provided by the market, e.g. baby food, baby clothes, 'meals on wheels'). Secondly, the definition captures what is common to different forms of care, in contrast to, for example, social policy literature where 'care' usually means most forms of care except child care.[21] Social policy literature in Britain may be seen to reflect the bias implicit in welfare state policies: while help may be given with, or the state may even take on, care of ill or elderly or disabled people, it is still implicitly assumed that child care will be provided by

---

[19] See my Introduction (sects. i and ii) and sect. ii below.
[20] See Ch. 1 sect. ii.
[21] See also the notion of 'community care' in the British policy discussion of the 1980s and 1990s: child care could not be relegated back to the community because it has never been taken on by the state to any significant extent in the first place, hence it was never included in the notion of community care. Some feminist authors in the social policy area avoid this bias (e.g. Thomas 1993, Ungerson 1990*a*, 1990*b*, Graham 1991). Other feminists, however, have stressed the differences rather than commonalities between different forms of care and raised doubts about the possibility of speaking meaningfully about care in

the parents, that is, usually the mother. Child care is thus separated out from most other forms of care, and this separation is reflected in the social policy literature. It does not, however, make any theoretical or conceptual sense to do so, and my own definition was developed so as to enable me to point to the commonalities between these different forms of care and also, by doing this, point to all the work hidden from the public eye that women do. Thirdly, then, as will emerge from my argument in this chapter and the rest of the book, my definition of care forms the basis of a materialist account of women's work as care which, in turn, allows me to tell a new 'story' of women's exploitation as carers. It thus focuses the discussion on a type of activities that has traditionally not been discussed in political theory, but that sorely needs discussion because it raises questions of social justice. More specifically, care is largely performed by women, it is mostly performed unpaid, and makes those who perform it, women, dependent on others, men.

(ii) *Care as an activity*

The definition of care that I have given in the last section has several immediate corollaries relating to the characteristics of the type of activities defined as care which I shall describe in this section.

First, one cannot care for oneself, since I have defined care as the kind of activity which meets needs which the cared for cannot possibly meet herself. This corollary might strike us as counterintuitive and in contradiction to normal usage of the word. Surely we can care for ourselves, too? Yes and no. According to the ordinary language usage of 'care', it would seem that we can care for ourselves. Note, however, that there is also a distinction in the way we use 'care': the most common usage of 'care'

general—see e.g. Ruddick 1989: 46–7. Unlike Ruddick, I think it makes eminent sense to discuss care in general and I also think that my definition specifies exactly those features that the different kinds of care have in common. This is not to 'confuse' these different kinds, as Ruddick suggests, but to talk at a more general level about their common aspects (Ruddick 1989: 47). (But see also Ruddick 1990, where it does seem to be implied that it is possible to generalize over various forms of care.)

in reference to care that benefits oneself is that of 'taking care of oneself' rather than 'caring for oneself', whilst 'caring for' tends to be used to refer to care that benefits others. This usage may reflect a subtle distinction that is made between the kind of serious and involved activity that is focused on others, 'caring for', and a more superficial kind of activity or even only protective attitude that one can endorse to one's own benefit and that of others, 'taking care of'. Once we admit that there is a distinction, however, it is clear that 'caring for' is the obvious candidate for referring to those activities which benefit others and for which we in turn depend on others. There is, then, at least some foundation in ordinary language usage for the narrow definition of care which implies that one cannot care for oneself.

Secondly, if it is true that one cannot care for oneself (in the sense explained above), it follows that care has an irreducibly social nature. Caring is done for others, hence each instance of caring involves at least two persons.[22] As such, it can be, and has been, taken as a paradigm case of social interaction.[23] Note also, as I pointed out when elucidating the definition of care, that the two positions or roles that are defined by care are not necessarily fixed nor long-term.[24]

---

[22] I do not address in my discussion the question of whether and in what sense one can care for non-human beings. My definition of care can easily be changed to allow for caring for animals, and possibly plants, but I do not think it is possible to care for inanimate objects or entities such as the environment, since it does not make sense to attribute needs to such entities, and my definition hinges on a theory of needs. Hence even a discussion of caring for animals, for example, would pose tricky questions about the needs of domestic as opposed to wild animals, as well as about our responsibilities as a result of altering the need structure of domestic animals. These questions are fascinating but beyond the scope of this book, since my focus is more narrowly on human society.

[23] See Held (1987b, 1993) who advocates mothering as a paradigm for political and moral theory; also Baier (1987b). Indeed, as I indicated in the introduction (sect. iii), the ethic of care debate can be understood to be debating, as one of the issues at stake, the adequacy of caring as opposed to other paradigms of social interaction (see Ch. 5 for a discussion of this debate). I do not think that Held's version is very successful, however, mainly because mothering is a special case which involves a marked and inevitable power hierarchy between carer and cared for over time. In caring in general, by contrast, such hierarchies can be reversible, e.g. in the case of equals such as friends. Caring, therefore, can model more social relationships than mothering. (Hoagland (1990) opposes mothering as a paradigm on normative grounds, notably because it cannot be fully reciprocal.)   [24] See sect. i.

If caring is done for others, it follows furthermore, and third-ly, that it benefits people other than the carer herself. It thus involves an asymmetrical transaction of material benefits. Unlike exchange or contracts, the usual paradigms in liberal social and political theory,[25] caring is not mutually beneficial, but consists of an activity engaged in by the carer which results in a benefit for the cared for. While the carer gives her time and energy, attention and skill, the cared for's needs are met. This asymmetry holds for all cases of care which are neither paid, recip-rocated, nor remunerated in other ways.

Hence, fourthly, unless the carer is remunerated in some way (in kind or paid), or the care she gives is reciprocated, she incurs a material net burden. It might be disputed that caring really is a burden. As I shall point out below, caring can be a very em-powering and rewarding thing to do, but it is nevertheless, and may equally well feel like, a burden.[26] The question therefore is in what sense caring can be said to be a burden. The answer, it seems to me, is that caring is a burden in the same sense in which work is a burden, and since it is commonly accepted that work is a burden, care will have to be recognized as a burden as well. (I also think that care actually is work, but rather than try to establish this claim, I will simply point out the respects in which care is similar to work, and thus similarly a burden.)[27]

There is a sense of work according to which activities have to be heavy and/or unpleasant toil before they qualify as work. This narrow sense, however, does not reflect the most common usage of the word and would exclude any activities that are interesting and rewarding.[28] One of the most common usages of 'work', by contrast, refers to all paid activities as work, and it is this sense that I shall base my discussion on. The question then is whether work in this wider sense can be said to be a

[25] See e.g. Nozick 1974 for a typical example of such a theory, and Pateman 1988 for a critique of contract theories.

[26] Arguably, different types of care involve more or less burdensome elements: compare child care with the care of a terminally ill person or a person with senile dementia. It is worth stressing, however, that even the 'easiest' type of care, whatever that is, may at times become a burden, and even the 'heaviest' type of care, whatever that is, may at times be rewarding.

[27] Richard Norman helped me clarify my argument about care being a bur-den.

[28] Interestingly enough, this sense would not exclude some of the 'heavy duty' physical tending tasks that form part of care.

burden, and if so, in what sense. One might reply to this question that not all work is literally a burden, as would seem obvious considering the 'work' of a philosopher, artist, or gardener. The point, however, of the claim that work is a burden is, maybe, not so much that all work is a burden all of the time, but that all work can become a burden any time for those engaged in it. More specifically, there are two respects in which work is burdensome. First, work imposes various kinds of strain on people. The strains that have traditionally been stressed in our understanding of work are either those of heavy physical work, of mindless, repetitive work, or the strains of responsibility. There are, however, other strains, too, such as the strain of intellectually demanding work, the strain of risk, or that of work involving constant interaction with and accommodation of the demands of other people. A major part of the strain imposed by caring is of the latter kind and is shared by clerical and service workers. It is no less real than physical strain, and is complemented by the strain of responsibility. Some caring moreover involves a lot of repetitive tasks such as physical tending. Care, in other words, involves strains of various kinds. The only basis for arguing that care is not burdensome would be to claim that only one particular type of strain, which is not typical of care, formed the ground of the burdensomeness of work. But this argument would clearly be difficult in the face of the various strains that are possible and potentially present in the manifold varieties of work we can think of. Hence in so far as work is burdensome because it imposes various strains in various combinations, care is burdensome, too, since it is no different from other types of work in this respect. In fact, it is these strains which make pay necessary: presumably most people would not incur the burden of these strains without their work also being a source of material benefits. Secondly, work is burdensome—as is care—in so far as it has to be done whether or not we happen to feel like doing it. In fact, unpaid care is more like paid work in this respect than most other unpaid activities that people engage in: it imposes demands on the carer that the carer does not necessarily have a choice about meeting. If an infant cries, or an incontinent patient has wetted her bed, they need attention, whether or not the carer feels like giving it to them. Care, then, is a burden in two important senses in which work is burdensome.

There is also an important difference between work and care, however: as far as work is concerned, it is the fact that we often do not feel like working that necessitates payment for work, since it is the material benefit linked to the work that makes us continue to do it, whether we like to or not. No such material benefit, however, is linked to unpaid care, nor does it produce benefits for the carer herself like other unpaid work such as housework or typically 'male' work such as repairing cars, decorating, or building.[29] Hence unremunerated or unreciprocated care is a material net burden, and further transactions are necessary to produce a situation in which burdens and benefits are in balance for the carer. As we shall see later, it is this characteristic of care that makes those who tend to take it on vulnerable to exploitation.[30]

Since caring takes place as a response to a certain type of needs—that is, needs the person in need cannot possibly meet herself—caring involves, fifthly, a one-sided dependency of the person in need of care on the prospective carer. Their relationship is not one between equals or of equal bargaining strength since the carer has the power to withhold care and the cared for's needs have to be met. This power differential is irreducible since the needs to be met cannot be met by those in need themselves: I cannot talk to myself if I need to talk a problem over with somebody—in the best case a person close and dear to me, in the worst case a helpline worker—nor can children bring themselves up, nor can a frail 90-year-old or a mentally disabled person survive without support by others. Again, this situation does not exemplify the usual assumptions made in liberal social and political theory, where people are typically conceived of as (ideally) autonomous, independent agents in control of their choices and their life plans.[31]

Hence, sixthly, the non-provision of care can involve serious harm or even death, and it is in the power of those who are in a position to care to let such harm happen by not caring (or not

---

[29] Why, then, do women engage in care? The answer to this question is complex and will emerge from sects. iii–v, as well as from Ch. 6.

[30] See sect. vii.

[31] To some extent, the fiction of people's autonomy and equal power—as opposed to dependency on others and equal powerlessness—is socially (and theoretically, see e.g. Dworkin 1981) maintained and perpetuated through the institution of insurance policies which turn people in need into people *entitled to*

caring adequately) or to prevent it.[32] In the case of need, then, inaction or the refusal to act are sufficient conditions for harm being incurred by the person in need. This aspect makes situations of need comparable to 'emergency' situations of houses on fire or people drowning, which are usually the only type of situations discussed in the literature where inaction will result in harm and action, conversely, has a peculiarly urgent quality. Cases of need, however, and the meeting of needs, are not chance cases where supererogatory actions are called for, but very mundane and everyday cases of being there and doing things for others who need us. They are not exceptional like emergency situations, but part of each of our lives. The reason, I suspect, why they have not been discussed in the literature until very recently, is because the meeting of needs has been and still is mostly done by socially invisible actors, i.e. women.[33]

Seventhly, given the importance of care for those in need and, especially, the harmfulness of inaction or inappropriate care, the

---

care, i.e. with the power to command care. This institution, however, is only accessible to those able to enter contracts and endowed with material resources, that is, adults with a more than basic income. Hence, on the face of it, given that it is a 'solution' only for some, it cannot possibly be a just solution. Moreover, it does not solve, nor even address, every human being's utter and absolute dependency at the outset of our lives, nor can it possibly cater for all the various needs that people have and that make them dependent on others, notably emotional ones. Note that this point is not about limits to people's autonomy such as social context and individual development that can be overcome in ideal circumstances: it is about absolute limits to anybody's autonomy. It is these absolute limits which lack recognition, let alone positive endorsement, in the liberal ideal of autonomy. (See Held 1993 for an argument in a similar direction.)

[32] Those who are 'in a position to care' are not necessarily the long-term carers of long-term dependants: if I see a crying child in the street I am in a position to care, even if this child is a stranger. As noted above, the roles of carer and cared for are not necessarily fixed.

[33] R. Goodin's *Protecting the Vulnerable* is a noteworthy exception in that he writes on the morality of rather everyday cases of inaction resulting in harm (Goodin 1985). Interestingly—and typically—enough, however, he does not address care in the sense discussed here at all, but the responsibility of those on whom others have come to rely or depend. His perspective is that of a benevolent patriarch on whom others depend for protection, and he himself calls his conception of obligations toward others who are thus dependent on one 'quasi-feudal'. The roles in his theory are clearly gendered: the bearer of obligations is male, the dependants are female or honorary females. There is also no acknowledgement of the needs that make *any* human being dependent on others, since his stress lies on created or at best grown relations of dependency, whilst the focus of a theory of care lies on inevitable dependency (see my fifth point above).

most important cognitive capacities, attitudes, and skills (and corresponding virtues) in carers are attentiveness or receptivity, responsiveness, and the ability to respond in the right way to the cared for and her needs.[34] The best illustration of attentiveness is the heightened attention in parents, even when asleep, to any noise indicating distress in their baby. Receptivity refers more generally to an attitude or a 'mode of consciousness' that, in Noddings's description, 'attempts to grasp or to receive a reality rather than to impose it'.[35] Thus unless a need is perceived to exist, care will not be a response, and the perception of need requires a person's openness to the signs or demands of need. Responsiveness, then, refers to the willingness and ability to respond to such perceived need. Last but not least, the ability to respond in the right way may involve considerable experience and knowledge in the carer: a parent not only has to realize that her baby is not well, she also has to know what to do in order to meet a need the baby (or, for example, the confused elderly person) may not even be able to express adequately.

Receptivity and responsiveness to the needs of others, that is, those cared for, imply, eighthly, that in a good carer the power she has over the person cared for is counteracted by her openness towards the cared for which means that she reacts to a perceived need as a demand on her to care. Consequently, the power balance between carer and cared for undergoes a characteristic reversal in favour of the cared for. Thus women often describe their lives as full-time mothers of small babies as 'dictated' by the rhythm of the needs of their babies, by their sleeping and waking periods.[36] Being 'on call' as a doctor or nurse in a hospital is an example of such availability in a more formal setting: it institutionalizes receptivity and responsiveness and thus makes doctors and nurses available to patients. This reversal of the

[34] See Tronto 1991*a*: 8, 1993, ch. 5, Noddings 1984: 16, 19, 22, 30–5, 122–3 and *passim*; Ruddick 1989. Ruddick 1989 focuses on mothering, but in so far as mothering is a specific instance of caring, her analysis is valid with regard to caring to the extent that it focuses on aspects that are general to any form of caring, such as the skills and virtues of receptivity and responsiveness (pp. 18, 24, 71–2, 119–23; see also her discussion of the relationship between mothering and care in general, pp. 46–7 and n. 21 above).

[35] Noddings 1984: 22. Noddings likens receptivity as characterized in the quote to that characteristic of aesthetic experience or creative work: creating art is a 'listening into' another reality, that of the work of art to be.

[36] See Gieve 1989*a*: 43 ff.

power balance may also explain many women's feelings of utter powerlessness and anger *vis-à-vis* their children or those of nurses *vis-à-vis* their patients (especially if the latter abuse the system)—feelings which would be difficult to understand if we looked only at the dependency resulting from need and the corresponding power in the carer. In an important sense, therefore, a person having the skills, attitudes, and virtues predisposing her to care is not really 'her own woman' to the extent that she cares and, even more so, to the extent that she takes on, or is simply faced with, long-term caring roles. She is other-directed and heteronomous, hence not the autonomous agent political and moral theory would have her be.[37] At any point in her life, caring responsibilities may impose themselves on her in a way which is not only not under her control, but which may also render her 'life plans' unrealizable in the form so far envisaged. Again we have to suspect that this form of heteronomy has so far not been discussed in political and social theory because the people affected by it were mostly women.[38]

Caring as an activity done by people is, lastly, situated in time and space and hence in particular social contexts. This is the

[37] Held makes a similar point in Held 1987b: 130–1; see also Held 1993. It might be objected that *plausible* conceptions of autonomy will allow a person to commit herself to caring activities whilst remaining autonomous. Two points need to be made in reply. First, the extreme case of autonomously choosing to devote oneself to the care of others can be compared to the case of freely choosing to sell oneself into slavery: both present a paradox indicating the poverty and limitations of content-neutral conceptions of liberty and autonomy. Secondly, and more importantly, people (typically women—see sect. v) may simply find themselves in a situation where they have to care because nobody else is there to do it, hence where the question of committing themselves to care is simply beside the point. Human life is more tragic—or more 'viscous'—than is (wishfully) implied in the liberal focus on choice.

[38] Kymlicka in his discussion of the ethic of care realizes the problem of 'heteronomy' in care, but shies away from its implications, reasserting the need for people to have some space in their lives where they are immune from the demands of others in order for them 'to be able to make genuine commitments to [their] projects' (Kymlicka 1990: 280–1). We might ask how this is to be possible: by not meeting their needs? By making others do the caring? At this point Kymlicka ends his otherwise quite perceptive discussion with a conjuring trick: by juxtaposing 'subjective hurts' to 'objective unfairness' as the grounds for moral claims he moves imperceptibly from referring to needs (as a species of subjective hurts) to referring to others' 'contingent desires' which he then argues can justifiably be overridden (p. 281). But he has helped himself to that conclusion rather unfairly and thus avoids asking the further questions that would have led him to appreciate the exact nature of this problem and its relation to questions of distributive justice (see Ch. 6).

most important point about caring as an activity, since it is the social context which determines where, when, by and for whom caring is done, and under what conditions. More specifically, the provision of care can be public, semi-public, or private. Public and semi-public care are provided by paid professionals, often in public or semi-public institutions such as hospitals, homes for elderly or disabled people, health centres or private practices, while private care is provided unpaid and in the private sphere.[39] It is this latter form, that of unpaid care, which is of specific interest to my argument for two reasons. First because the bulk of unpaid care is done by women,[40] and secondly because it is their performance of unpaid care which makes women vulnerable to exploitation.

Take the example of child care as a typical case of full-time care, i.e. where a carer has to be available and potentially involved in caring tasks all the time, in a society divided into public and private spheres. Assume furthermore, as is the case in Great Britain, that child care is not provided publicly so that parents have the choice between buying child care on the market or engaging in it themselves.[41] In such a situation, any parent who cannot afford to buy child care is reduced to a more or less exclusively private person, since she has to be available all the

[39] By 'public' I refer here to state provided care, by 'semi-public' to private sector care, that is, to care provided either by professionals as self-employed workers or by professionals employed by commercial or voluntary organizations. This slightly awkward terminology is forced by the fact that there is a third kind of care which is unpaid and provided in the 'private sphere' of people's homes usually by people related to those they care for either as kin or as friends or neighbours (see Ch. 5 sect. vi for an analysis of the differences between care in the private and public spheres; see Okin 1991 on the ambiguity of the public/private distinction which forces such terminology). Of course, semi-public and public care can be provided by professionals or paid workers in the homes of those cared for, hence the distinction I make does not coincide with the distinction between differently located spheres, that is, the private or domestic sphere of the home and the non-domestic public sphere. Rather, it is a distinction between different modes and social relations of provision which are, however, also associated with notions of public and private.

[40] See sect. v.

[41] There are two further alternatives, which are, however, both not very common: one could try to arrange for others to provide child care unpaid, either on the basis of exchange, as in child care groups, or on the basis of kinship relations. While child care groups are difficult to organize and maintain, members of the family are often not easily available in a society based on nuclear family units or 'defective' family units where only one adult is a full member of the unit. Where extended families are more common, as in some ethnic minority communities, unpaid child care is more easily available.

time. This in turn means she will not be able to go out to work.[42] Moreover, since child care does not produce any material benefit for the carer, the carer will have to depend on her husband or partner, her family, or the state for her own survival. Full-time carers are thus full-time burdened without receiving any material benefits for their care, their lives are dictated by the needs of others while their own livelihood and well-being are dependent on others. On top of all this, they are virtually excluded from participation in the public sphere. With regard to the balance of material benefits and burdens as well as more general considerations of self interest, then, full-time care in societies where the main source of income of most people is waged work is the kind of activity no self-interested individual in her right mind would ever choose to do. Why, then, is it done at all, why do women do it, and why is it mostly women who do it?

One answer to these questions is to point to the economic pressure on women to become full-time carers, or, more euphemistically, the economic rationality of women 'choosing' to stay at home as carers.[43] Given that they are in most cases the poorer earners, their withdrawal from the labour market combined with their husband's continued and/or increased participation in it allows the maximization of household unit income.[44] Now while this explanation seems to make (some) women's continuing role as full-time carers intelligible, it cannot be the whole story since it confounds economic rationality with gender specificity. First, there is evidence from 'cross-class' families and from families with employed wives and unemployed husbands that men do not seem to 'choose' to become full-time carers in situations where it would make economic sense for them to do so.[45] Secondly, given that men in comparable situations seem to rank self-interest higher than household rationality, why is it that women do not? Why is it, in other words, that women take

---

[42] She might take on home work, but home work is even worse paid than typical 'women's jobs' and will not be a valid alternative unless the carer cannot find any better paid work or is otherwise committed to staying in her home (see Allen and Wolkowitz 1987).

[43] Of course, many women are not in a position to 'choose' to stay at home because their income is needed to support their family.

[44] See e.g. Becker's 'New Home Economics' (Becker 1981).

[45] See McRae 1986 and Morris 1990.

on the role of unpaid carers, regardless of whether it is in their self-interest or not? And why is it, we may further ask, that even in situations where both men and women engage in waged work it is still women who typically do most or more of the unpaid caring?[46]

In conclusion, the discussion of the various features of care as defined in the last section has allowed me to point to the peculiarities of this type of activities which, because they run against the grain of most work in mainstream social and political theory, also highlight various presumptions in such theory. The most pressing question emerging about care, given its peculiar features, especially the material disadvantage involved in engaging in unpaid care, is why it is mostly women who do it. In order to answer this question, we have to look at the three remaining aspects of care.

(iii) *The psychology of care*

The psychological aspects of caring stand in curious contrast to its material conditions. Whilst involving a material net loss, caring is also often one of the most meaningful and rewarding kinds of activity that anyone could engage in. Witness Noddings in her description of caring:

I am also aided in meeting the burdens of caring by the reciprocal efforts of the cared-for. When my infant wriggles with delight as I bathe or feed him, I am aware of no burden but only a special delight of my own . . . many of the 'demands' of caring are not felt as demands. They are, rather, the occasions that offer most of what makes life worth living.[47]

---

[46] See the data from time budget studies: Hartmann (1987) and Pleck (1985) provide a useful discussion and overview. Time budget studies are not necessarily reliable indicators of the performance of care, however, because they mainly aim at measuring time spent on housework. Thus some definitions of housework exclude child care, whilst others include it but do typically not include other types of care. Some housework tasks, however, will be caring activities according to my definition. It may be argued, therefore, that the amount of housework women do as compared with men is a good indicator of how much care they do as compared with men. This argument is further supported by the fact that both care and housework are traditionally and stereotypically 'women's work' (see sect. v). [47] Noddings 1984: 52.

Caring, from this perspective, is not necessarily, nor even usually, the kind of zero-sum game that a focus on its material
aspects such as I endorsed in the preceding section makes it out
to be. It is more a situation of mutual giving and taking, and
the gratitude in the eyes or words of the cared for, their well-
being and happiness, may constitute more of a reward for the
carer than any material benefits ever could.[48] Hence the cared
for's benefit does not imply a net loss in the carer, and the caring situation is not really asymmetrical. Caring is a labour of
love and rewarding in itself, even if it does not generate any
material returns for the carer. The latter seem to recede in the
minds of many carers in favour of feelings of love and caring
about this particular person and wanting to maintain, restore,
or improve her well-being—as long, at any rate, as carers can
afford not to worry about material conditions.

Caring, moreover, can be an extremely empowering kind of
activity and is certainly less alienating than a lot of the paid
work that women are offered as an alternative or other unpaid
services that women are expected to do.[49] Helping others, looking after them and their welfare, meeting their needs, is one of
the most important, if not *the* most important, sources of empowerment for many women. The power a carer feels, however, is
subjective, a positive sense of ability and energy,[50] and it is this
sense of power that underlies the peculiar logic of care whereby the more one gives, the more one is given in return.[51] Women
are very susceptible to this kind of power: women's self-respect
and feelings of self-worth do not necessarily depend so much
on any of the public indicators of power such as success, powerful positions, or control of material resources, but often on
their being needed by and being able to help others.[52]

---

[48] For an argument that the language of 'economic man' is particularly inappropriate to caring relationships see Held 1987b, 1993.

[49] See Finch 1983 and Delphy and Leonard 1992 on the variety of services that
wives provide for their husbands. Note that not all activities that Delphy and
Leonard describe as 'services' would count as services under my definition which
distinguishes care from services (see sect. i).

[50] See Gilligan, reporting McClelland's research on the meaning of power
where men interpret power as 'assertion and aggression' while women 'portray
acts of nurturance as acts of strength' (Gilligan 1982: 167–8).

[51] See Alibhai 1989: 35; see also Gilligan's more extensive discussion of interdependence (Gilligan 1988b, esp. p. 16) and Noddings 1984: 52.

[52] See sect. v.

Note also that this subjective empowerment deriving from 'making others well and happy' is not linked in any straightforward way to the very considerable power and influence a carer has over the cared for's welfare and it may also be felt side by side with feelings of powerlessness.[53] Thus an overprotective mother may think she is not powerful enough really to care for her children (because their well-being does not entirely depend on her), but doing the best she can for them by meeting all their needs (in a way which keeps them dependent on her and which is not in their best interest). The empowerment as well as powerlessness she may feel contrast with her power over her children's welfare and her abuse of this power, neither of which she may even be aware of.

Note, furthermore, that the empowerment deriving from care is not as such specific to care. We may feel empowered in the same sense of ability and energy by engaging in other activities which are rewarding in themselves. Any hobby or sport may produce similar feelings and some of these feelings may even be derived from the fact that the activity is social and shared with others. What is specific to care, however, is its essentially other-directed and other-beneficial nature and the fact that the sense of empowerment derives from exactly those features: it is *because* and to the extent that a carer can make others happy and well that she feels powerful. Sports, by contrast, are social in so far as they are team sports, but they are not engaged in in order to produce benefits for others, nor are they determined by the needs of others.

There is, however, another side to the psychology of caring which contrasts with the positive and glowing picture that has been presented so far. Thus we may understand what has been said so far as the 'best case scenario' of the psychological aspects of care. There is a corresponding 'worst case scenario' which I shall present in the following. The feelings of real—as opposed to ideal—carers may then be understood to vary along the dimension between the two scenarios.

A carer can easily feel exhausted by the seemingly or often actually never-ending demands of others and by the fact that her efforts are directed towards looking after others' well-being.

---

[53] See sect. ii above.

Worse than this, she may even feel used by those she cares for, like cheap labour or even like a servant or slave, neither of whose lives are their own. She may feel this way because, in fact, she does not have a life of her own, because her life is filled with caring for others. She may feel completely out of control and powerless because as a carer she is at the constant beck and call of others. These feelings may be seen to be linked to the fact that, as a carer, a person will be extremely vulnerable to others' demands because of the peculiar skills and virtues of receptivity and responsiveness that caring involves. They are, moreover, linked to the fact that care *is* asymmetrical in that, unless it is paid, it implies benefiting others and burdening oneself.[54] The worst case scenario of the psychology of caring thus reflects the material asymmetry noted above, while the best case scenario with which I started off at the beginning of this section stands in contradiction to it. How, then, do carers experience caring? The best answer to this question is probably that carers will experience instances of both the best and the worst case scenario and will usually find themselves somewhere in between the two.[55]

How caring is experienced, whether it comes easily or not so easily to people, furthermore depends to some extent on how this activity fits in with their conceptions of themselves and the structures of their personalities. An individual who sees herself as defined in relation to others, as part of a network of relationships, will be more predisposed to relate to others, perceive their needs, and respond to them than a person who sees herself as separate from others and basically defined by the projects she engages in, the positions she holds, the power or money she has.[56] These differences in self-conception and identity have been found to be gendered: it is women who tend to have the former and men who tend to have the latter type of self-conception. The differences themselves have been explained by reference to the fact that it is women who mother.[57] I cannot discuss the details of this account here, however. What is important to note for the purposes of my own argument is that if this account is valid it provides an important and very fitting part of the

---

[54] See sect. ii above.   [55] See Ungerson 1987.
[56] See Gilligan 1982, Chodorow 1978.   [57] See Chodorow 1978.

micro-explanation of why it is that women continue to do most of the caring.[58]

There is one further and crucially important factor which systematically influences the experience of carers. One implication of the best case scenario is that carers will probably not experience an acute conflict between meeting the needs of others by caring and meeting their own needs, while the worst case scenario will probably involve awareness of such a conflict and may also involve resentment of the fact that carers cannot meet their own needs as they perceive them. Now to the extent that women are raised to be *selfless* carers they are taught the denial of their own needs because this will make them less likely to be aware of a possible conflict between meeting their own needs and those of others.[59] This means that their experience as carers will be systematically biased towards the best case scenario. Even more dramatically, if their needs structure can be changed in such a way that the meeting of the needs of others will also meet their own needs—e.g. their need to feel empowered and important by being indispensable, or their need to engage in meaningful activities—the problem of a conflict of needs will not even arise and their experience will not even be in danger of approaching the worst case scenario. The difference in self-conception between a relationally and non-relationally defined self may be seen to imply such different need structures as well. These considerations, if valid, imply that women's awareness of their own needs— supposing we know what these are—may be fundamental to their experience as carers, and that the tradition of raising girls to become selfless wives, mothers, and daughters may have done much harm in preventing women from being aware of their own needs.[60]

(iv) *The ethic of care*

The activity of care does not only involve specific skills, but may also be seen to involve a particular moral outlook which has

[58] See sect. v for an overview of the various parts of the 'story' of why women care. The validity of Chodorow's account does not preclude the causal efficacy of other factors such as social pressure and constraints.

[59] See sect. v.   [60] See Miller 1988 and my discussion in sect. v.

recently been discussed extensively under the heading of the 'ethic of care'.[61] Since Nel Noddings has provided feminists with the so far most sustained attempt at elaborating the moral values, virtues, and dilemmas arising from caring, I shall base my presentation on her account.[62]

Noddings acknowledges caring as an activity—to which she sometimes refers as 'caretaking' or later as 'caregiving'[63]—but insists that 'in the deep human sense that will occupy us, I cannot claim to care for my relative if my caretaking is perfunctory or grudging'.[64] In her ethic of care, Noddings focuses on caring as an attitude rather than as an activity and the sense of caring that she is concerned with is psychological-cum-moral. By thus contrasting caring as an attitude with caring as an activity, it might seem as if she sees the two as independent of each other, since she not only insists that 'caretaking' which is grudging is not care, but also claims that caring as an activity is not necessary for caring as an attitude to exist.[65] This may be seen to pose a problem for my account: how can Noddings's ethic of care be part of a general theory of care as an activity if she sees care as an attitude as so clearly distinct from the activity? The problem posed is not serious, however. First, it is worth stressing that both aspects of care usually go hand in hand, and certainly in the most typical cases of care, both attitude and activity would be present. Secondly, and more importantly, it seems to me that

[61] It is Carol Gilligan's work that started the whole discussion about the ethic of care (Gilligan 1982). For collections of essays on this discussion see e.g. Kittay and Meyers 1987, Hanen and Nielsen 1987, Card 1991, and Larrabee 1993. Held, herself an important participant in this discussion, refers to many of the ideas and arguments from the discussion in her elaboration of a feminist morality (Held 1993).

[62] Noddings 1984. Other book-length works on the ethic of care, broadly speaking, have been published since, such as Ruddick 1989, Held 1993, and Tronto 1993. These, however, either focus on mothering (Ruddick, Held) and/or have a much broader scope (Held, Tronto). Noddings therefore remains the main point of reference for a discussion of the ethic of care. Her version of the ethic of care also has instructive shortcomings which I shall discuss in the following two chapters. Noddings 1989 uses the previously elaborated care perspective in her discussion of conceptions of evil. Her construction of the ethic of care does not seem to have substantially changed in this later work (see my references to both works below, and esp. Noddings 1989: 184 ff.).

[63] Noddings 1984: 9 and Noddings 1990: 125, respectively.

[64] Noddings 1984: 9.   [65] Ibid. 22.

in such typical cases the attitude of care is systematically related to the activity, that is, that the attitude reflects the demands
or exigencies of the activity. In fact, this correspondence is exactly what we find. The skills that I pointed out earlier as required
of a good carer correspond very closely to the virtues that
Noddings postulates as central to care.[66] Hence there is no real
problem, only a slightly looser connection between care as an
activity and as an attitude than we might have wished for for
the sake of a neat fit between the two.[67]

The attitude of caring then, according to Noddings—and the
activity of caring, we might add, too—involves most importantly
a close attention to the feelings, needs, wants, or ideas of others. It consists of an 'engrossment' into their lives and reality
and of a focus away from one's own world, point of view, and
preoccupations:

When my caring is directed to living things, I must consider their
natures, ways of life, needs, and desires. And, although I can never
accomplish it entirely, I try to apprehend the reality of the other.

This is the fundamental aspect of caring from the inside. . . . there is
invariably this displacement of interest from my own reality to the reality of the other.[68]

Note that such apprehension of the reality of the other is not
specific to care. It is also necessary for good management practice or, on a more sinister note, important for anybody who
wants successfully to manipulate others. We therefore have to distinguish between the caring attitude and the cognitive function
that is part of it. The cognitive function of 'apprehending another person's reality' may be common to these various purposes,

---

[66] See sect. ii.

[67] In giving a materialist account, in fact, I have to presume that there is a
systematic connection, and furthermore, that it is the activity of care which determines the moral outlook rather than the moral outlook which delineates the
activity (see Marx and Engels, *GI*). I do not want to make any strong deter-
ministic claims, however, but merely draw attention to the fact that I am at least
committed to a weak version of a causal link from the activity to the moral outlook. This commitment contrasts with Noddings's clearly idealist version of the
ethic of care. This idealism is maintained and, if anything, even more explicit
in Noddings 1989: see e.g. her discussion of marxism (pp. 107–9) and of wom-
en's oppression and exploitation (pp. 174–6).

[68] Noddings 1984: 14; see also pp. 16, 19 and Noddings 1989: 185.

but the attitude itself is distinct: in managing or manipulating others the cognitive function is used for different purposes, usually for the purposes of people other than those whose reality is thus apprehended, while in caring such 'receiving' of others, as Noddings often calls it, is part and parcel of a benevolent relation between carer and cared for which compels the carer to act on behalf of the other person rather than in her own interest. Moreover, receiving others, according to Noddings, is not exclusively cognitive or rational, it is, more importantly, *feeling* with others: 'It is not at bottom a matter of knowledge but one of feeling and sensitivity. Feeling is not *all* that is involved in caring, but it is essentially involved. . . . in the receptive mode itself, I am not thinking the other as object. I am not making claims to knowledge.'[69] Engrossment in others, then, is both a cognitive and an emotional state of apprehending and feeling with others, a state which Noddings describes as absolute. The other, when she is received, 'fills the firmament'.[70]

The cognitive aspect of caring is further qualified by Noddings as 'receptive-intuitive' as opposed to 'objective-analytic', the latter being a cognitive mode 'in which we impose structure on the world' instead of 'listening, looking, feeling'.[71] The receptivity characteristic of caring is comparable to the aesthetic receptivity of artists creating works of art.[72] The role of reason and rational considerations is thus circumscribed. Reason is harnessed to the service of caring and becomes dangerous and counterproductive if it ceases to be thus circumscribed. Hence rational thought is not necessarily opposed to caring and at points more than necessary in order to determine the right course of action. The danger, according to Noddings, lies in the fact that our thoughts may run away with us:

It is not that objective thinking is of no use in problems where caring is required, but it is of limited and particular use . . . The rational-objective mode must continually be re-established and redirected from a fresh base of commitment. Otherwise we find ourselves deeply, perhaps

[69] Noddings 1984: 32; see pp. 16, 30.
[70] Ibid. 74. This is a formulation which Noddings takes over and quotes several times from Buber's *I And Thou* (Buber 1970; see e.g. Noddings 1984: 176). Noddings is heavily influenced by Buber and by existentialist thought more generally. These influences also illustrate the idealism of her approach.
[71] Noddings 1984: 34.   [72] Ibid. 22.

inextricably, enmeshed in procedures that somehow serve only themselves; our thoughts are separated, completely detached, from the original objects of caring.[73]

More specifically, the idea here is that a carer may move in
thought from a concrete situation to a more abstract and principled way of thinking about this particular situation, but that
she always has to return to the particular situation before she
decides to act. The primary imperative for a carer, therefore, is
to remain 'tuned in', as it were, with the other person:

We keep our objective thinking tied to a relational stake at the heart of
caring. When we fail to do this, we can climb into clouds of abstraction, moving rapidly away from the caring situation into a domain of
objective and impersonal problems where we are free to impose structure as we will. If I do not turn away from my abstractions, I lose the
one cared-for. Indeed, I lose myself as one-caring, for I now care about
a problem instead of a person.[74]

Abstract thought, in other words, always has to be circumscribed
by receptivity. It may be instrumental in caring, but it cannot
replace receptivity, nor can it be the ultimate or even main focus
of the carer.[75]

The receiving of others, in its turn, leads to a 'motivational
shift'.[76] Instead of being concerned with her own aims, the carer
sees those of the cared for as if they were hers and wants to act
to meet them: 'My motive energy flows toward the other and
perhaps, although not necessarily, toward his ends, ... I allow
my motive energy to be shared; I put it at the service of the
other.'[77] Feeling with the other arouses in us 'the feeling, "I must
do something." When we see the other's reality as a possibility
for us, we must act to eliminate the intolerable, to reduce the
pain, to fill the need, to actualize the dream.'[78] This motivational

---

[73] Ibid. 26.   [74] Ibid. 36; see pp. 25, 35.
[75] In stressing receptivity or sensitivity and the development of such an attitude in moral agents as the main focus of the ethic of care, Noddings's argument is parallel to arguments defending virtue-based morality as against rationalist
arguments: see McDowell 1978, 1979 and Lovibund 1994: 794 for a similar observation. McDowell's focus, of course, is not exclusively on care although he typically uses examples of caring to illustrate his position (McDowell 1978: 19–20
and 1979: 343). See also Ch. 5 sect. iii.
[76] Noddings 1984: 33; see Noddings 1989: 185.   [77] Noddings 1984: 33.
[78] Ibid. 14.

shift is either 'natural' or morally induced. That is, the impulse to care for others is either an immediate, spontaneous reaction to the perception of need in others, or it is a reaction that is based on a commitment of the carer to maintain herself as 'one-caring', as Noddings calls what I termed carers. Thus not in every situation will a person's first impulse be to care. If that person holds an ethic of care, however, she will have to stay true to her ideal of 'maintaining and enhancing caring', and it is this ethical ideal that will induce her to care.[79]

This indicates the sense in which Noddings's ethic is 'psycho-logical-cum-moral': caring, according to her, is in many cases a 'natural' or immediate reaction to the apprehension of others' reality.[80] Caring as a moral attitude and ideal supervenes on the 'natural caring' without which it would be an impossible ideal. An ethic of care 'strives to maintain the caring attitude and is thus dependent upon, and not superior to, natural caring.'[81] Two natural, pre-moral sentiments thus underpin the ethic of care, that of sympathy with others as well as a longing for related-ness with others.[82] The 'ethical ideal' is based on these senti-ments in that the good to be achieved answers to these sentiments, both in their natural and moral forms: this good is the related-ness with others that care creates, maintains, and enhances.[83] It is not clear from the text whether this good is supreme and how it relates to other goods, but we may conclude from the central position she accords it that at least in an ethic of care it figures as the supreme good.[84] Again, this good is both natural, in so

[79] Noddings 1984: 42. Again, there are striking parallels to a virtue-based morality which accords a central position to the conception of the good life in determining moral action: see McDowell 1979: 343–4.

[80] She also believes that it comes 'more naturally' to women than to men and describes the virtues characteristic of caring as well as her ethic of care as 'fem-inine' (Noddings 1984: 1–3, 40–6, 128–31 and *passim*; see also Noddings 1989: 186–7 and *passim*). She also claims, however, that it is possible for both men and women to develop this 'feminine' side or part of themselves (1984: 6, 44). Cf. my discussion of the gendered nature of care in sect. v.

[81] Noddings 1984: 80; see also Noddings 1989: 184–5.

[82] Noddings 1984: 104.

[83] This is one of the points where Noddings's idealism is telling: her ethic is focused on the agent, the carer, rather than on the activity or the outcome it produces. It is worth pointing out, however, that there is another good that is achieved by caring: the meeting of the needs of the cared for. This good is not addressed in her discussion—certainly a significant omission on her part.

[84] It is thus comparable to human flourishing as the supreme good in Aristotle's ethic. The characteristic and telling difference between the two ethics, however,

far as we experience it as a good in our lives without having to have reflected upon and endorsed it, and moral, in so far as we can endorse it as the ideal we try to achieve in our lives and which guides our actions.

A further aspect of this ethic must be stressed. In correspondence with Gilligan's findings about women's tendency to think about moral dilemmas in context rather than abstractly, caring for Noddings is always a response to concrete situations and cannot be reduced to any rules or principles:

To act as one-caring, then, is to act with special regard for the particular person in a concrete situation . . . she acts in a nonrule-bound fashion in behalf of the cared-for . . . [An ethic of care] does not attempt to reduce the need for human judgment with a series of 'Thou shalts' and 'Thou shalt nots'. Rather, it recognizes and calls forth human judgment across a wide range of fact and feeling, and it allows for situations and conditions in which judgment (in the impersonal, logical sense) may properly be put aside in favor of faith and commitment.[85]

What is morally right or wrong can thus only be determined in reference to particular situations: actions are evaluated 'with respect to how faithfully they conform to what is known and felt through the receptivity of caring'.[86] Hence the ultimate decision can only be made in particular situations on the basis of a caring person's perception of this situation. Cases cannot be decided abstractly, nor can we come up with any abstract rules. Rules can at most serve as 'guidelines toward desirable behavior',[87] as 'economies of a sort' which help us deal with everyday situations.[88] The danger, however, is that they make a person insensitive to real people, and in so far as they do this, they distract from rather than guide moral action: 'I may come to rely almost completely on external rules and, if I do, I become detached from the very heart of morality: the sensibility that calls forth

---

is that care and relatedness are goods dependent on the interaction with other people while in Aristotle the superior virtues that achieve more complete happiness are those whose practice is possible without dependence on others (Aristotle 1980 (*NE*), x. 7).

[85] Noddings 1984: 24–5; see also p. 96. Cf also Tronto 1987 and Blum 1988 on the conceptualization of an ethics of care as 'particularist' or 'contextualised' and my discussion in Ch. 5.   [86] Noddings 1984: 92.
[87] Ibid. 200; cf. pp. 55–6.   [88] Ibid. 47; see also Ch. 5 sect. iii.

caring.'[89] It is crucially important, therefore, that a caring person 'must know when to abandon rules and receive the cared for directly'.[90]

Similarly, justification does not refer to principles or rules, but to a person's apprehension of the situation and feelings. It is a mistake to think that caring could ultimately be justified by reference to principles or be argued for on the basis of principles:

> In arguing from principles, one often suppresses the basic feeling or longing that prompts the justification. One is led to suppose that reason produces the decision. This is the ultimate and tragic dishonesty, and it is the one that we shall try to avoid by insisting upon a clear-eyed inspection of our feelings, longings, fears, hopes, dreams.[91]

Reason and rational argument thus have a rather circumscribed role in this ethic of care, while natural and moral sentiment play a much more important and crucial role together with the virtues of 'receptivity, relatedness and responsiveness' which are crucial to a carer's moral outlook and action.[92]

By way of a summary, we can understand Noddings's ethic of caring as an elaborate and more systematic version of the moral concerns and values that the women in Gilligan's original research expressed. Gilligan claims about the 'different voice' she describes that a concern with relation with others, rather than separateness and autonomy, is central to it, and she stresses the interdependency of carer and cared for. Noddings states similarly that 'relation will be taken as ontologically basic and the caring relation as ethically basic'.[93] Noddings, like Gilligan, also stresses the need to make moral judgements in the context of particular situations and the impossibility of deciding cases in the abstract.

There is, furthermore, a similar distinction in both authors between a masculine and a feminine approach in ethics. Both identify reason, abstract thought, rules, and principles as masculine and intuition, feeling, receptivity to others, and contextualized thinking as feminine. Noddings, however, puts more stress on women's supposedly natural capacity to care, while

[89] Noddings 1984: 47; cf. pp. 51–2.   [90] Ibid. 52; see also p. 56.
[91] Ibid. 57.   [92] Ibid. 2.
[93] Ibid. 3; see also p. 51 and Noddings 1989: 183 ff. and *passim*, Gilligan 1982, ch. 2, and Houston 1989: 86.

Gilligan adopts Chodorow's psychodynamic explanation of this difference of moralities and moral identities in men and women.[94]

Noddings's ethic of care and Gilligan's original research on women's 'different moral voice' thus complement each other perfectly: Noddings can be seen, and probably sees herself,[95] as giving the kind of account of an ethic of care which Gilligan's women subjects would have given had they been philosophers and given themselves enough time to consider and explicate their moral thinking in detail.[96] At the same time, however, it should be stressed that Noddings's ethic of care is just one possible version of such an ethic. Her idealist version is very influenced by existentialist philosophy, an influence which is most obvious in the focus on attitudes as opposed to, for example, outcomes, as well as in the focus on the moral agent, the carer, as opposed to, for example, care as an activity or practice.[97] It is thus worth noting that other versions of an ethic of care are possible, but have generally been presented in rather more programmatic outline.[98]

(v) *The gendered nature of care*

In this section I shall discuss more explicitly than I have so far what I have had to refer to throughout this chapter already: the

[94] Noddings 1989 tends slightly more to a social constructionist position about 'feminine caring', but leaves the question ultimately open (pp. 186–7).

[95] See Noddings 1984: 8 and 42, which are two of many places where she quotes Gilligan or reports her findings.

[96] Gilligan's later position is that care and justice are two moral perspectives that both men and women know how to use, but that there is a clear gender difference in terms of what perspective provides the main focus for moral thought and deliberation in men and women: see Gilligan 1988*a*, p. iii and Gilligan and Attanucci 1988: 82. See also Ch. 5, sect. i.

[97] See also Noddings 1989. Ruddick 1989 is a good example of a version of the ethic of care (restricted to mothering) that avoids agent-centredness by focusing on mothering as a practice.

[98] See e.g. Tronto 1987, 1989, 1991*a*, 1991*b* and Blum 1988. Tronto 1993 is an interesting new development of her previously published work on the ethic of care which probes its possible extension into the public sphere. Ruddick 1989 and Held 1993 are also more elaborate versions, but of an ethic based on mothering rather than care more generally. As I argued above, these accounts are interesting to the extent that mothering exemplifies the general characteristics of care rather than the specific characteristics required by mothering. I shall discuss Noddings's and other possible versions of the ethic of care in Ch. 5.

gendered nature of care. Whilst I have so far sketched what we might call a 'general theory of care', looking at care as an activity and the psychology and ethic of care, it is now time I focused fairly and squarely on the fact that the 'general' theory has a rather particular application. The theory mainly reflects women's lives, psychologies, and morality. This should not really surprise us since it is mainly women who care. Caring in all its aspects is thus deeply gendered. I shall elucidate this claim in the following.

Caring as an activity, disposition, and attitude forms a central part of probably all cultural conceptions of femininity and is virtually absent from, or even incompatible with, conceptions of masculinity. In these conceptions, woman the carer or nurturer is opposed to and contrasted with man the hunter or fighter. Caring is part of what it is, or even entirely what it is, to be a woman: caring supposedly comes naturally to women, hence the care for husband, children, parents, relatives, neighbours, and more generally the needy is supposed to be the ultimate fulfilment in women's lives. Men, by contrast, are supposed to be fighters. If they are not involved in physical fight or war and can express their masculinity in this way, they express it by being competitive and more generally by having, and being in, power.[99] The economy and the state are the predominant spheres where they can prove their manhood. If they are not successful in these spheres, they have at least power in the private sphere over their wife and children, and this power manifests itself in their getting looked after and served at home.[100] Women thus have to serve and care for men so that masculinity as power can stay intact, and their serving and caring for men is ideologically explained and justified by their being just the kind of persons who are good at and love doing that. This gendered contrast also conveniently obscures what lies behind it, namely a systematic power hierarchy.[101] Last but not least, these interdependent

[99] See Connell 1987, Hearn 1987, Brittan 1989, Segal 1990, and Clatterbaugh 1990 for recent research on masculinity.

[100] Of course, some men may be unfortunate in that it is their wives who 'wear the trousers', but this saying only proves the point that it is usually those who (used to be the only ones to) wear the trousers who have the power. As long as this saying is in use, i.e. seems meaningful to people, it is referring to a gendered hierarchy of power in the family whose beneficiaries are men.

[101] See Connell (1987), who stresses the fact that masculinity and femininity are defined so as to 'fit' each other. He calls the version of femininity that 'fits'

conceptions of masculinity and femininity are not only maintained and reproduced in everyday discourse, literature, and the mass media, they are also given credibility by pseudo-scientific and scientific theories, sociobiology being only the latest example of a steady flow of 'scientific explanations' of gender difference.[102]

Femininity and masculinity are also associated with different social spheres: the former with the private sphere of the home as a haven in a heartless world, the latter with the public sphere, i.e. the heartless world itself, consisting of both the competitive sphere of the economy and the site of political power and war, the state. The contrast between the two spheres is not simply one between spheres where one is most likely to find members of one or the other sex predominate,[103] but turn on the distinction between masculine, self-interested competition and fighting 'out there' and the feminine caring response to the demands and needs of everybody in the home. Women as carers have the magic ability to heal and undo in the home whatever wounds the bad world has left on those who are entrusted to her.

Note, however, that this contrast contains a rather skewed representation of the private sphere:[104] not *everybody's* needs are met if it takes a selfless wife and mother with unflinching commitment to meet all the needs there are. The home can only be such a haven if there is no conflict between the needs of the carer and those of the others. In order for the haven to be possible as an ideal picture, therefore, the needs, wants, and desires of the person who is to be this magic carer have either to be presumed to be non-conflictual or have to be eclipsed altogether. Hence the carer has to be either self-less or self-fulfilled as a carer.[105]

masculinity 'emphasized femininity' and argues it is 'defined around compliance with [the global] subordination [of women] and is oriented to accommodating the interests and desires of men' (p. 183).

[102] See Brittan 1989, ch. 4.

[103] There are parts of the public sphere where women predominate, such as those sectors of industry which mainly employ women. There, too, however, women's presence is gendered and explained by the supposedly feminine types of work they do.

[104] It also biases thought about the public sphere. This, we might speculate, shows particularly strongly in the difficulties many have in imagining that care in the public sphere can be genuinely good care. (See my discussion in Ch. 5 sects. iv–vi; see also Dalley 1988.)

[105] By the self-less carer I mean a person who is literally without a self defined by needs, wants, and interests that could conflict with those of others, by the self-fulfilled carer I mean a carer whose caring for others also fulfils her own

The image of the haven in the heartless world thus depends on the self-less or self-fulfilled carer who *makes it* such a haven. The idyll can only be maintained at the cost of turning women into (or forcing them to be) such ever available carers, whether that corresponds to women's needs, wants, and interests or not. It is, moreover, also part of this picture that self-interested action can only be compatible with masculinity, i.e. men's work and wheeling-dealing or politicking in the public sphere, but not with femininity. If women were represented as acting self-interestedly in the sphere into which they are inscribed by this picture, there would immediately arise the danger of conflicts of interests and the necessity for dealing with them either by fighting it out or by negotiating and this, remember, was a mode of interaction that belonged to the public, but not to the private sphere, the supposed haven. Women's self-interest, and women's needs, wants, and desires, therefore, have to be eclipsed altogether in this picture or have to be made to fit—or, arguably, distorted—via the figures of the self-less or the self-fulfilled carer.

Now there is a sense of caring that applies specifically to men, namely that of 'providing for'. Traditionally, men are caring husbands and fathers if they are reliable breadwinners,[106] but they do not have to change their children's nappies or sing them lullabies in order to be said to be caring fathers. Correspondingly, a caring son would not be expected to care for his frail parent himself, but rather to provide the material resources to pay for care if needed, i.e. if his sister or wife did not agree to, or could not, do the actual caring herself.[107] Caring sons are those who do not forget their parents and maybe give them a hand, drive them when needed, and do some repair works or maybe shopping, but not necessarily or even usually do they do any of the actual tending that care as an activity involves.[108] Such care, that

needs, wants, and interests, i.e. a carer whose self is defined by other-regarding rather than self-regarding needs, wants, and interests to the extent that self-regarding needs, wants, and interests would conflict with those of others. Notice that both the self-less and the self-fulfilled carer would, by definition, not feel the strain of caring (see sect. iii).

[106] On the association of masculinity with paid work and the image of the breadwinner see Brittan 1989, ch. 4.

[107] The 'normal' expectation is that daughters or daughters-in-law will care for frail elderly persons in preference to sons (see Qureshi and Walker 1989).

[108] See Qureshi and Walker 1989: 90–2; Parker 1990: 46–7.

is, care in the sense of 'looking after' or 'tending' is a woman's thing to do. Caring in the sense of 'providing for' thus confirms the breadwinner role that is attributed to men,[109] while the actual unpaid care-taking is one of the few things that women are seen and recognized as being good at: 'men aren't very good at . . . looking after people. Well *I* wouldn't be any good at it anyway . . .' says a man in a recent study of carers whose frail parents are looked after by the only daughter in the family.[110] Thus, of course, speak many men—an admission of 'failure' which serves both as an explanation and justification of the fact that they do not, need not, cannot, or even should not get involved in any actual care. Caring as providing thus confirms rather than contradicts the gendered identities and roles of men and women and reinforces gender difference in the private sphere in conformity with the general conceptions of masculinity and femininity.

There are, nevertheless, actual exceptions to this gender lore. First, as many men care for their elderly wives as wives care for their elderly husbands.[111] This is an important exception in that it means that men can and do engage in care in the sense of looking after and tending others. However, in this case, it is not necessarily *qua men* that they care but arguably *qua husbands or lovers*. At least some men see themselves as fulfilling the vows they have incurred when marrying their wives, and most men see their care as motivated by their love for their wives.[112] The care is thus not necessarily given on the basis of their 'male nature', but more significantly on the basis of their social and / or emotional relation to the cared for. Women, by contrast, but according to the same gender lore, are supposed to be carers *qua women* and naturally, often regardless of their actual social and / or emotional relation to the cared for. A daughter who has a tense or conflictual relationship with her mother or father would still be expected by others, and feel obliged, to care for her parent,

---

[109] The breadwinner role also *excuses* men from taking on time-consuming unpaid care, see Finch and Mason 1993: 119 ff.   [110] Ibid. 108.
[111] See Parker 1990: 46.
[112] See Ungerson 1987: 86, 91–2. According to some gender lore, it is only the civilizing influence of women that makes naturally aggressive man-the-hunter sociable (and capable of caring, we might add). What better way, then, of taming man than via the love of a woman (see Clatterbaugh 1990: 17). What better way also of blaming women for (not being better at containing) all the violence committed against them?

and similarly daughters-in-law are roped in, even if not to the same degree.[113] It is also interesting to note that some men carers interpret their care along professional lines, thus making another profession or second calling out of it, which they systematize and think of using in other contexts.[114] Effectively, what they do in thus reinterpreting it is to masculinize the highly 'feminine' activity of care.[115]

Secondly, at least some men do seem to get more involved as fathers than they used to do before.[116] There are even 'lone fathers' and some men who take on significant or even the main responsibility in a couple for the care of their children. Significantly, however, Segal notes about them that *'men who are less rigid about appropriate gender roles . . .* are the fathers most at ease with, and most likely to engage in, active parenting'.[117] Such fathers also seem to learn the required skills such as sensitivity and responsiveness,[118] although it may not come easily to them. Here is what a full-time father says about his experiences:

When I became a father, I came up against the limits of my masculine upbringing . . . *My emotional life had been geared around having things done for me.* Suddenly the tables were turned and I found myself resentful and with precious little to give. For the first few months I was angry and self-pitying, not only because it was isolating and hard work, but because I was expected to give unconditionally.[119]

If being a man means being cared for and serviced by others, especially, but not exclusively, by women, this difficulty would be expected.[120] On the other hand, however, it can also be expected that men can change and can learn to care. Both exceptions thus confirm the gendered nature of care as an activity in pointing out the specific difficulties that men encounter when they

---

[113] See Qureshi and Walker 1989; also the fact that some care performed by women neighbours, friends, or cousins, often based on good relations between them and the cared for, see Ungerson 1987.   [114] See Ungerson 1987: 108.

[115] See also Segal 1990: 46, on gender differences in 'mothering'. Men carers are also perceived as needing more support by the social services and are given more home help (see Ungerson 1987: 60 and Bobbington and Davies 1983).

[116] For a discussion of changing conceptions and practices of fatherhood and of their import see Segal 1990.   [117] Ibid. 45, my emphasis.

[118] Ibid. 46.   [119] Rutherford in Segal 1990: 42, my emphasis.

[120] See Miller 1988 on the psychodynamics of the difficulties men have engaging in caring and nurturing. Note also the fact that men in service positions are traditionally seen as feminized and often suspected to be homosexual, hence are seen not to be 'real men'.

do engage in care, and the gender-specific coping strategies and explanations of their care that they may endorse in contrast to the 'naturalness' of care for women.

Nonconformity of men and women to this gender lore, not surprisingly, meets with considerable social pressure and resistance. Thus women who display a healthy dose of self-interest by securing their own independent income and refusing to cede control over their lives are still easily accused of being selfish—an accusation it would be difficult to make to men—and might feel guilty about it or be made to feel guilty about it. They are still in danger, when pursuing the same careers as men do as a matter of course, of being labelled honorary men, cold or uncaring, lacking somehow in 'femininity'.

The social institution of heterosexuality plays an important role in enforcing these gendered contrasts, too, in so far as it labels deviance from the norm of heterosexuality—which almost invariably implies deviance from femininity and masculinity—as abnormal, perverse, or sick. Hence the enforcement of gender difference is intimately linked with and supported by the enforcement of heterosexuality. Thus lesbians who on the basis of their political and/or sexual choice do not relate intimately to men, hence do not care for or service them in significant ways, are still accused of wanting to be men, or straightforwardly of being unnatural or perverse. Similarly, men who show emotions or who engage in caring or servicing activities are easily called wet or labelled sissies or pansies. Moreover, the ever virulent homophobia expressed in (virtually always male) violence against gay men and lesbians shows the degree to which masculinity is fragile and has to be maintained by labelling as perverse, and 'punishing', those men who do not conform and those women who encroach on their territory.

Masculinity may be even more fragile than femininity and conformity to it may have to be policed more strongly because there is so much more at stake in losing it: women do not have much power or privilege to lose *as women*. This fragility also means that men have to repress whatever 'feminine' aspects they experience in themselves—unless they define and understand themselves as deviant—and will have to police other men to do the same. Hence a lot is stacked against men developing the 'caring' side of themselves. This pressure may also explain why unemployed men find it hard to do any caring work or more generally 'women's' work in the home, even if their wives have full-time jobs: unemployment does already pose a threat to their male identity and purchasing power as breadwinners, but the prospect of 'playing housewives' may add insult to injury and would probably make them fear the loss of respect from their mates. Conversely, the explicit non-identification with masculinity, as in many gay men, makes the acceptance of 'feminine roles' and characteristics easier: witness the development of a specific form of male-to-male care, that of 'buddyship', in the gay community as a response to the AIDS epidemic and the consequent need for significant amounts of care.[121]

Caring, however, is not just part of a gender stereotype and a corresponding gender lore or ideology. It is also, as an activity, a main component in the sexual division of labour which is still prevalent in most or even all societies: most care, whether paid or unpaid, and certainly most of the unpaid caring work, is done by women. Despite exceptions, the rule still is that it is women who are engaged in child care, and in a recent survey of British social policy literature on care excluding child care, Parker concludes that there has been no real shift in the performance of all varieties of care. It is still women who 'provide the bulk of care'[122] in caring for the elderly, especially outside the bounds of marriage,[123] and for physically disabled children and adults.[124] As mentioned above, the only significant exception to this rule is elderly husbands caring for their wives. The sexual division of labour with regard to care is thus confirmed in one study after another, and even the authors of a recent study whose analysis stressed individual choice and commitment and the fact that caring responsibilities are negotiated rather than automatically incurred state in their conclusion that 'women in general do seem to be more firmly locked into sets of responsi-

---

[121] We might also conjecture that the assumption of a caring role by a husband for his wife is much easier after a lifetime of activities conforming to gender roles. Husbands caring for their wives are mostly past retirement age, hence have already shed the breadwinner role (Parker 1990). Unlike younger, unemployed men, they are not under pressure to prove their manhood anymore. (And, of course, they are free to care because they do not engage in paid work anymore—but so are unemployed younger men.)　　　　[122] Parker 1990: 55.
[123] Ibid. 46.　　　[124] Ibid. 50, 54.

bilities to relatives and men are more peripheral'.[125] They also find that women's excuses for not being able to care are less readily accepted,[126] that women are seen as the '"obvious" people to take responsibility', partly because they are seen as more competent and partly because they have less to lose if giving up their jobs,[127] and that women tend to do what they call the 'personal caring', i.e. physical tending, especially if there has not been any open or explicit negotiation about it.[128] Thus even a study which set out to look at negotiated agency and the flexibility of arrangements has to acknowledge the constraints of a highly gendered structure in the sphere of care.[129] Women moreover, but not surprisingly, bear the main costs of unpaid caring, both in terms of performing the actual care and in terms of forgone income and emotional strain: 'generally, female carers [are] more likely to give up their jobs, lose more money and to experience more stress than are male carers'.[130] It is clear, then, that the sexual division of labour is highly unequal in that it imposes the burden of unpaid care to a large degree on women whilst it frees men to take up more profitable types of work.

The sexual division of labour finds its correlative in differences between men and women with regard to the psychology of caring and carers. Thus women's identity tends to be more often defined in relation to others than in terms of separateness from others.[131] More specifically, their sense of self and self-worth is 'traditionally built . . . on activities that they can manage to define as taking care of and giving to others'.[132] Women are more likely to feel powerful when involved in caring for others while men tend to see giving to others or even co-operating with those

---

[125] Finch and Mason 1993: 165.   [126] Ibid. 119.   [127] Ibid. 76.

[128] Ibid. 77.

[129] This structure is presupposed and often actively supported by the social policies of the modern welfare state. In Britain, the recent move of care back into the 'community' is only one of many policies which *de facto* rely on women to provide that care unpaid that it has become too expensive for the state to provide paid. Similarly the continued refusal of most welfare states to provide public child care keeps the burden of unpaid child care (or payment for child care provided by others) firmly placed on women's shoulders.

[130] Parker 1990: 93.   [131] See Gilligan 1982, Chodorow 1978, Miller 1988.

[132] Miller 1988: 54. It should be noted that this sense of self may be more shared by middle-class than by working-class women: see Walkerdine and Lucey 1989, Fisher and Tronto 1990: 156.

who are supposed to care for and service them as opposed to their self-interest and their own life plans[133] or even as a loss.[134] Men also tend to associate power with assertion and aggression rather than with care,[135] while women not only feel powerful as carers, but also 'have a much greater sense of the pleasures of close connection with physical, emotional and mental growth than men'.[136] Thus women are much more likely to define themselves in relation to others and more specifically as carers,[137] and they are more likely to enjoy caring as an activity, that is, they are more likely to find themselves closer to the best case than the worst case scenario of caring.[138]

It is important to stress, however, as several authors do, that women's perception of their own needs will be systematically distorted in a society where their prescribed role is that of caring for others and servicing their needs:

In a situation of inequality, the woman is not encouraged to take her own needs seriously, . . . First, [women] are diverted from exploring and expressing their needs (which would threaten terrible isolation or severe conflict not only with men but with all our institutions as they are arranged and, equally importantly, with their inner image of what it means to be a woman). Secondly, women are encouraged to 'transform' their own needs. This often means that they fail, automatically and without perceiving it, to recognize their own needs as such. They come to see their needs as if they were identical to those of others—usually men or children. If women can manage this transformation and can fulfill the perceived needs of others, then, they believe, they will feel comfortable and fulfilled. Women who can do so will seemingly be

---

[133] See Kymlicka's juxtaposition of care demands and projects: this implies that care cannot figure as a project—whilst, of course, it does for countless women (Kymlicka 1990: 280–1).

[134] Miller 1988: 43. As Miller points out, in so far as men are used to having things done for them, even the request for co-operation with those who are supposed to be there for them will be experienced as a loss or diminishment of their autonomy and independence (p. 43). Note, by contrast also with Kymlicka (see previous note), Noddings on whether caring means loss: 'Since I am defined in relation, I do not sacrifice myself when I move toward the other as one-caring. Caring is, thus, both self-serving and other-serving' (Noddings 1984: 99). In other words, if a person defines herself and her projects as in relation to others caring cannot represent a loss; if, however, one's self-definition and the definition of one's projects are self-regarding caring will be seen as a loss and as opposed to one's own interests.   [135] Gilligan 1982: 167–8.

[136] Miller 1988: 40.   [137] Finch and Mason 1993: 160; see Ungerson 1987.

[138] See sect. iii.

most comfortable with social arrangements as they now are. The trouble is that this is a most precarious transformation.[139]

By identifying their own needs with those of others, Miller suggests, women may be able to be happy with their caring and servicing lives, but they are not able to develop themselves and their own potential to the full.[140] Nor, we might add, do they necessarily make the best sort of carers: not only are they in danger of making children too dependent on them, but they will also not be able to perceive needs in others correctly that they have had to deny in themselves.[141] Moreover, as the existence of both best and worst case scenarios in caring testifies, it may not always be possible to identify one's own needs successfully with those of others and at points it may just be obvious that one's own needs conflict with the needs of others. The self-less and self-fulfilled carer, in other words, are a dangerous fiction that is imposed on women at their own cost.

Last but not least, as mentioned in the last section, the ethic of care is highly gendered as well.[142] This is not surprising, either as a cultural stereotype or as an actual fact, if caring is associated with femininity, if the sexual division of labour is such that it is mainly women who care, and if women's psychological structure predisposes them more than men toward endorsing such a perspective and value system. It is, therefore, more women than men who endorse such an ethic of care, and even if the actual difference is not as clear-cut as the original research suggested—that is, even if women are also capable of and often engage in moral thinking from the 'rights and justice' perspective and some men endorse a caring perspective—the difference remains to be pointed out.[143] Thus even if we cannot speak of a strict 'division of moral labour' between women who endorse an ethic of care and men who endorse an ethic of rights and justice, there is a remarkable difference, both at the level of actual differences between men and women as well as at the level of conceptions of femininity and masculinity. Care dovetails with femininity and its emotional connotations, but jars with masculinity

---

[139] Miller 1988: 18–19.

[140] For an extensive discussion of the distorting effects of the oppressive structures within which women care on women themselves, their relationships, and the nature of their care, see Blum *et al.* 1976, also Houston 1989.

[141] See Miller 1990.   [142] See Friedman 1987*b*.   [143] See Gilligan 1987.

and its preoccupations with reason, power, and conflict. A 'real man' might think in terms of fair play and 'being good mates' or friendship, but he would not be expected to think in terms of 'receiving others' and caring for them, being there for them, meeting their needs. As stressed above, it is femininity that is about being there for others, that is, caring for, nurturing, and servicing others, and it is precisely for this reason that Noddings calls her approach a 'feminine' approach to ethics.

One last clarification about what has been said in this section is in place. I have listed four ways in which care is gendered: first, as a concept it is gendered and fits into gender lore in so far as it marks out what is feminine and contrasts with what is masculine; secondly, as an activity it is firmly located in the women's half (or more than half) of the sexual division of labour; thirdly, as an outlook and activity it matches women's psychology more closely than men's; fourthly, the ethic of care tends to be endorsed by women rather than men. The picture that arises from these four aspects is one of deep division between men and women not only in terms of gender lore, but also in their psyches and activities, as well as in terms of their actual commitments and values. Hence the question arises about this picture whether these differences are explained by men's and women's different natures—as gender lore would have it—or whether they are socially constructed and enforced, or, if they are both, which explanation points to the predominant causal factor. Arguments may be and have been put forth on both sides.[144] I cannot discuss this question in detail here, but would like to point the reader to an old and, it seems to me, still valid argument. At this point in time, not having enough evidence of societies where women are or were equal to men, there is no way of telling whether it is women's nature to be caring or whether it is a 'nature' that has developed in response to their being forced to be the carers in society, at least partly by being excluded from other spheres, since we do not know what kinds of things women would choose to do were they really free to choose, how they would think, and how they would conceive

---

[144] Note that not all feminists fall on the side of social construction, however—witness Noddings and some radical and psychoanalytic feminists—while most sexist and conservative arguments are to be found in the essentialist camp, which asserts natural and inevitable differences.

of themselves.[145] The answer in the twentieth century remains very much the same as Mill gave in the nineteenth century: we are in no position to know, but we do know that there are elements of restriction and force—even if not of the obvious legal kind that Mill was arguing against—and as long as there are, we can assume there have to be. This in turn must make us conclude that men and women would be capable of the things they are said not to be capable of since restrictions and (structural) force would not be necessary otherwise. It seems to me, then, that the burden of proof lies in the essentialist camp and that the social construction position is more plausible. However, since we cannot know, either position can be asserted.

(vi) *The circle of care*

So how are these gendered aspects of care related? It looks as if they fit together like matching and mutually reinforcing parts of a whole or structure. They do not fit exactly and very neatly, but they are clearly linked, and they are clearly mutually reinforcing. They form a nexus of material practice and corresponding psychology and ideology which it has proved hard for women to escape and for men to enter. I shall call this nexus the 'circle of care'.

The circle of care represents women's part in the sexual division of labour in our societies. Thus women's actual work as carers is reinforced by their gendered identity, the strong sense of empowerment and self-realization which they draw from it, and by their ethic of care which compels them to care where they feel needed. The fact, on the other hand, that it is still mostly women and not men who do the caring continuously works to reproduce and develop women's skills and knowledge as carers and thereby to increase their openness and readiness to respond to needs. Both attention and skills are improved by the actual caring of women and predispose them towards further caring while men's lacking involvement keeps them inattentive to the demands of those in need and to the need to respond by

---

[145] See Mill's very elaborate argument in *The Subjection of Women* about this question (Mill 1985).

caring. Thus if men's preferred response to need continues to be the provision of material resources, in correspondence with their roles as breadwinners, they continue to get around actual care and fail to develop the skills needed to care well.

Corresponding to this continued division of labour and skills, the gender stereotypes of the caring, nurturing woman and the brave, strong, and self-interested ('knows what he wants') man are reproduced in daily reality: the link between care and femininity is maintained and strengthened as long as it is mainly women who do the actual caring and men who provide the material resources. Furthermore, women's perception of their own needs is likely to be distorted in a society in which they grow up to be carers. This, together with the fact that it *is* women who mother—if we believe Chodorow's account of the formation of psychological difference between men and women—increases women's predisposition and capacity to care and their sense of self-realization in caring while it decreases these factors in men.[146]

Thus when we ask why women continue to do the caring, the answer will have to refer to all four aspects of caring: women's material activity as carers is not only reproduced through the economic pressure of wage differentials, but also through psychological dispositions, emotional rewards, moral outlook, and cultural and moral norms and values and social pressure. Women do not only respond more easily to needs, but their moral values correspond to and strengthen this basic attitude of receptivity and responsiveness to others, and social pressure as well as public policy will do their part to make those women who are not 'caring' mothers, wives, or daughters toe the line. For much of history and in much of the world, women were made to do the caring because they were excluded from participating in other spheres of life. At the end of the twentieth century and

---

[146] See Chodorow 1978. As indicated above, I wish to remain uncommitted as to the truth of Chodorow's account. *If* it is valid, it fits in neatly with the rest of the picture I am drawing here by explaining psychological difference by reference to the sexual division of labour (rather than, say, by reference to inherent structures of the human psyche). If it is not valid, a different explanation may be presumed to be possible at least in principle. Such an explanation would provide the link between psychical difference and the other gendered aspects of care. It would thus provide part of the microexplanation that underpins the macro picture of sexual divisions in society.

in the developed countries, however, legal and open exclusion of women from the public sphere of politics and well-paid work has ceased to be a causal factor in this circle of care. This is why Delphy and Leonard's account of women's exploitation is antiquated and inappropriate for exactly those societies they mean their theory to apply to. If women continue to care in these societies, it is despite the fact that men have lost the direct power over them that they used to have *qua* husbands.[147] The explanation of why they do, therefore, has to refer to a more complex picture. The circle of care arguably provides a more adequate story in answer to this question.

Note, however, that there is one part of my theory of care that so far does not fit this picture of mutually reinforcing aspects of care. This is the possibility of care being experienced as a burden rather than as self-fulfilling and empowering. To the extent that care is experienced as a burden it must make women think about why they do it and whether they want to continue doing it the way they have been so far. It may also make them ask the questions that I have been asking in this chapter, i.e. why women do most of the unpaid caring in the first place, and it may make them realize the burden and injustice that the sexual division of labour imposes on them. The worst case scenario thus can have the function of an 'outlaw emotion' in that it has the potential of making women question their own role in society as they have seen and accepted it so far by making them sorely aware of their own needs which are not being met.[148] It may make them ask: and who cares for me? why do I bother? It may make them insist on getting a better deal than they have had so far. Of course, things are not that simple, and it takes a lot more than simple questions to start changing one's life. But these kinds of questions may form a beginning. The worst case scenario may thus hold the seeds of protest for women, the seeds of a more conscious conception of their own role in the sexual division of labour, and possibly the seeds of doubt about the justice of life as they know it. However, such an experience may also lead women to feel inadequate as carers. It may make them try harder and deny their own needs even more than they have so far.

[147] See Ch. 3 sects. v and vi.
[148] For an account of 'outlaw emotions' and their value to feminist theory see Jaggar 1989.

In the latter case they would be reinscribing themselves as carers, in the former case they would have the chance to break out.

The point I mean to make is that the circle of care is not as closed as it may seem from my description above even though all of its aspects contribute strongly to its closure. One of these aspects is the distortion of women's needs in the process of making them into carers. Another one are the blind spots or myopias inherent in some versions, notably Noddings's version, of the ethic of care which prevent women from conceiving of and recognizing injustice where it is done, even at their own cost. In the following section I shall look at the myopias in Noddings's ethic of care and argue that because of them, it functions as an oppressive ideology which contributes to women's exploitation: by trying to be perfect carers, women lose sight of their own needs and their own interests.

(vii) *Care and justice: the myopia of Noddings's carers*

Carers' myopia derives from the fact that Noddings's ethic of care, as I have stressed before,[149] is extremely context-bound. I shall illustrate how this contextuality derives from the demands of care as a practice and how it is developed by Noddings in her version of the ethic of care before presenting the three types of myopia that her version of the ethic of care suffers from.

Note, to begin with, that carers are good carers to the extent that they are 'swayed' by the demands of need, want, or desire in others, that is, to the extent that they are open and responsive towards them.[150] The centrality of the virtues of attentiveness and responsiveness in the ethic of care obviously derives from the other-directed and other-beneficial nature of care as an activity. Noddings is thus correct in highlighting these virtues. One who is not open in such a way fails as a carer since she will fail to care if she fails to apprehend the reality of the other. Given such an attitude of openness or receptivity towards others, however, a carer runs into what has elsewhere been described as the 'problem of boundaries' in relation to utilitarianism:[151] since there are always unmet needs somewhere, can a good carer

---

[149] See sect. iv.   [150] Noddings 1984: 56; cf. p. 19.   [151] Williams 1981.

ever stop caring? Or to put it differently, given unlimited needs, are there any boundaries to the caring responses of carers?[152]

Noddings's response to this problem is as follows. First, the carer is justified in not responding to need if she is in danger of exhausting herself and needs time off to recover in order to maintain her ability to care in the future.[153] This constraint is internal to any ethic of care since it derives from the overriding ideal of care itself.[154] Secondly, a carer's caring response is consequent not merely on the perception of need, but also on the existence and nature of the relation between carer and cared for. Thus the closer the relation, the stronger is not only the impulse, but also the obligation to care.[155] Thirdly, care is bound by 'proximity' and the possibility of completion of care: a carer may have to respond to the need of the homeless person she passes by in the street, but not to the needs of a hungry child in a refugee camp in Ethiopia.[156]

The second and third boundaries are an expression of Noddings's very strongly contextualized interpretation of an ethics of care, and it is this strong contextualization which is responsible for

[152] See also Noddings 1989: 186, where the problem is only treated very cursorily, however, and comparatively played down.

[153] Noddings 1984: 98–100.

[154] No carer, according to Noddings, can be completely other-directed, hence completely oblivious to self-interest. Self-interest is only important, however, first, in so far as it allows the carer to have experienced her own needs and wants and the good consequent upon their being met by caring others (ibid. 50, 151) which, in turn, is required for the natural and moral striving for relatedness and care; and secondly, in that it justifies the carer in protecting herself against being harmed (p. 115), where harm is either harm to the physical or ethical self. The former case of harm is a case of self-defence, the latter the case most important to Noddings's ethic, i.e. that of protecting oneself from moral exhaustion and the consequent 'diminution' of one's ethical ideal (see also pp. 98–100).   [155] Ibid. 47, 85–6.

[156] See ibid. 47, 86, 152. Noddings uses different examples, but the point is the same: it is physical proximity that allows relation between carer and cared for and that also allows the caring to be completed. By this, Noddings refers to both, the actual caring activity as well as the acknowledgement of that care by the cared for. Only if care is acknowledged is it completed (ibid, ch. 3). The child in the refugee camp suffers because she or he cannot make physical proximity happen—a well-off potential carer could by going there, but Noddings seems to think that this option is not necessarily justified because it would mean ceasing to care for those to whom there are already existing close relationships and therefore corresponding strong obligations (p. 86). For a critique of the 'proximity criterion' see Card 1990: 102 ff. Noddings 1990 slightly revises this criterion by introducing the possibility of 'establish[ing] caring chains' based on *trust* rather than actual relationship. She insists on this being 'risky', however (p. 121).

the first type of myopia. Given that care will be a response not to any case of need, but will depend on whether somebody in need happens to be in the right place (where there are real carers) at the right time (when carers are or can be receptive to the needs of others) and in the right circumstances (where carers do not have prior or overriding obligations to care and have the resources needed), the actual provision of care for those in need will be very uneven. It will depend on factors which are completely irrelevant to the distribution of care which should be consequent on the existence of need and need only. Hence, given that the distribution of care to those in need of care will not provide equal care for cases of equal need, it is unjust.[157] Now carers who endorse Noddings's version of the ethic of care may perceive this as a problem, but they are not in a position to change their own caring response since the latter is determined contextually rather than by abstract considerations or general principles.[158]

Noddings's ethic of care renders carers myopic not only with respect to the distribution of the benefits of care, but also, and secondly, with respect to the distribution of the burden of care to carers. Consider, to start with, the following case of free riding: in a 'community of carers', the egoist is king! The egoist will always be in a position to be cared for when in need since he can rely on others' caring response whenever he needs care, whereas he himself does not care for others because it is not in his interest to do so.[159] Carers, on the other hand, cannot

[157] This point has been made by others, see Tronto 1987, Held 1987*b*, and Friedman 1987*b*.

[158] The most explicit reference to justice in Noddings occurs in the following quote: 'Caring . . . limits our obligation so that it may realistically be met. It will not allow us to be distracted by visions of universal love, perfect justice, or a world unified under principle' (Noddings 1984: 100–1). See also my exposition of Noddings's discussion of the role of principles in sect. iv and my discussion of the ethic of care in Ch. 5. Noddings (1990) admits in response to various critics, with respect to the injustice caused by racism, that 'we may indeed need a concept of justice' (p. 121), but she is hopelessly vague on what this implies and points instead to the 'tendency to bog down in endless abstract wrangling over procedural rules and definitions instead of listening and responding' (p. 122). This is a move very typical of Noddings's style of argument as well as of her conception of abstract morality which avoids any real discussion of certain more general problems—see my presentation of the third kind of myopia below and also the discussion in Chs. 5 and 6.

[159] An egoist, by definition, has only self-regarding needs, wants, and interests. Care to an egoist thus is obviously a burden rather than self-fulfilment (see sect. v).

qualify their caring response by considerations of deservingness since this would be to allow care to be influenced by considerations or principles external to their ethic of care.[160] As long, then, as the egoist can make sure he is in physical proximity to carers when he needs them—or, even better because more reliable: as long as he has some sort of relationship with one or more carers—he can get away with free riding on their care. Again it is obvious that this is a case of blatant injustice: the egoist is exploiting the carers by way of taking advantage of their receptivity and other-beneficial activities. Noddings type carers, however, have no way of preventing him from doing so for the same reasons as those in the first case of myopia: they would let principles override their caring response and, even worse, diminish their ideal by refusing to care where they could.[161]

The egoist king among carers can, of course, be generalized to the case of a society split into a class of egoists and a class of carers. We all know this case: it is that of a society characterized by a sexual division of labour, morality, and skills between male fighters and female carers, that is, a society in which care is deeply gendered.[162] Like the egoist, the fighters will be able to exploit the carers in virtue of the latter's receptivity and responsiveness to need, provided they can invent and enforce a social institution whereby individual carers cannot help but be faced with the needs of individual fighters and their offspring. This institution is heterosexual marriage.[163] Note that men do not even

---

[160] Desert is a concept that Noddings does not discuss at all, but I am fairly certain that she would treat it along the same lines as justice, that is, as a principle which should not deflect a carer from trying to maintain and enhance her ideal of caring.

[161] In fact, the second type of myopia is even harder to resist in Noddings's ethic precisely because a refusal to care for somebody who is proximate is bound to affect the 'ethical self' negatively, while not caring for somebody who is not proximate is perfectly justified. The latter does not even count as a failure, let alone as a refusal to care because it is simply beyond a carer's reach (which is restricted by proximity). On failing to care see Noddings 1984: 115: 'There can be no greater evil, then, than this: that the moral autonomy of the one-caring be so shattered that she acts against her own commitment to care.' (See also pp. 113–20 and my renewed discussion of this myopia in Ch. 6 sects. i and ii, and Noddings's seriously meant question: 'How can we remain in caring relations with those who seem clearly to be doing wrong?' (Noddings 1989: 187).) Houston (1989) deals with a slightly different, but related aspect in Noddings's treatment of the obligation to care.

[162] See sect. v. Baier (1987a) and Houston (1989) have made similar points.

[163] Heterosexual monogamous marriage and equivalent forms such as common law marriage and cohabitation maximize contact between individual fighters

have to be fighters or uncaring for such an exploitative situation to obtain systematically. Given the crucial importance of receptivity and responsiveness in the carer, it suffices that men are in general less open and responsive to the 'demands' of care than women for a fairly strict division of labour between caring women and non-caring men to reproduce itself.[164] Hence anything short of equal and equally strong care orientation among men and women—anything short of the abolition of the sexual division of labour, morality, and skills with regard to care—will imply the exploitation of women as carers.[165]

It follows, moreover, that in any society which burdens one group exclusively with the main bulk of care a Noddings type ethic of care will function as an oppressive ideology and a catalyst for exploitation by preventing those who endorse it from taking seriously or even realizing the fact that they are being exploited. It will channel those who endorse it, that is, women, into actual care while freeing men to pursue materially more beneficial kinds of activities such as paid work or enterprise or even simply leisure. The second kind of myopia, then, engendered by the ethic of care (as interpreted by Noddings), lies at the heart of women's exploitation as carers.[166]

and carers and spread the benefits of care in a more egalitarian fashion than polygyny, where married men benefit vastly more than, and at the expense of, unmarried men.

[164] Women mostly have to go to women friends for emotional support while men get their emotional support mostly from women (see Bartky 1990: 99–100; see also 135 n. 7 for further references; Bartky raises the interesting question just how supportive women as social inferiors can be of men—a problem parallel to Hegel's master–slave dialectic).

[165] I am telling an extremely simplified story in this paragraph, but it needs to be told as starkly for the point to be made. I am far from wanting to imply that there are for women no benefits whatsoever deriving from heterosexual marriage (or equivalent forms). They may be 'given' everything they need 'in return' for their care—or so the official, seemingly egalitarian, story goes (see Delphy and Leonard 1992 and Ch. 3). In fact, their living standard will usually be higher than they could have afforded themselves relying on their own income. What I do mean to stress by making this point is that women are extremely vulnerable to being exploited in this institution and have the fewer resources for resistance to exploitation the more they identify themselves as carers and the more the ethic of care informs their actions (see also sect. viii and Ch. 6 sects. i and ii).

[166] Card (1990), Hoagland (1990), and Houston (1989, 1990) have all criticized Noddings's ethic of care for making women vulnerable to exploitation, but their notion of exploitation is broadly moral, intending a lack of respect and/or reciprocity, not material inequality. Their critique is, therefore, quite different from

The third kind of myopia relates to the rejection of 'abstract principles' and, more generally, the radical contextuality of Noddings's ethic of care. Any context-transcendent considerations, like, for example, the kind of considerations I have indulged in in discussing the first two varieties of myopia, may at best be used as 'rules of thumb' in the process of moral deliberation, but it is the actual situation and the receptivity towards the real needs of real people in it which ultimately determines the carer's response to it. An ethic of care 'puts persons before principles', or, more technically, accords lexical priority to considerations of care over more abstract considerations of any kind.[167] Consider the example Noddings uses to illustrate the point: as a caring person, Ms A cannot 'go to the barricades' to fight on the side of black civil rights activists—despite her strong belief in the validity and justice of their cause—if her (bigoted) loved ones fight on the other side. She may try to argue with them to change their opinions, but ultimately the obligations deriving from her actual relationships override any action in accordance with her 'abstract' convictions.[168] It is this myopia which prevents carers from taking seriously the considerations of justice I have introduced in this section in order to criticize the first two types of myopia, since considerations of justice may not override considerations of care and hence may not lead a carer to leave a situation exploitative of her caring skills and values.

In conclusion, the discussion of Noddings's ethic of care in this section has thrown into relief two main sets of issues. First, and rather indirectly, it has provided us with a new exploitation story regarding women as carers which it is worth relating to the discussion of the preceding chapters in order to highlight its merits. I shall do so in the last section of this chapter. Secondly, it has focused on the three types of myopia which arise from

mine, tending to focus on the question of care in *abusive* relationships rather than the more everyday and more systematic type of material injustice that I am concerned with.

[167] See sect. iv and my more detailed discussion in Ch. 5.

[168] Noddings 1984: 109–10. Note that this ordering of obligations is perfectly rational and consistent even if it implies a rather parochial set of priorities for action. As I tried to make clear in sect. iv, Noddings is not opposed to principles as such, but to the priority that is accorded to them in relation to the more contextualized considerations of care with respect to concrete individuals that a carer is faced with in particular situations. See also Noddings 1989 *passim*.

the radical contextualism of Noddings's ethic of care and which prevent carers from addressing in any serious way issues of distributive justice that arise with regard to care: practically about the distribution of the benefits of care to those in need and about the distribution of the burden of caring as an activity to carers or potential carers, and theoretically about the compatibility between considerations of justice and considerations of care. More specifically, I have argued that the second type of myopia lies at the very heart of women's exploitation as carers and that Noddings's version of the ethic of care, if endorsed by women, actually functions as an oppressive ideology which blinds them to their exploitation. The question therefore arises whether an ethic of care is necessarily radically contextualized and thus excludes considerations of justice or whether we can reject Noddings's conception as a misconceived version of the ethic of care whilst maintaining the general attempt to formulate an ethic of care. More specifically, what needs further discussion is how care and justice are related to each other and whether there necessarily is a conflict between these values and considerations. I shall address myself to the 'ethic of care vs. the ethic of rights and justice' debate and the more specific question of how considerations of care and considerations of justice are related in Chapter 5 before returning to Noddings's myopias and drawing final conclusions in Chapter 6. Before I can move on to this new set of questions, however, I shall bring the argument of the first two parts of the book to a close by looking one last time at the story of the exploitation of women as carers.

(viii) *The exploitation of women as carers*

I left the discussion of women's exploitation at the end of Part I with negative conclusions regarding Delphy and Leonard's theory of women's exploitation *qua* wives, but with more positive conclusions about what was required in a 'story' about women's exploitation to make it a plausible story. Most crucially, I argued, a story about women's exploitation had to be able to point to the mechanism whereby women are exploited since there was so much variability in women's material lives that generalizations about their material status—hence their exploitation status—were problematic if not downright impossible. What, then, is the exploitative mechanism, and how reliably does it work? The exploitative mechanism, as should be obvious from the argument in this chapter, is what I have called the circle of care, an interlocking set of constraints and practices that channels women into doing the bulk of care that needs to be done in any society. Or, to put it in terms of the sexual division of labour, it is the social institution of the sexual division of labour which constructs women as carers and thus systematically 'extracts surplus labour' in the form of unpaid care from them (to harken back to Marx's definition of exploitation).[169] Unlike in Delphy and Leonard's story, however, women may not ever be subjected to any direct force and yet be exploited. The circle of care works more subtly and on many levels, social and individual, situational and psychological, conscious and unconscious, whilst Delphy and Leonard's story focuses exclusively and, as I have argued, implausibly, on the relations of production in the family, especially on the power the head of family has to extract work from other members of the family and on the benefit he draws from women's work. In my story, women may care for reasons completely unrelated to their husbands: usually, care is a response to a perceived need, that is, is motivated both from within the carer and by the situation she is in, and it is precisely for this reason that women who are open to the demands of need cannot easily stop caring.[170] Force, in my story, is exerted mostly more indirectly by all the social norms and institutions which channel women into care, including their self-conception and ethics, but not at the point where they actually engage in care, and even if there is force at this point, it is more likely to be exerted by the social services or the family at large rather than, or as well as, the husband by himself.

Similarly, the question of who benefits from women's exploitation as carers is answered rather differently in Delphy and Leonard's and my story. Whilst Delphy and Leonard again point exclusively to the husband, the beneficiaries in my story are men in general (as well as women who have opted out from caring): given that so and so much care needs to be done in any society, and that there is no particular reason why some rather than

---

[169] See Ch. 2 sect. vi.
[170] See Ch. 6 sect. ii for further discussion of this point.

others should do it, all those who do not do it benefit from the fact that others have taken it upon themselves to do it.[171] Given, moreover, that most of this care is performed unpaid, hence that those who perform it incur a material net burden whilst at the same time freeing the others to pursue materially more beneficial types of activities (income generating as well as leisure), it is clear that non-carers are materially better off than carers. Hence non-carers are 'extracting surplus labour'—unpaid labour which does not benefit those who perform it—from the carers, hence benefit from the exploitation of carers.[172]

The story of the exploitation of women as carers, then, avoids the problem of the variability in women's particular material conditions by focusing on the mechanism whereby care is 'extracted' from carers.[173] This mechanism also explains the continuing material inequality between men and women by reference to two facts: (1) the fact that most care is unpaid, hence a material net burden for those who care, and (2) the fact that the shouldering of that burden by women frees men to pursue materially more beneficial types of activities, notably income-generating ones.[174] Note, however, that women do not have to be poor to be exploited as carers, since the notion of exploitation is relative,[175] although it is also true that women are poorer than men,

[171] Delphy's earlier work is more structural than Delphy and Leonard's, and there is at least one earlier paper where Delphy takes a more structural line in answer to the question of who benefits from women's exploitation and the exploitation of ethnic minorities (Delphy 1984, 'Our Friends and Ourselves', esp. 114 ff.).

[172] There is a slight complication in this exploitation story compared with more traditional ones: the *immediate* beneficiaries of care—those whose needs are met— are third parties, but not exploiters. This is unlike in the more traditional case of exploitation where the benefit from the work of the exploited accrues to the exploiter. The exploiters, in the case of care, then, are those persons whose time is freed by not having to care. There are therefore two kinds of benefit involved in care, hence two types of beneficiaries: (1) the meeting of needs benefits a person in need incapable of meeting this need herself, and (2) the caring by carers implies a time gain for those not having to do it. It is the second type of benefit which marks the exploiter, not the first.   [173] See Ch. 3 sect. iii.

[174] If *time* were focused on more explicitly as a material resource, the difference would be even more obvious, since carers lose out on material resources as well as time, whilst non-carers gain both time and thus also the opportunity to engage in activities which will generate material resources (paid work) and in activities which will increase their potential to generate material resources in the future (education; skill and knowledge enhancement through work).

[175] Noddings, in a later discussion which is probably a response to criticism such as mine in the preceding section, does refer to women's exploitation, but

especially with respect to both material resources *and* time—a fact which becomes especially visible after divorce.[176] Thus even though there is variability in women's material lives as well as a general difficulty to determine their exploitation status[177]—and some women escape exploitation altogether by refusing to care—the exploitative mechanism is in place as long as the sexual division of labour with regard to care persists, that is, as long as the circle of care exists. This, in turn, means that even if not all women are exploited all of the time, women in general are exploited in this specific way, and therefore each woman is highly vulnerable to being actually exploited *qua* carer.

Two more clarifications may be necessary to complete the picture. First, I do not mean to claim that women are *only* exploited as carers. They may be exploited as wage workers as well, for example, but I do mean to claim that women's exploitation as carers is the main form of exploitation that applies specifically to women. Secondly, I should add a note about unpaid work that women do which, according to my definition, is not care, but a service.[178] According to this definition, a lot of work that women do for their husbands or adult children cannot be counted as care because it does not meet a need that those in need could not possibly meet themselves. Given that such work is a service and not care, how does it fit into the exploitation story, if at all? In response to this question, I need to point to what we might call the centripetal tendency of the circle of care: whilst the circle of care is most centrally about care as I have defined it, it also 'pulls in' other types of work, notably other unpaid work that is a service according to my definition. The reasons why such work is performed are several, but are crucially related to the specific features of the circle of care. Once the sexual division of labour with regard to care is established—once the circle of care is functioning—differentiation between men and women is established in various ways. As I have argued above, women typically acquire the other-directed and other-beneficial

is desperately vague in referring to 'the exploitation and oppression of women forced to perform tasks that bring them neither compensation nor recognition' as a 'cultural evil' (Noddings 1989: 175), and moreover mistaken in thinking that exploitation implies poverty (pp. 174–6).

[176] See Weitzman 1985 and Okin 1989 on 'vulnerability by marriage'.
[177] See Ch. 3, sect. iii.   [178] See sect. i above.

virtues and skills that are required in any good carer, notably a readiness to respond to the demands of need. Given that these virtues and skills open women up to the demands of others, it becomes difficult to restrict responses to care only, since both care and services meet needs and since it is sometimes difficult to establish whether a need is absolute in the sense of not being meetable by the person in need herself or a need which can be thus met.[179] Also, given this care-based gender differentiation, women's self-conception, fulfilment, and happiness are often dependent on being important or even irreplaceable for others, hence will tend to make them want to 'do things for others' regardless of whether they are really needed, or whether they are merely providing a service.[180] Furthermore, the social roles of 'wife', 'mother', 'daughter', and especially that of 'housewife' include both care and services, and once women have adopted those roles, they will understand them as including both and encounter social pressure if they do not conform. Lastly, femininity is characterized by both care and services for others, by 'being there for others', and although it is easier to refuse to conform to the stereotype as far as services are concerned, the confusion nevertheless remains and may be deeply internalized.

All these factors, then, contribute to the widening of the circle of care to include unpaid services as well, but at the heart of the circle of care remains women's performance of care, and it is women's performance of care, not of services, which poses the most difficult problem as far as the abolition of women's exploitation as carers is concerned. I shall return to this question in Chapter 6. Before I can do so, however, I have to discuss more specifically the nature and function of the ethic of care. The ethic of care—as interpreted by Noddings and discussed in the previous section—functioned as part of the circle of care and thus as an oppressive ideology further predisposing women towards caring whilst at the same time either blinding them to the fact that their care implied their exploitation or at least rendering them morally incapable of acting on that perception. Can the ethic of care be conceived in a way which pre-

---

[179] See sect. i above.
[180] See sect. iii above, and also the point that a lot of women tend to perceive men as more needy than they really are (see sect. i, pp. 134–5).

vents it from having this oppressive function? I approach this question in the next chapter by looking at the ethic of care debate as a whole and specifically at the question whether considerations of justice—hence ultimately of exploitation—can form part of an ethic of care.

PART III

5

Considerations of Care and Considerations of Justice

In this chapter, I shall discuss at length how considerations of care and justice are related to each other, and more specifically whether they are compatible. Given, in much of the relevant literature, the unfortunate representation and/or understanding of the ethic of care as not only contextualized but also 'particularist' and therefore opposed to, or even incompatible with, a universalist ethic of justice, I shall spend most of this chapter arguing that principles of justice do have an important place in an acceptable ethic of care. Thus I argue, by looking at Gilligan's own writings on the ethic of care as well as her interpreters, that the important distinction between the ethic of care and the ethic of right and justice is one of content rather than form (in a sense to be explained) and that this opens up a detailed enquiry into how considerations of care and justice are related to each other (section i). I then argue, by taking a close look at Noddings's version of the ethic of care, that considerations of justice cannot fail to arise in and about the practice of care (section ii) and, furthermore, that Noddings does not have any metatheoretical grounds for rejecting principles of justice as part of an ethic of care (section iii). I then argue that the radically particularist position which refuses to accept the possibility of general considerations as part of the practice (and therefore the ethic) of care altogether is untenable (section iv) and address a further argument that particularity, based on relatedness, is constitutive of care (section v). Having dealt with all these objections to the possibility of combining considerations of care and justice, I look at how they are in fact related in both public and private care (section vi) before drawing my conclusions (section vii).

(i) *Content and form in Gilligan's ethic of care*

Since the publication of Gilligan's *In a Different Voice*,[1] in which she argued that women tend to speak and deliberate in a 'different moral voice', there has been a lively and controversial debate about the possibility and shape of what she called the 'ethic of care', its relationship to what she called the 'ethic of right and justice',[2] and about whether such an ethic would be specifically feminine—as Noddings, for example, would claim—or feminist—as other authors have argued.[3] One of the characteristics, and problems, in this debate, however, is that the contrast between the two ethics has been interpreted in very different ways by different participants in the debate. These varying interpretations may be traced back to Gilligan's original argument which used a number of dichotomies and dimensions with which to contrast and thus define the two ethics. It is, unfortunately, not very clear which contrast(s) she meant to be basic, nor is it therefore clear how exactly the two ethics are defined. As a consequence, different dimensions and dichotomies delineating the contrast are focused upon by different contributors to the debate. More specifically, it is useful to distinguish the interventions in this debate by certain moral and political philosophers from the rest by looking at their very specific reception and understanding of it. I shall refer to this specific reception as the *particularism debate*[4] and distinguish it from the *ethic of care debate* which is much broader and which has branched out into many disciplines. In fact, one might argue that Gilligan's book did not just

---

[1] Gilligan 1982.

[2] Quite how the two ethics are defined by Gilligan is as unclear as is the contrast between them (but see n. 33 below). I will argue for what I think is the most plausible interpretation of Gilligan's claims, but my general strategy will be to avoid discussion of the two 'ethics' and instead concentrate on a more micro-level of looking at considerations of care and justice in the practice of carers. This circumvents both the need for defining the two ethics and the need to indicate at this stage what the relationship between them is.

[3] See Tronto 1987, 1989, 1991a, 1991b, 1993, Fisher and Tronto 1990, Held 1987a, 1987b, 1993. Most feminist contributors to this debate have been less committed to endorsing and developing an ethic of care and more in favour of some revision or even integration of both ethics: see Baier 1987a, Friedman 1987b, Kroeger-Mappes 1994.

[4] I have taken the notion of particularism from Blum 1987. Blum is one of the most long-standing 'particularists' in this debate. (See n. 8 for references.)

start a debate, but initiated a new research paradigm by opening up new and promising lines of enquiry in the vast interdisciplinary field of gender studies and feminist theory.[5] The particularism debate, by contrast, addressed itself to a very specific problem, namely the question to what extent and how particular moral concerns and commitments could figure in moral theories whose basic structure was universal and impartial. These latter theories are usually referred to as impartialist theories, and the metaethical approach of these theories as impartialism.[6]

This debate started independently in moral philosophy,[7] but at least one of the critics of impartialism, Blum, subsequently used Gilligan and her ethic of care as one good example of such a particularist ethic whose distinct features could not be done justice to by incorporation into an impartialist framework.[8] Other participants in this debate, such as Noddings and Tronto, used Gilligan's ethic of care as a good illustration of the need for a new metaethical approach.[9] Now the reason why I have to mention the particularism debate is because, unfortunately, it seems to have monopolized the ethic of care debate at least in moral philosophy and has thereby marginalized other possible uses that could have been made of Gilligan's findings and insights.

[5] According to one source, there were over 1,100 references to Gilligan in a 5-year period alone (from 1986 to 1991, see Tronto 1991a: 3). Gilligan herself seems to have moved on from studying moral development and the two moral voices to studying adolescent development in girls with an approach inspired by her earlier research (Gilligan *et al.* 1990).

[6] See Blum 1988: 472, and Blum 1987; see also the July issue of *Ethics*, 101 (1991), and various contributors to Kittay and Meyers 1987 and Hanen and Nielsen 1987 as well as Friedman 1989 and Rooney 1991 among many others. Blum characterizes impartialism as a 'moral outlook or orientation' which is 'based on impartiality, impersonality, justice, formal rationality, and universal principle' (Blum 1988: 472). The notion of 'impartialism' is taken from Darwall 1983, and seems now commonly accepted (see the above mentioned issue of *Ethics*, 101 (1991) which was based on a conference on 'impartiality'). The most important branches of impartialism are utilitarian, neo-Kantian, and contractarian approaches or theories.

[7] For early critics see Williams 1981, Stocker 1976, Blum 1980, Cottingham 1983, Dancy 1983, Kekes 1984.

[8] This argument is to be found in Blum 1988, but Blum has been developing a critique of impartialism since his book *Friendship, Altruism, and Morality* (Blum 1980); see also Blum 1986, 1987. Dancy (1992) is another particularist who intervenes in the ethic of care debate.

[9] See Noddings 1984, *passim*, and Tronto 1987: 657–8. Noddings does not call herself a particularist, but she obviously, and more radically than any other theorist, falls into this category. See also Friedman 1987a.

More specifically, it has focused discussion on formal, metaethical aspects at the expense of a discussion of the different *content* an ethic of care might have.[10] In virtue of this focus, care and justice have tended to be posited as incompatible because based on different metaethical frameworks.[11]

Now, as far as the metaethical issue is concerned, I want to remain agnostic at this stage of my argument,[12] mainly because I think that issues arising about the content of an ethic of care and considerations of justice within it are much more straightforward, interesting, and moreover have not been discussed in any detail yet. What I am interested in, therefore, in this chapter, is to explore in detail how considerations of care and justice arise from the practice of care and whether and how they fit together. Before I start on this task in section ii, I would like to take a short look at Gilligan's own characterization of the two ethics over the years in order to substantiate my point that Gilligan's concern is not only, or not even mainly—and even not at all in her later work—with differences in form between the two ethics, but with differences in content, even if it sometimes looks as if differences in form were quite central to her distinction between the two ethics. This discussion of Gilligan does obviously not serve as an argument for looking at the content of the ethic of care, but it illustrates how a stress on (supposed) formal distinctions between the two ethics can eclipse some of the most interesting points in her work.

The particularism debate does not only distract from questions about the content of the ethic of care and about how considerations of justice and care are related to each other, it is also based on a fairly one-sided and to some extent misleading representation of Gilligan's own claims. While it is true, on the one hand, that Gilligan stresses the particularity and contextuality of women's moral judgements and their refusal to cite any principles—a stress that has been made much of by both the 'particularists' and the 'impartialists' in the particularism debate—she

---

[10] Most authors do not make this distinction and mostly take the ethic of care to involve differences in both content and form. Authors who are more interested in the different content of the ethic of care are e.g. Held (1987*a*, 1987*b*, 1993), Baier (1987*b*), Friedman (1987*b*), Noddings (1989), and Tronto (1993).

[11] This argument is strongest in Noddings 1984.

[12] See sect. vii for a short discussion of it.

also envisages, on the other hand, the possibility of *generalizing* the care perspective. Thus on the one hand, one finds quotes such as the following:

[Claire's judgement] is a contextual judgment, bound to the particulars of time and place, contingent always on 'that mother' and 'that unborn child' and thus resisting a categorical formulation. To her, the possibilities of imagination outstrip the capacity for generalisation.[13]

On the other hand, however, Gilligan refers to care in the highest stage of development as a 'universal injunction' against hurting others,[14] as 'the most adequate guide to the resolution of conflicts in human relationships',[15] and as the 'principle of judgment' that is 'universal in its condemnation of exploitation and hurt'.[16] The question therefore arises how seriously Gilligan meant her assertions of the particularity of her subjects' moral judgements.

Furthermore, and very much in contradiction to the metaethical oppositions of the particularist ethic of care and the impartialist ethic of justice which were asserted by contributors to the particularism debate, Gilligan does not see considerations of justice and care as incompatible or fundamentally opposed.[17] Thus it is worth noting that Gilligan attributes women's transition from the second, self-eclipsing to the third (and highest), self-inclusive stage of the ethic of care at least contingently (that is, for college-educated women in the 1970s) to the influence of considerations of rights and justice: the ideal of selflessness and selfless care for others—which is typical of the second stage—is

[13] Gilligan 1982: 58; see also p. 22 where she asserts that women's 'greater orientation toward relationships and interdependence implies a more contextual mode of judgment'. It is the notion of contextualization that has been focused on by particularists, see especially Tronto 1987, but also Noddings 1984.

[14] Gilligan 1982: 90; see also pp. 95, 100.   [15] Ibid. 105.

[16] Ibid. 74. Note that Gilligan usually stresses the 'moral injunction' to avoid harm or hurt (specifically the hurt of being excluded or left out) in her early work. Her mentioning of exploitation would seem an unfortunate mistake in this context because the wrong done by exploitation may not only (or not even necessarily) be that of harm to a person, but also, and more importantly, the wrong of unfair treatment or injustice. Gilligan does not seem to be aware of this slippage into essentially a justice mode of evaluation since she repeats this mistake several times.

[17] This is true at the level of *considerations* of care and justice, but more difficult to ascertain at the level of the compatibility of the justice and care perspectives: see my distinction below between considerations and perspectives and n. 25 below.

called into question by the concept of rights, by the assumption underlying the idea of justice that self and other are equal . . . [T]he concept
of rights entered into their thinking to challenge a morality of self-
sacrifice and self-abnegation . . . [T]he concept of rights changes women's conceptions of self, allowing them to see themselves as stronger
and to consider directly their own needs. . . . Thus changes in women's
rights change women's moral judgments, seasoning mercy with justice
by enabling women to consider it moral to care not only for others but
for themselves. The issue of inclusion first raised by the feminists in
the public domain reverberates through the psychology of women as
they begin to notice their own exclusion of themselves.[18]

Gilligan thus seems to have no qualms about asserting that considerations of justice and women's rights can be crucial factors
in enabling women's moral development to the highest stage of
the ethic of care by including their own needs in their moral
deliberation. Considerations of justice and care for Gilligan are
therefore not as fundamentally opposed as her particularist interpreters would have it.

Furthermore, and even more importantly, although Gilligan's
assertion is contingent and seems to imply for her that women
can reach this stage *without* explicitly considering their rights,
her assertion of contingency with regard to considerations of
moral equality of the self with others is mistaken. It is obviously
necessary rather than contingent that women consider themselves as deserving of equal moral concern, respect, or consideration if they are to move from the self-less second to the
self-inclusive third stage of the ethic of care: how would they
come to include themselves in their considerations of care if not
because they consider themselves as equally worthy of such considerations, or because they consider their own needs as much
as they do those of others? Now in so far as this type of consideration is a consideration of justice—and I will argue below
that it is[19]—at least one consideration of justice is in fact a necessary condition, logically and psychologically, for reaching the
highest stage of the ethic of care as Gilligan conceives it. This is
an important point, however, not only because it corrects distortions of Gilligan, but also because, more generally, it shows
that considerations of justice are at the very heart of what to any

---

[18] Gilligan 1982: 149.   [19] See sect. ii.

feminist, surely, must be a version of the ethic of care which is preferable to the self-less version.[20] Gilligan's ethic of care in its highest stage has therefore ceased to be a 'pure' ethic of care such as Noddings would have it.[21]

Now one might object to this argument that Gilligan is simply inconsistent. However, while it is true that Gilligan is not interested in philosophical subtleties and is at points annoyingly vague or even contradictory, it is more interesting to interpret this particular point as indicative of an understanding of the relation between the ethic of care and the ethic of justice which is crucially different from that of a full-blown particularist. For the latter, considerations of justice are not compatible with considerations of care because of the metaethical divide between them.[22] For Gilligan, by contrast, justice and care are compatible in one respect, but not in another. Thus if a distinction is made between *considerations* of care and justice and *moralities* or *ethics* of care and justice, it is clear that what may be true at the level of moralities or moral frameworks may not be true at the level of specific considerations or conceptualizations. In fact, Gilligan makes just that distinction in a later paper where she points out that we need to distinguish 'care as understood or construed within a justice framework'—that is, considerations of care as they figure within a morality of justice—and 'care as a framework or a perspective on moral decision'.[23] From this paper on, Gilligan refers to care and justice as different perspectives each of which 'frames the problem in different terms'[24] and which 'denote different ways of organising the basic elements of moral judgment: self, others, and the relationship between them'.[25]

---

[20] By saying that the self-inclusive version must be preferable to the self-less version for feminists I do not mean to imply that it is the best version. As I shall argue below, an acceptable ethic of care needs more than this one minimal consideration of justice, and it has to incorporate considerations of justice much more explicitly.

[21] Noddings 1984; see also sect. ii. Ironically enough, this argument also applies to Noddings's version of the ethic of care, given that it is a self-inclusive version, even if the self of the carer is included in a rather attenuated way.

[22] See Noddings (1984), for whom considerations of care and justice involve distinct modes of thought (see Ch. 4 sect. iv).   [23] Gilligan 1987: 24.

[24] Ibid. 23.

[25] Ibid. 22. The language of 'perspectives' instead of moralities indicates her interpretation of the two frameworks as modes of thinking akin to the *Gestalt* organization of the perceptual field into figure (those aspects which are seen as

The difference between the perspectives is that care and justice appear within very different contexts in the two perspectives or occupy different places in the overall construction of the perspectives:

Within a justice construction, care becomes the mercy that tempers justice; or connotes the special obligations or supererogatory duties that arise in personal relationships; or signifies altruism freely chosen . . . ; or characterizes a choice to sacrifice the claims of the self. All of these interpretations of care leave the basic assumptions of a justice framework intact: the division between the self and others, and the logic of reciprocity or equal respect.[26]

Care as a moral framework, by contrast,

is grounded in the assumption that self and other are interdependent, an assumption reflected in a view of action as responsive and, therefore, as arising in relationship rather than the view of action as emanating from within the self and, therefore, 'self governed'. . . . Justice in this context becomes understood as respect for people in their own terms.[27]

While Gilligan's notion of justice from within a care perspective is different from the idea of equal rights that she stresses in her earlier book, and while both representations of considerations of justice as well as her idea of the presumptions of the justice perspective are questionable and severely limited, the distinction itself is crucially important, since it opens the way for a more detailed investigation of how considerations of justice may relate to considerations of care from within an overall perspective of care (or justice), instead of focusing on the formal or

salient and focused upon) and ground (those aspects which recede in importance or are not taken in at all): see pp. 22–3. With ambiguous perceptual objects, perception jumps between the two possible alternative interpretations, but the two alternatives cannot be integrated visually. This parallel thus leads her to be doubtful, but ultimately agnostic, about the possibility of integrating the two perspectives (see pp. 26, 30). There is some empirical evidence that most people have a marked preference for one of the perspectives although they are capable of endorsing both (see Gilligan and Attanucci 1988; see also Gilligan 1988a, 1988b). Gilligan's usage of 'perspectives' may, unfortunately, again suggest formal contrasts, but as will be clear from further quotes below, her stress is nevertheless on substantive differences which are characterized by a combination of both, different concepts and ideas and a different organization of these into a coherent whole.   [26] Gilligan 1987: 24.

[27] Ibid.

metaethical differences between the two moralities. Furthermore, this distinction also clarifies where, for Gilligan, the main difference between the two moralities or perspectives lies. Note that I asserted earlier that it is not clear from Gilligan's book what contrasts between the two ethics are basic for her, and that I remarked that the contributors to the partialism debate focused on the formal or metaethical dimensions of the contrasts.[28] The nearly exclusive focus on formal contrasts might have been avoided, however, by a closer, and ultimately more accurate reading of Gilligan, starting with her very first introduction of the ethic of care at the beginning of her book—'The different voice I describe is characterized not by gender but *theme*'[29]—and proceeding with attention to the many places where she characterizes the contrast in terms of *content* rather than form. Thus notice, in particular, that the description of 'two different constructions of the moral domain'[30] recurs frequently, and that it does not refer primarily to different formal features, but to substantially different claims about specific moral problems as well as different moral frameworks.[31] Furthermore, a recurring contrast of Gilligan's is the contrast between the two perspectives in terms of their basic premisses, foci, principles or 'injunctions', or ideals:

A justice perspective draws attention to problems of inequality and oppression and holds up an ideal of reciprocity and equal respect. A care perspective draws attention to problems of detachment or abandonment and holds up an ideal of attention and response to need. Two moral injunctions—not to treat others unfairly and not to turn away from someone in need—capture these different concerns.[32]

The two frameworks thus provide, according to Gilligan, and in more technical parlance, different conceptualizations of the moral

[28] Sher (1987) provides a list of five contrasts all of which are quite successfully undermined in his ensuing discussion: abstract vs. concrete or contextualized, principled vs. non-principled, impersonal vs. personal, duty vs. care, rights vs. responsibilities (pp. 179–80). Dancy's list of eleven contrasts is a mixture of formal and substantial criteria, but he takes one of the formal contrasts, principled vs. non-principled, as ultimately distinctive (Dancy 1992: 458).

[29] Gilligan 1982: 2, my emphasis.   [30] Ibid. 69; see also p. 105 and *passim*.

[31] Ibid. 28, 32, 59, 62, 69, 105, 160, 164.

[32] Gilligan and Attanucci 1988: 73. This is the most recent characterization I have read, and, it seems to me, also the most plausible. See earlier similar characterizations in Gilligan 1982: 32, 69, 160, 174; Gilligan 1987: 24, 31.

realm. Hence Gilligan has been misrepresented in the particularism debate, and with this misrepresentation a detailed enquiry
into the relationship between considerations of care and justice
was left out, too.[33]

In what follows I shall start to redress the balance. This is all
the more important since, while a lot has been said, at least pro-
grammatically, by impartialists eager to defend themselves against
the particularist critique by spelling out how particular considerations of care are compatible with an impartialist framework
or ethic, there has been a comparative lack of argument by theorists of care with regard to how considerations of justice fit into
an ethic of care.[34] This is partly due to the very small number
of authors who have worked on spelling out an ethic of care,[35]
and partly to the metatheoretical construction of the ethic of care
as particularist.[36] Thus, as I shall argue in the following section,

[33] It may be worth noting as well that the definition of theoretical concepts
in empirical psychology is very different from a philosophical definition in that
it often proceeds through an enumeration of characterizations along various
dimensions. What is annoying to philosophers about Gilligan's definitions, therefore, is not necessarily a point of criticism within empirical psychology.

[34] Examples of impartialist 'defences' are to be found in the following: Adler
1989, Hill 1987, Baron 1991, Barry 1995. The main defence strategy of impartialists has been to claim that particular considerations such as considerations
of care are compatible with universal principles because universal and impartialist justifications can be given for people acting according to particular considerations based on particular relationships. The crucial move by impartialists
in this argument is the distinction between two levels of moral thinking: the
level of justification of principles and values and the level of moral deliberation
in specific situations leading to action in people's day-to-day lives. Within such
a two-level framework, it is argued, acting according to 'partial' concerns, as
they are then labelled, is perfectly justifiable, and the ethic of care can thus be
'fitted into' an impartialist framework. For a detailed discussion of various 'incorporation' claims see Blum 1988, for a more general discussion of gender bias in
impartialist moral theory see Calhoun 1988.

[35] Authors whom I am aware of and who have worked on theorizing care
(within moral or political theory) at book length or in any detail greater than
one article's length number just two: Noddings and Tronto (see Noddings 1984,
1989, Tronto 1987, 1991a, 1991b, 1993). Blum is another possible candidate, but
I am not sure he would consider himself a care theorist rather than, say, a particularist who is also interested in care. Others, such as Ruddick (1989) and Held
(1987a, 1987b, 1993), have focused on mothering rather than care, although Held's
latest work also synthesizes many of the arguments of the ethic of care debate
into her own version of a feminist morality (Held 1993).

[36] See Noddings 1984, 1989 and Tronto 1987. Unlike Noddings, Tronto has
always asserted the need for considerations of justice, but did not discuss these
claims in any detail (Tronto 1987: 659–60, 1991b: 33). In her latest work, Tronto
withdraws from the metaethical opposition between the two ethics (Tronto 1993:

Noddings blinds herself to the recognition of principles of justice arising from within the practice of care by interpreting her ethic of care as radically contextualized.

In conclusion, much more needs to be said, and in much more detail than has hitherto been provided, about how considerations of justice fit into a perspective of care. The particularism debate has not only misinterpreted Gilligan, but also done a disservice to the development of the ethic of care and the discussion of the role of considerations of justice within it, by focusing on the formal contrast between the ethic of care and the ethic of justice to the virtual exclusion of a detailed discussion of their differing contents. This has also eclipsed the more specific discussion of how considerations of justice are related to considerations of care. I shall address myself to this task in the remainder of this chapter.

(ii) *Considerations and principles of justice in Noddings's ethic of care*

Whilst Noddings is not absolutely opposed to admitting principles in general—and therefore should not be opposed to admitting principles of justice in particular—into her version of the ethic of care, she accords them a very circumscribed role.[37] There are other points in her discussion, however, where she presents an even stricter view. In what follows, I shall discuss two cases at length where, it seems to me, Noddings dodges the question of considerations of justice where they are at least implicitly at work. The first case will serve as an occasion to derive two principles of justice which are part of an ethic of care, as I shall argue. The second case raises the question of justice with regard to the justice of a carer's burden of care. Both cases thus point up the need for considerations of justice.

Consider, then, the first case: the example of a 'dilemma' for

211 n. 45). She also argues for the integration of considerations of justice as well as other impartialist values such as equality, democracy, and pluralism in a political theory based on a care perspective whose main advantage is that its grounding in care leads to the accommodation of difference much more organically than traditional universalist theories (Tronto 1993, ch. 6).

[37] See Ch. 4 sect. iv.

a carer given by Noddings herself in the course of her discussion of the role of principles. Ms Brown has promised to go to a concert with her husband, but her child has fallen ill. So she has to decide whether to stay at home with the child or to accompany her husband. Here is Noddings's description of the carer's difficulty:

Sometimes the decision is easy: the child is obviously too ill to leave, or the child is hardly ill at all and happily engaged in some activity. But often the dilemma is real, and we struggle with it. There is fever, and, while there is no real danger, the child keeps asking, 'Mother, *must* you go?' The solution to this sort of conflict cannot be codified. Slogans such as 'Put your husband (child) first!' are quite useless. There are times when he must come first; there are times when he cannot.[38]

Note, first, that the situation described here is an instance of what is commonly termed the 'circumstances of justice'.[39] What makes it a dilemma for Ms Brown is the fact that there are two mutually exclusive demands on her care and that she cannot satisfy both. Her care, in other words, has become a scarce resource for which two persons compete.[40] In making her decision, she cannot help but make a decision which is either just or unjust, since she cannot help her circumstances, which are circumstances of justice. Noddings renders her decision as follows:

When she decides, if she cares, she decides not by formula, nor by a process of strict 'rational decision making'. There is . . . a turning point.

---

[38] Noddings 1984: 52.

[39] See Hume 1888: 494–5, and 1975: 183–4: if care were always abundant *and* if 'every man [had] the utmost tenderness for every man' (1975: 185), there would be no need for principles of distribution of care. So far, Hume is correct. However, even if everybody were inclined to care circumstances of justice could still arise where care *as an activity* rather than as a sentiment has become scarce. Principles of justice thus do not presuppose selfishness in people, nor do they presuppose self-interested competition (see the following note). What they do presuppose is scarcity of resources. The resource in question is either the activity of care itself, or a carer's time or energy.

[40] The sense in which people in situations of need can be said to compete— if they can be said to compete at all—is purely technical. Unlike in cases of market competition or, even more extremely, cases of Hobbesian competition leading to mutual aggression and violence, persons in need (children, invalid or frail elderly persons, etc.) may not even be in a position to engage in any competitive activity against each other.

She turns away from the abstract formulation of the problem and looks again at the persons for whom she cares. Perhaps her child is still anxious and irritable; she receives his pain clearly. Perhaps her husband is merely annoyed, not hurt; perhaps, at some deeper level, he too wants only support for his best (i.e. caring) self. If she sees this, having received both persons, she decides to stay with the child ... [Her decision] is right or wrong according to how faithfully it was rooted in caring— that is, in a genuine response to the perceived needs of others.[41]

What Noddings describes in this passage is a typical example of a decision-making process. There are two mutually exclusive alternatives between which she has to choose: meeting the needs of her child or those of her husband.[42] Now any decision-making process of this kind, it would seem, involves two steps. The first step is the collection of as much information as is needed about the current situation, i.e. information about the respective needs for care, and, by inference, about the prospective outcomes. This is the step that Noddings would describe as 'receiving both persons'. But a correct and detailed enough assessment of the needs of both persons does not by itself generate a decision. As a second step, the carer has to compare their needs and decide to respond to one of them, since action can only ensue after one alternative among the two has been chosen as the right, desirable or, as in this case, the just one.

In a situation of conflicting needs and demands on the carer, the carer cannot avoid some harm from occurring, given that the failure to meet needs results in harm. The situation is thus not only conflictual for the carer, but *dilemmatic* because she cannot avoid harm from arising whatever she decides.[43] She can,

[41] Noddings 1984: 53.

[42] Note that Ms Brown's needs or wants do not seem to be relevant in this example. We know from Noddings's description, though, that she would have liked to go to the concert, too (ibid. 52). Would she be caring for her husband if she herself enjoyed going to the concert, indeed if going to the concert fulfilled a need of hers, too? She would, according to my definition, if her presence were necessary for her husband to be able to enjoy the concert and if his emotional balance were at least somewhat disturbed without those occasional concert outings with his wife. Whether or not going to the concert also meets her own needs is thus irrelevant to the question whether or not this is an instance of caring for her husband: caring does not have to be incompatible with the interests or desires or even the needs of the carer. Note, however, that Noddings's definition is much less strict than mine (see Ch. 4 sects. i and iv).

[43] See Gilligan 1982: 80, 103.

however, try to minimize the harm by responding to the greater need. In fact, this is what Ms Brown does according to Noddings: her perception of the situation is clearly—though not explicitly according to Noddings's description—that the child needs her attention and care more than her husband, and this is why she decides to stay with the child.[44] Of course, she would not put her husband always first, nor her child, because what she 'puts first'—the way she prioritizes exclusive alternatives—is the person who has the greater need. Now this 'principle' of responding to needs in order of their magnitude not only involves the kind of 'calculus' that Noddings denies her carers engage in, but it is also a principle of distributive justice. More specifically it is a principle of *harm minimization*: given that some harm will result from her not meeting one of the demands for care, the best a carer can do is to minimize the harm she cannot prevent from occurring. But the harm minimization principle is also and at the same time a distributive principle of justice which allows the carer to decide whose needs to meet in preference if and when she operates under circumstances of justice.

Such a principle may not be explicitly endorsed by Ms Brown, but as a carer she responds to situations of conflicting needs in correspondence with it. Indeed, as a response pattern, the strategy to minimize harm could probably be observed in any good carer under similar circumstances.[45] Now since no carer can avoid circumstances of justice, i.e. conflicting demands on her care, every carer has to have some sort of strategy of dealing with such situations. Given that caring consists of the meeting of needs, that is, given that caring as an activity is geared towards avoiding harm being incurred by others, a harm minimization principle would seem the most obvious candidate for such a strategy. An ethic of care, in other words, will not be complete

[44] She may, and probably will, try to reduce the harm done even more by promising to her husband (and to herself?) that next time, come what may, she will accompany him to the concert. Dilemmas in care call for creativity and imagination. See the example of the girl who, when finding herself disagreeing with her friend about what to play—her wanting to play next door neighbours, him wanting to play pirates—suggests that they play 'the pirate who lives next door' (source could not be located); see also the case below of the mother of the sick boy and the bored girl for a more mundane example of carer's imagination.

[45] Gilligan suggests a similar way of dealing with such dilemmas when discussing how one of her subjects resolved a particular dilemma (ibid. 95; see also p. 65).

unless it contains guide-lines for circumstances of justice, and the harm minimization principle is the best and most obvious option. Carers may endorse such a principle explicitly or only tacitly, but it is impossible for them, short of acting uncaringly, not to endorse it at least tacitly, since they cannot help but encounter circumstances of justice. Noddings, then, is mistaken in thinking that an ethic of care does not contain any principles of justice. The first principle of justice in care that I have derived in this section is the harm minimization principle. There is (at least) one more principle of justice that I believe carers endorse and act by: the principle of equality.[46]

Consider the following example. A mother spends the whole afternoon with one of her children, playing and chatting with him because he is ill in bed. Her other child complains that she hasn't played with her. 'It's not fair', the girl says, 'if you play with him but not with me. I'm bored.' What her daughter raises here is an issue of distributive justice: she questions her mother's spending more time with her brother than with her. Now the mother might respond like this:

Look, as you know, your brother is ill and he just needs me more at the moment than you do. You won't be too sad if you play by yourself for a while, but your brother would be very sad if I didn't cheer him up right now. I tell you what, though. I can see it's no fun being all by yourself. Why don't you join us for a bit, and we'll play a game that all three of us can play together.

In this response, although the mother asserts implicitly a version of the harm minimization principle as a justification of her spending more time with the ill boy at the expense of the girl, she bases her 'compromise' solution on what I shall call the principle of *equality in care* (or principle of equality, as a short version): she takes her daughter's need for company into equal consideration with the needs of her son.

The principle of equality is not always compatible with the principle of harm minimization. It might look in the above example as though it is, because meeting the needs of both the daughter and the son surely must reduce harm more than meeting the

---

[46] There may be more distributive principles of justice, such as a principle of urgency, but the two principles that I discuss in this section are, I believe, the main and most important ones.

(admittedly greater) need of one child at the expense of the other child. But assume, further, that the daughter's need is really to have her mother's exclusive attention, as is her brother's. The mother can therefore not satisfy both children's needs. Assume, furthermore, that the need of the daughter is not that great and that of the son very great so that spending exclusive time with the daughter would make the son suffer much more than the daughter suffers not spending any time with her mother (sick children are much needier of love and attention than healthy children). In this case, her compromise solution is not necessarily an optimizing solution (hence does not necessarily minimize harm), since both children suffer some harm not having the exclusive attention of their mother. But it is a solution that satisfies the equality principle since the needs of both children are taken into consideration and to some extent met.[47] The principle of equality thus takes account of and, to the extent that it is acted upon, expresses, the fact that the mother loves both children and that the welfare of both of them matters to her.[48]

As with the harm minimization principle, not acting accord-

---

[47] Putting numbers—indicating the level of harm caused by absence of care or care which is less than what is needed—to the different alternatives may make the point more succinctly. There are three alternatives:

(1) Mother spends time with son: S 0   D 2
(2) Mother spends time with daughter: S 10   D 0
(3) Mother spends time with both: S 3   D 1

Alternative (1) minimizes harm, but alternative (3), although not optimizing, would be preferred by the principle of equality.

[48] This example is somewhat artificial—but not, I think, unrealistic. It is necessary, in any case, to help us distinguish two possible interpretations of the equality principle. The first and weaker interpretation is, in fact, implied by the harm minimization principle, whereby people are treated equally if everybody's needs are counted for one and nobody's needs for more than one in the harm minimization calculus. This interpretation follows standard utilitarian interpretations of equality. According to the second, stronger interpretation, however, equality of consideration is independent of the harm minimization principle and can be incompatible with it, as in my example. 'Equality of consideration' may, in fact, not capture precisely the meaning of the principle, since it requires not only that everybody's needs be considered, but that they continue to be considered and, maybe, to some extent be met *even if* they would remain unmet according to the harm minimization calculus. It might be better understood as a principle of equality of inclusion in care (see n. 50 below), although putting it like this suggests a stronger interpretation than is in fact correct at least for private care (see sect. vi below). I will therefore keep the ambiguous unspecified formulation of the 'principle of equality', hoping that the intended interpretation is clear.

ing to the principle of equality would not be very caring nor very just. If it is part of the concern of a carer to maintain or enhance relationships and care—a concern that both Noddings and Gilligan stress[49]—then meeting even small needs or doing even small things for those with the lesser need may be important precisely because this is a way of affirming and confirming the existence of a caring relationship, whilst the neglect of lesser needs at the expense of meeting greater needs—as an unmitigated harm minimization principle will dictate at least in some situations—may be a most uncaring and ultimately destructive thing to do.[50] The aim of maintaining relationships thus arguably imposes the principle of equality as a distributive principle in addition to the principle of harm minimization. Again, upon reflection, this principle can be seen at work in carers' practice, implicitly if not explicitly, and, as with the principle of harm minimization, there is no good reason for not accepting it as part of an ethic of care.

To summarize my argument so far, two principles of justice can be derived from the practice and general framework of values of care, the harm minimization and equality principles. These principles are a necessary part of an ethic of care since a carer will invariably find herself in circumstances of justice and will use such principles to inform her action. Note that my argument is different and, in fact, stronger than any of the arguments about the need for principles of justice in an ethic of care in the literature. Typically, arguments for principles or considerations of justice are made on the basis that an ethic of care has undesirable features or consequences without them, or that there are dangers in the practice of care which need to be held in

---

[49] Noddings 1984: 42 and *passim*; Gilligan 1982, ch. 2, esp. pp. 59, 62, and *passim*.

[50] The equality principle might also be understood to capture—but against Gilligan's understanding of justice—what Gilligan thinks is a concern central to the ethic of care, that is, the 'problem of inclusion': 'morality is seen . . . as arising from the experience of connection and conceived as a problem of inclusion rather than one of balancing claims' (Gilligan 1982: 160, see also pp. 32, 63.) According to my argument, there is no opposition between considerations of care and justice as far as the equality principle is concerned precisely because the equality principle makes a carer include in her consideration and action the needs of all persons concerned. For further discussion of who does and/or should get included (and thus count as 'a person concerned') see Ch. 4 sect. vii and sect. vi below.

check by such principles.[51] My contention is that (at least some) principles of justice form in fact an organic part of the practice of care, and therefore the ethic of care. Far from being extraneous impositions, as in the usual arguments—a view which continues to imply an opposition between justice and care—considerations of justice arise from within the practice of care itself and therefore are an important part of the ethic of care, properly understood.

I now come to the second case which points up the relevance of considerations of justice for Noddings's carers, and which conforms more to the argument that considerations of justice are needed to hold in check dangerous tendencies in the ethic of care (as understood by Noddings): the case of what Noddings calls caring 'deteriorat[ing] to cares and burdens'.[52] As in the first case, Noddings does not seriously consider the possibility that this type of case may call for considerations of justice. I have argued above that the worst case scenario of feeling care as a burden may be an important situation for a carer in that it may make her question whether her burden is just.[53] Noddings, by contrast, discusses such situations in very different terms. Either they are, for her, situations which do not raise questions of justice at all, not even potentially, but situations where the carer herself needs to be cared for, either by herself or by others so as to be able to restore her caring capacity: 'There exists in all caring situations the risk that the one-caring will be overwhelmed by the responsibilities and duties of the task and that, as a result of being burdened, he or she will cease to care for the other and become instead the object of "caring."'[54] Or they are situations which threaten to import mistaken notions of care. Thus Noddings reverts to the strategy of rejecting principles and rules when discussing an example where a man does raise questions of justice with regard to his care burdens:

What we do depends not upon rules, or at least not wholly on rules—not upon a prior determination of what is fair or equitable—but upon a constellation of conditions that is viewed through both the eyes of the one-caring and the eyes of the cared-for. By and large, we do not

---

[51] See, among others, Tronto 1993: 170–1, Held 1993: 75.
[52] Noddings 1984: 181.   [53] See Ch. 4 sect. vi.
[54] Noddings 1984: 12; see pp. 100, 125–8, 181–2.

say with any conviction that a person cares if that person acts routinely according to some fixed rule.[55]

The implication seems to be, for Noddings, that anybody who would act according to what she sees as principles of justice would at least be questionable as a carer. In this passage very early on in the book, the relevance of considerations of justice with regard to the 'burden' of care is thus swiftly ruled out of court for the rest of the book.

Hence Noddings either dismisses considerations of justice with regard to the burden of care, or she does not even consider them in the first place. Instead, she treats situations where carers feel burdened as situations which threaten to undermine the ethical ideal, since a carer who feels burdened will not care as well, will not be as receptive and responsive, as a carer who cares joyously. The response to this situation thus has to be that a carer needs to look after herself in order to restore and maintain herself as a carer. While this is certainly a correct analysis of the situation, the difficulty with it is that it treats the problem as entirely subjective, i.e. related to the carer's capabilities and feelings, instead of *at least equally* as potentially an objective problem: if the carer feels burdened that may be because, in fact, she *is* burdened too much and probably, or at least possibly, unjustly.

The place where this failure becomes most obvious and most telling is when Noddings discusses domestic work which, for her carers, is an occasion to 'celebrate the ordinary, human-animal life that is the source of [their] ethicality and joy'[56] and is 'filled with opportunities for receptive and creative encounters'.[57] While Noddings does ask herself why it is that many women 'feel . . . overworked and underpaid' doing it,[58] the answer she comes up with is equally telling: women may feel they need recognition for this work which they do not get publicly, nor often privately, but strong women do not need such recognition. Hence women must 'learn how to maintain themselves as ones-caring through a general strengthening of self-image'.[59] What is potentially an occasion for a critical discussion of women's unjust material benefits and burdens—the recognition of women feeling overworked and underpaid—is thus turned into an exercise of blaming the

[55] Ibid. 13.   [56] Ibid. 125.   [57] Ibid. 126.   [58] Ibid.
[59] Ibid. 128.

victim. Women who feel burdened are counselled to strengthen their self-image as carers instead of made to question their situation presumably because by questioning their situation they would put 'principles above persons' and thus fail as carers.[60] It is thus in her idealist treatment of the 'burdens of care' that Noddings fails most appallingly, and that the root of the problem with her version of the ethic of care lies. It is her idealism which blinds her—and carers who endorse her ethic of care— to potential objective wrongs, and which makes her version of the ethic of care an oppressive ideology. I do not intend to deal with this case at the required length here, but let me stress that this second case—unlike the first, which illustrated the fact that (at least some) considerations of justice in fact were part of the practice of care—points up the need for further considerations of justice and the inadequacy of Noddings's idealist version of the ethic of care, in parallel to the free-rider case discussed in the last chapter.[61]

To conclude, then, both cases, the 'carer's dilemma' and the 'carer's burdens', illustrate that considerations of justice are either implicit in an ethic of care or are needed to complement it. While the first case has served as a springboard for the derivation of the two principles of justice in care, the second case has served to illuminate the dangerous limitation of an idealist, agent-centred version of the ethic of care.

(iii) *Principles of justice and metaethical positions*

As a way into exploring how Noddings might respond to my argument that considerations of justice form part of and are needed in an ethic of care, and more specifically, to my derivation of the two principles of justice in care, let me note that there is, at least by the look of it, a puzzle about her claims about the role of principles, rules, or calculi.[62] Thus, on the one hand,

---

[60] See sect. iii below.

[61] See Ch. 4 sect. vii. I shall discuss both cases, the free rider and the 'carer's burdens' case further in Ch. 6.

[62] I shall concentrate my argument in this section on the stronger claim that principles of justice must form part of an ethic of care and shall assume that the weaker claim about the need for considerations of justice more generally is subsumed in the defence of the stronger claim.

Noddings does not reject principles completely and agrees that deliberation at a more abstract level might be important for carers.[63] On the other hand, as her treatment of Ms Brown's dilemma as well as that of other cases shows,[64] she does refuse to accept that the decision-making of a carer can be done on the basis of or by reference to principles. She also often contrasts two ethical 'approaches' which she clearly thinks are exclusive in the sense that one cannot endorse both at the same time and that they involve opposite mind sets, as it were: one approach putting 'principle above person', the other, caring one, putting person above principle.[65] Can these two positions be reconciled? They can, if we distinguish between the role of principles in an ethic *tout court* and the role of principles in the process of moral decision-making. Thus notice that Noddings repeatedly points to what she calls the 'turning point' in decision-making which, for her, is a point where a carer moves her attention from the consideration of principles back to the situation in order to 'receive' or ascertain it again.[66] If principles cannot straightforwardly 'dictate' a decision, but play some sort of role in the process of coming to a decision, then it is possible for principles to have a place in an ethic of care, but to have a less prominent place than they have in 'principled' ethics such as Kantianism or utilitarianism.[67] We can then understand the contrast of the two 'approaches' in Noddings as a contrast referring to the process of moral decision-making rather than to the role of principles in an ethic as such, and the existence or non-existence of the 'turning point' back to the situation at hand (which implies a weakening of the role of principles in the process) is what distinguishes the two approaches.

If this is a correct interpretation of Noddings, the puzzle is solved and she is consistent, but she is then not in a position to maintain what I described in the last chapter as her myopia with regard to principles: she could not reject them *tout court* because the rejection of the prominent role of principles refers not to the

---

[63] See Ch. 4 sect. iv; for a typically vague formulation see Noddings 1984: 13.

[64] Noddings 1984, *passim*. See also the example I discuss in Ch. 4 sect. vii.

[65] Noddings 1984: 36–7, 57, 107, 110.

[66] Ibid. 53, and her section on turning-points, pp. 35–7.

[67] See Dancy's more elaborate discussion of the differential role of principles in various ethics (Dancy 1992).

ethic of care as such, but primarily to the process of decision-making. She could therefore not reject my derivation of principles of justice in care on the grounds that they are *principles* of justice either, since it is perfectly legitimate to discuss such principles as long as it is not presumed that decisions about the distribution of care are made simply by subsuming such situations under those principles of justice. Nor, as I have argued in section ii, could she reject them because they are principles of *justice*, because it is obvious that, in circumstances of justice, a carer will engage in considerations of justice either implicitly or explicitly.

There are at least three metaethical positions which have historically been endorsed and which Noddings could endorse in order to spell out more clearly exactly what place she thinks principles do have in an ethic of care, both in the abstract and in the process of decision-making. The first position, endorsed by Ross, understands principles or duties, as 'prima facie'.[68] This means that whilst it is possible to come up with a list of duties or principles which are clearly valid and evidently true,[69] the world is too complex to provide us with situations which can clearly be subsumed under one of these duties or principles. In fact, there are always several under which any particular situation can be subsumed, and this is why duties can only be 'prima facie': it is up to the moral deliberator in particular situations to weigh the various duties in a way appropriate to the situation at hand.[70] Noddings does endorse Ross's conception of 'prima facie duties' as an illustration of a metaethical position like hers which, according to her, 'admits that (principles) yield no real guidance for moral conduct in concrete situations',[71] but it seems clear to me that Ross's position is too committed to the validity of principles *as such* to be a model that Noddings could endorse.

---

[68] Ross 1930, 1939. I present the three positions in order of the importance that is accorded to principles.

[69] See Ross 1930: 29–30: the truth of moral statements about prima-facie duties is self-evident as mathematical axioms are and such duties constitute a moral order which is 'just as much part of the fundamental nature of the universe as is the spatial or numerical structure expressed in the axioms of geometry or arithmetic' (pp. 29–30).   [70] Ibid. 30–1, 41–2.

[71] Noddings 1984: 85. This formulation is at any rate too loose as an account of Ross, since Ross does not deny that principles yield guidance: he only denies that they yield immediate guidance, that is, guidance unmediated by reflection on the particular case. (Thanks to Sabina Lovibond for drawing my attention to this point.)

The second position, held by Aristotle, is more radically doubt-ful of the possible role of principles. Strict rules and laws from which inferences can be made are simply not adequate to the domain of moral deliberation and action, which is the domain of the particular.[72] Principles can only play a limited role because 'among statements about conduct those which are general apply more widely, but those which are particular are more true, since conduct has to do with individual cases, and our statements must harmonize with the facts in these cases.'[73] Unlike Ross, then, Aristotle questions not only the role of principles in moral decision-making, but also their status and validity as such in any ethic. Principles can only be guide-lines or rules of thumb, rough guides rather than ultimate points of reference, not just in moral deliberation, but *as such*.[74] It follows from this, and illus-trates this point, that young people can be excellent mathe-maticians or geometricians—simply by following the rules, as it were—but they cannot be good moral deliberators because they lack the experience of the manifold particular situations and deci-sions that those with practical wisdom have, including the abil-ity to generalize over those situations, and this experience is needed in order to form the disposition to respond to situations in the right way.[75] Moral deliberation, as in Ross, is likened to perception rather than rational deduction[76] (of which it would be a species if principles played a central role), and it is the quasi-perceptual appraisal of the particular situation that yields the decision.[77] Hence it is not the role accorded to principles in moral decision-making which distinguishes Aristotle's position from that of Ross, but their epistemic and ontological status in an ethical system: while Ross likens them to self-evidently true mathematical axioms, Aristotle likens them to much less certain and much less reliable 'rules of thumb'.

Now, surprisingly enough, Noddings does not refer to Aristotle at all, but it seems to me that the tenor of her statements on principles would suggest her endorsing the Aristotelian rather

---

[72] Aristotle 1980: 146, 148 (*NE* vi. 7, 8); see also p. 3 (*NE* i. 3).
[73] Ibid. 40 (*NE* ii. 7; see ii. 2).
[74] See Nussbaum 1986: 299–305, and Nussbaum 1990.
[75] Aristotle 1980: 148 (*NE* vi. 8); see pp. 3–4 (*NE* i. 3).
[76] Ibid. 148 (*NE* vi. 8).
[77] Ibid. 47, 98 (*NE* ii. 9, iv. 5). See Ross's reference to these two passages in his discussion of moral deliberation (Ross 1930: 42).

than the Rossian model. Thus note especially her treatment of principles as 'guidelines' and 'economies of a sort'[78] that a carer 'formulates and holds . . . loosely, tentatively' and will be 'wary of'.[79] The point, however, is that even if Noddings is best understood to endorse the more radically 'non-principled' Aristotelian position, she still has no good reason to object to a discussion of principles of justice in care, since even on the Aristotelian model such a discussion is illuminative of good practice. Certainly Aristotle himself had an interest in rules and principles, and especially in justice.[80]

There is a third and even more radical position with regard to the role of principles that Noddings could take. Thus she might reject as inadequate the construction I have given above of the moral deliberation that carers engage in when responding to dilemmas (and other situations calling for a caring response).[81] More specifically, what I suggested in reconstructing the principles of justice was that there are two stages to any process of decision-making—the taking in of information about the situation, and the processing of that information to yield a decision—and that the working of the principles of justice comes into play in the second stage of this process. Noddings might retort, however, that no distinction can be made between the perception of a situation or the ascertaining of the facts about a situation and the moral evaluation or 'moral processing' of these facts. For a carer, she might say, the process of perception itself yields an interpretation of what is morally salient and there is no second stage at all, hence no further process of deliberation is necessary. To become a good carer thus involves most crucially the formation of a certain sensitivity or perceptivity which, once developed, ushers in reasons for action without there being a need for further deliberation. What is stressed in this reply, then, is the centrality of perception, even more so than in the Aristotelian position. Perception, or, as Noddings would put it, the 'receiving' of others, is so crucial precisely because it is all there is.[82]

---

[78] Noddings 1984: 200, 55.   [79] Ibid. 55.

[80] See Nussbaum 1990: 68, Aristotle 1980 (*NE*), book v.   [81] See sect. ii.

[82] This position has been elaborated by McDowell (1978, 1979). Dancy (1992) seems to suggest a similar position as the 'genuine feminist' one (p. 464), but does not elaborate it in any detail. See also Dancy 1983, Kekes 1984, and McNaughton 1988.

Noddings herself has not actually taken this line, but she could do so in order to resist admitting that there are principles of justice. However, even on this model, it is not clear to me that it would be impossible to insist that such morally interpreted perception can be reflected upon and that what would be reflected upon would precisely be the patterns that such perception ushering in action follows. Those patterns could be described as following 'rules of care' or even 'principles of care'—allowing for the required degree of flexibility, of course—some of which would be principles of justice. Thus short of denying that anything can be said generally about caring as a (good) practice, I do not see how even the third position could ultimately defeat the quest for reflection upon the principles that inform caring as a practice. Thus even if 'generalizations will be approximate at best, and examples will need to be taken with the sort of "and so on" which appeals to the cooperation of a hearer who has cottoned on',[83] that is, even if, when discussing principles, there is an understanding that they are not written in stone, one can nevertheless discuss them.

I conclude, then, that Noddings has no good reasons for rejecting the discussion of principles of justice that arise from within the practice of care, nor that of considerations of justice more generally. What is worth stressing again is that, short of refusing to consider any generalizations about care, there is no position which would provide the metaethical grounds for refusing to discuss principles of justice. I furthermore conclude that there is no need to take a metaethical stand in order to discuss considerations of justice because any metaethical framework except one that is completely non-principled will allow for principles of justice and this 'allowance' is all I need for the purposes of my discussion. I therefore remain neutral about the three metaethical positions that I have discussed in this section, although the second or third seem to me more plausible. What I have been concerned to show in this section is that regardless of what metaethical position short of a complete rejection of principles Noddings might endorse she does not have any arguments for ruling the discussion of principles of justice in care out of court. Since it seems clear that Noddings does not endorse a completely

---

[83] McDowell 1979: 343.

non-principled metaethical framework,[84] I conclude that her objections against principles, rules, and calculi in considerations of distributive justice are mistaken.[85]

(iv) *The generalized and the concrete other*

In the last section I have pointed to several metaethical positions which fall short of the strictly principled types of ethics such as Kantianism and utilitarianism and which Noddings and ethic of care theorists more generally might endorse. There is an extreme position, however, that I mentioned in my discussion, but did not seriously consider because it was clear that it would not be endorsed by Noddings: the position that general considerations, let alone principles, have no place whatsoever in an ethic of care. I am not sure anybody actually holds this position, despite the programmatic claims that can be found in the literature, so I might be thought to waste my time and the reader's time by building up a strawwoman and then destroying it.[86] I shall nevertheless discuss this position in this section for two reasons: first, because there is a lingering tendency among ethic of care theorists to voice such extreme particularist intuitions and, secondly, because it seems to me well worth going into the reasons for resisting such intuitions.

Benhabib may be seen as referring to such an extreme position in her distinction between two different 'standpoints', that of the 'generalized' and the 'concrete other', which 'delineate both moral perspectives and interactional structures'.[87] While the

[84] As the existence of the puzzle with which I began this section illustrates, Noddings does not reject principles as such.

[85] The mistake probably occurs because of a slippage from the criticism of the prominent role of principles in decision-making to the rejection of the prominent role of principles as such. As I have tried to illustrate with the three metaethical models, however, these two aspects are distinct and it is possible to endorse principles as such whilst rejecting their prominent role in decision-making (as Ross, for example, does). My guess is that this confusion has contributed considerably to the metaethical opposition of the particularist ethic of care (where there is a strong stress on particular situations of decision-making as part of the practice of care) to the impartialist ethic of justice (where there is an opposite stress on the role of principles as such) and thus to the eclipse of a discussion of considerations of justice in the ethic of care.

[86] But see Dancy (1992), who might fill in as a strawman.

[87] Benhabib 1987: 86. Benhabib herself argues that this distinction has to be transcended, but, in using it, implies that there are two distinct standpoints.

standpoint of the generalized other implies that 'we abstract from the individuality and concrete identity of the other' and see her as a 'rational being entitled to the same rights and duties we would want to ascribe to ourselves',[88] the standpoint of the concrete other 'requires us to view each and every rational being as an individual with a concrete history, identity and affective-emotional constitution'.[89] As a consequence, if the standpoint of the generalized other contains, among other considerations, considerations of justice, and if the standpoint of the concrete other is that of care, it might be said that considerations of care and justice are incompatible, since the standpoints themselves are clearly incompatible. Corresponding to this distinction, considerations of justice are general in that they are about people as instantiations of a generalized other, given that considerations of justice refer to principles or general categories, while considerations of care are particular in that they are about people as the individuals they are, that is, about concrete others.[90]

Now to start, I need to mention (in order to set aside) an inconsequential sense in which 'care is particular'. As has been insisted by many, care as a practice is particular in that if we care for people we always respond to and care for particular others in particular situations of need. We cannot care for a generalized other because the latter is an abstraction like the 'average person'. There is, therefore, a corresponding sense in which considerations of care are particular, too: they are particular in the sense that they refer to the particular persons we care for. But by the same token, we cannot be just to a generalized other either, since justice or injustice is never done to abstractions but to concrete, real people. Consequently, considerations of justice can be particular in exactly the same sense, i.e. in that they refer to particular persons, even if they refer to particular persons as instantiations of general categories. If one looks at considerations of care and justice in particular situations of moral action

---

[88] Ibid. 87.   [89] Ibid.

[90] See also Tronto 1989 and Blum 1988. Blum is very careful in formulating, in rather Kantian terminology, the particularist position that he ascribes to Gilligan: 'The moral agent must understand the other person as the specific individual that he or she is, *not merely* as someone instantiating general moral categories such as friend or person in need' (Blum 1988: 474–5, my emphasis). In Blum's formulation, the question of compatibility is not prejudged because considerations of care are not presumed to be exclusively particular.

and deliberation, therefore, they are particular in the same sense in that their object is particular. This sense, however, is inconsequential, since it does not distinguish considerations of care from considerations of justice.

It might be insisted, though, in response to this, that there is a sense in which considerations of justice are general and in which considerations of care are not. Thus considerations of justice generalize over a vast range of possible situations and people and are about people in so far as they are instantiations of abstract categories such as 'a person in need', 'a holder of rights', 'a beneficiary of distributive principles', or even simply 'a person'. By contrast, considerations of care do not use any general categories, according to this response, and are therefore particular in the much more radical sense that no general categories can be used, nor can generalizations be made in considerations of care. This response thus spells out the extreme position which I mentioned at the beginning of this section. I shall argue in the rest of this section that this response is mistaken about the nature of care as a practice, and therefore about the nature of considerations of care.

Let me concede, first, that the suspicion held by many feminists of general claims, rules, and principles which are also often very abstract is not groundless, given that the history of social and political thought is littered with the usage of general terms in ways which conceal, obfuscate, or deny actually existing differences. Thus the concepts of 'man', 'human being', or 'person' have been used in general claims that obviously abstract from men's experiences, perspectives, and circumstances only and generalize them falsely as those of men and women.[91] What feminists should object to here, however, is not abstraction or generalization as such, but false generalization and unwarranted abstraction. Abstraction is unwarranted whenever it disregards differences which matter or are relevant to the question at hand, but is acceptable when disregarding irrelevant details. Accordingly, generalization is false when characteristics true of a subclass (men) are attributed to the whole class (human beings)

---

[91] For a recent example see Rawls's conception of justice on the basis of the views of (male) heads of households in the original position and the bias resulting from this false generalization (Rawls 1971, and see Okin 1989 for a critique of Rawls along these lines).

without being true of all instances of that class (men and women). More specifically, then, with regard to the conceptualization of care and justice, I must be aware of the possibility of false generalization. As such, however, abstraction and generalization should not be rejected and, indeed, are necessary tools for feminist theory and argument. Furthermore, those who completely reject general and/or abstract claims commit the very sin of generalization that they accuse their adversaries of: they do not examine specific cases of generalizations with regard to their correctness, but reject *all* possible cases as incorrect, a rejection which is not even possible a priori.

Secondly, it seems to me that one of the points that my discussion of the 'carer's dilemma' case in section ii has illustrated is not only that care is a practice that follows certain patterns that can be described by rules or principles, but also that dilemmas force carers to think more explicitly about the rules and principles that they follow implicitly or tacitly in their normal practice. It is precisely when habitual patterns fail to point unambiguously to the right thing to do that a moral agent is forced to reflect on how to reconcile them, and this, in turn, means becoming aware of what they are in the first place. The very fact that a carer normally may not be aware of the rules and principles she follows, but is only aware of focusing her attention on this particular situation or this particular person, can thus not be taken as evidence that carers do not engage in more general considerations, or do not follow rules and principles. Indeed, as I have argued above, it would be morally irresponsible for carers not to reflect on their practice more generally in such dilemmatic situations.

Thirdly, general considerations also form part of considerations of care every time the carer uses the practical knowledge she has as and when it is relevant to the particular situation at hand. Thus any knowledge which informs a carer's response applies to the cared for as an instantiation of a general type. Take the case of a mother taking care of an ill child. If she knows what can and cannot be done about flu—i.e. engages in considerations of care about her child as an instantiation of a flu sufferer—she will presumably provide better and more adequate care than if she has no idea about how to care for flu sufferers. General considerations about flu, and more generally considerations about various types of need, conditions, or even types of persons, thus do not interfere with, but on the contrary, if sensibly used, improve the actual care provided.[92]

Fourthly, any practice which one can learn and get better at usually has standards of good practice and rules to follow. Care is most certainly such a practice, since it does not come 'naturally' to anybody,[93] although it may come more easily to some than to others.[94] Some of these standards refer to the appropriateness of the practice and to the corresponding dispositions which have to be acquired, such as attentiveness and responsiveness,[95] and these standards will be learnt from those deemed to be good practitioners—in our case, good carers.[96] Distributive

---

[92] A particularly striking illustration of this point is the lack of care for children who were sexually abused before the occurrence of such abuse, its effects, and symptoms were generally known, as compared to the possibility of adequate care now, based on such knowledge. Ignorance in a carer is without consequences at best, but positively harmful at worst.

[93] The sexual division of labour between 'carers' and 'fighters' cannot be taken as evidence for this claim because the explanation of that division itself is disputed between those who think it natural and those who think it social.

[94] There is ontogenetic evidence that the more adequate the care somebody has received as a child, the better a carer that person will be able to be in her later life (see Miller 1990). Those deprived of care altogether, if they survive at all, are often unable to relate to others and thus lack an ability which is a prerequisite for care, i.e. the ability to be attentive and responsive to others. Thus note the famous 'maternal deprivation' studies of Rhesus monkeys in the 1950s. It is worth pointing out, however, that what the infant monkeys were deprived of was not maternal care, but care as such. The experiments thus proved not the necessity of maternal care, but the necessity of care.

[95] See the virtues and skills that are required in carers as presented in the previous chapter (sects. ii and iii).

[96] I call carers 'good practitioners' because care has features of both *poiesis* (making) and *praxis* (action), according to Aristotle's distinction (our modern notion of 'practitioner', despite its roots, suggests *poiesis* rather than *praxis*). It is thus both an art and moral action or neither: it has an end other than itself—in so far as its end is the meeting of needs in others—and would by this criterion be *poiesis*, which is judged by its outcomes, but it is also clearly an activity which is *morally* evaluated with reference to itself (see Aristotle 1980: 142–3, 34 (*NE* vi. 5, ii. 4)). While Noddings, in typically idealist vein, concentrates exclusively on that aspect of care which is *praxis* in insisting on the evaluation of care with reference to its inherent aspects, I think that care should be evaluated with regard to both its inherent characteristics and its outcomes: good carers not only care in the right way (for the right reasons, with the right attitude, etc.), but are also good at meeting needs (as opposed to meeting them badly or not at all). The insistence on evaluating carers with respect to how good they are at meeting needs is all the more important in a world where those dependent on care do not have a voice, or are not heard, to protest against insufficient, bad, or abusive care (see n. 121 below).

considerations, however, will have to be part of such standards of good practice, too, given that circumstances of justice will be encountered by any carer, and there is no good reason to think that distributive considerations would be more general or abstract than other considerations of good practice.

Fifthly and lastly, care in the public sphere illustrates more clearly how general considerations enter considerations of care, in that it necessarily involves the more explicit use of general knowledge and standards and is furthermore subject to the requirements of impartiality governing the public sphere. With the rise of the modern welfare state and the corresponding expansion of the caring professions, more and more care takes place in the public sphere mediated by either an exchange relationship between the caring professional and the cared for or by the state which pays the caring professional to care for persons in need.[97] Now one of the main differences between public and private care is that public care fails to meet the conditions which would allow for fully individualized, 'particular' care: it is not motivated by existing particular relationships and an impulse to act on behalf of the other on the basis of this relationship and the emotions appropriate to it, nor can it use the individualized knowledge that persons who know each other typically have of each other. It is nevertheless a response to needs, informed by general knowledge and motivated by a general commitment to care for those in need.[98] Standards of good practice are also much

[97] Of course there has always been care mediated by exchange or power relationships such as care given by domestic servants, nurses, nannies, or slaves. Such carers are typically from lower classes than those who receive the care and/or they often are from different racial or ethnic and less privileged groups. The personalized nature of such care and its location within households, however, approximates private care more than institutionalized care in the public sphere, such as care in any national (or international) system of health care provision.

[98] It would be difficult to imagine anybody would choose a caring profession unless they had some sort of commitment to care at least initially. Of course, this commitment may be difficult to maintain as the phenomenon of 'burn out' in the caring professions proves. An interesting border-line case is very prestigious and well-paid caring professions such as medicine, dentistry, surgery, psychoanalysis: these professions may be chosen for their prestige and income rather than out of a commitment to care. A recognition of the possibility of commitment being replaced by desire for prestige and/or income with regard to these professions is implicit in the difficulty many patients have in trusting these professionals to have the patient's well-being rather than their own purse or status at heart. Conversely, trust is much less a problem with regard to much less well-paid professionals such as nurses (although their commitment, conversely, may be feared to be undermined by their low pay).

more explicitly part of public care in that they are spelt out in professional codes of practice and the learning of these standards as well as the knowledge required for good care forms part of the professional or vocational training. Lastly, care in the public sphere meets the general requirement of impartiality by which the public sphere functions at the expense of personalized relationships. Accordingly, the principles of justice in care that I introduced above take a much more prominent role in care in the public sphere. Thus care in the public sphere consists of the meeting of needs in people under the constraint of the two principles of justice which I introduced above and in explicit disregard of existing relationships between people. The favouring of 'one's own people' in the public sphere is favouritism or nepotism and as such an instance of malpractice precisely because everybody's needs are to be considered equally (and to some extent met) in the public sphere, while the basic rationale of public health and social services can be understood as that of harm minimization.[99]

Public care can thus be seen as a major challenge to any conception of the ethic of care which insists on the particular nature of care and of considerations of care, whilst it provides support for those interpretations of the ethic of care which do accept the possibility of general considerations and principles as part of the ethic of care. Indeed the fact that the latter kind of interpretation manages to bring out the commonalities between care in the private and the public sphere instead of obfuscating them is a further point in its favour.

I conclude, then, that the extreme position which denies the existence or appropriateness of any general considerations in the practice of care is clearly mistaken. I would like to add, how-

---

[99] The principle of equality in care is thus generalized to include all citizens (or all residents of a country, or even all persons) in its scope, while the harm minimization principle has the same scope. I elaborate the features of public care further in section vi. Given chronic scarcity of resources in any national health system, other distributive 'principles'—some of them questionable with regard to their justifiability—are operative in addition to, and thus modify the application of, the two principles of justice in care: there is discrimination against mainly elderly people who need expensive treatments, the raising of charges for various types of treatments or tests (which discriminate against those who are not poor enough to be entitled to these benefits free of charge, but not well enough off to pay easily for them themselves), and the preferential ordering of treatments and operations according to urgency. Only the latter principle (of urgency) is in my view justifiable as arising from the practice of care.

ever, a sense in which the insistence on the contextualized and particular nature of care can be accommodated. As I stressed in the last section, the fact that general considerations and principles are endorsed as part of the ethic of care does not imply the endorsement of a strictly principled metaethical position. There are various ways in which the role of general considerations and principles can be weakened without denying them a role altogether.[100] One important factor that I have not mentioned yet is the role moral sensitivity, imagination, and intuition may play in the practice of care. Thus, as is stressed by holders of even the most principled of ethics, principles cannot be applied mechanically: the application of principles requires sensitivity to the features of the particular situation as well as imaginative sympathy. Intuition may come into play in the appropriate ordering of principles for particular situations. It is even possible that principles provide only very rough guidance and that a large part of what makes caring good caring and a moral practice is the acquisition of a 'responsiveness and yielding flexibility, a rightness of tone and a sureness of touch',[101] a capacity to be 'ready for surprise' and 'resourceful at improvisation'.[102] But the affirmation of some or even all of these claims does not imply that general considerations and principles are not also important.[103]

In conclusion, then, the practice of care, while consisting of a concrete activity involving particular individuals interacting with each other, does not exclude and is arguably even defective without general considerations, standards, or principles forming part of considerations of care. The distinction between the standpoint of the generalized and the concrete other hence does not line up with the contrast between general and particular considerations, nor with that between considerations of justice and care. Hence the extreme position with regard to the 'particularity' of considerations of care and the ethic of care is mistaken.

(v) *Care and relatedness*

Before I can move on to consider the relation between considerations of care and justice in further detail, I have to address a

---

[100] See the different metaethical positions that I discussed in the last section.
[101] Nussbaum 1986: 304.   [102] Ibid. 305. See also Nussbaum 1990.
[103] As Nussbaum, not a care theorist, but one whose interpretation of Aristotle might provide a very interesting metatheoretical model for ethic of care theorists, does acknowledge: Nussbaum 1986: 306; see also Nussbaum 1990.

last objection that some die-hard particularists might make to my argument in the last section. They might argue that the very fact that I had to use public care in order to make my point about general considerations as part of the practice of care illustrates that I have misunderstood the nature of care. According to this objection, care undertaken by 'caring' professionals does not qualify as real care: it takes place because the caring professional is paid, either by the person cared for or by the state or some other third party. It is a market or public sector relationship of service. *Real* care, by contrast, takes place between persons who know and care about each other.

I shall introduce the term *'relatedness'* to refer to this kind of personalized relationship between people. Thus by 'related' or 'relatedness' I mean to refer not only, and not even necessarily, to kinship relations, but to the kind of relationship that exists between individual people who have personal knowledge of each other, have a shared history between them, and who feel emotionally close and involved with as well as committed to each other on the basis of and because of their mutual knowledge and shared history.[104] Hence I can be related in this technical sense to people—friends, loved ones—who are not relatives in the sense of kin, and conversely, the mere fact of people being relatives does not imply relatedness. Now it is this kind of relatedness, the objector might insist, which makes people concrete and real to us, more real than strangers on the street, and it is because we are related to some but not others in this way that we care about them and know how to care for them.[105] Relatedness, according to the objection, is therefore constitutive of care.[106] Public care, then, parades as care, but is not care at

---

[104] Giddens's recent theorization of the 'pure relationship' (Giddens 1991) attempts to spell out the individuality of personalized relationships as well. In contrast to my notion of 'relatedness', however, which allows of degrees of intimacy, shared history, commitment, and mutual knowledge, his conception of the 'pure relationship' is ideal typical, i.e. captures a particular type of relationship which is intimate, equal, reciprocal, and self-reflexive. It thus describes not only an extreme, but is also much narrower than my concept in that it imposes quite stringent conditions (equality, reciprocity, self-reflexivity) for its realization. A lot of caring relationships do not meet any of these conditions.

[105] Noddings has been construed as endorsing this position by Tronto (1989: 182), but this is mistaken since Noddings does discuss caring for (proximate) strangers as well as education as an instance of care in the public sphere (Noddings 1984).

[106] Again, I might continue to be constructing a strawwoman in characterizing this position. Even if I do, however, arguing against it allows me to make

all because carer and cared for are not related, and it is there-fore a service like many other services provided in the public as opposed to the domestic sphere.

This objection, however, does not strike me as very strong. First, it makes unintelligible why public care is called care in the first place. As I pointed out in the previous section, it is the same as care between related persons except for the lack of related-ness: it meets somebody's needs, it involves the same skills and virtues, the same standards and principles, and the same forms of general knowledge. The crucial question therefore is whether relatedness is as central to care as it is made out to be in the objection. Now it is true that relatedness calls forth feelings of 'caring about', and that in turn, it seems, is what impels people to act on behalf of those they are related to.[107] The absence of relatedness, however, does not necessarily imply the absence of any impulse to act on behalf of others who are (more or less) unknown strangers. It seems to me that attentiveness and will-ingness to respond with care to those in need—the two main requirements in a carer—are dispositions which, if they are devel-oped in a person, will make her care *generally*. In other words, caring is a disposition that has no inherent boundaries. Conversely, if there is no such disposition, caring even for those one loves is going to be boring, a chore, or a drag.[108] Thus a crying child may be a stimulus for some to ask her what is wrong while it may cause the reaction of 'brat' in others and may make them want to tell her to shut up, whether parent or unknown stranger. Similarly, somebody's depressed face may be boring to some whilst calling for concern and care in others, whether friend, teacher, or stranger on the bus.[109]

It might be objected that my claim about the generality of the

what I feel are important points, so the point of the section is not lost. Also, the force behind this objection, feeding on vague intuitions and feelings most of us probably share, points to the need to look more closely at what is at stake.

[107] Aristotle pointed this out in his criticism of Plato's idea of 'universalizing' familial bonds in order to create unity in the Republic: Aristotle 1988: 23–5 (*Politics*, ii. 3–4).

[108] See also the characterization of people as 'having a heart for others' (i.e. caring) as opposed to their being 'insensitive' or hard which confirms the fact that the disposition to care is perceived as generally present or absent (in degrees) in people.

[109] Noddings does acknowledge that care will not end with relatedness, since she envisages 'ones-caring' to care for anybody in need who is proximate, whe-ther stranger or related (in my sense), thus agreeing with my point that the

disposition to care is contradicted by the well-known fact that people make very rigid distinctions between 'their own' whom they care for and 'others' who are left to look after themselves. My first response to this is that it may be true, but it does not prove that the disposition to care is not general, nor does it prove that people are 'naturally' selfish or 'naturally' only disposed to care for their own. With regard to the first point, it seems to me that boundaries to people's willingness to care are imposed through belief and value systems extraneous to the practice of care such as racist, classist, religious, nationalist, 'familialist',[110] and other discriminatory attitudes which *prevent* the care disposition from getting activated. To the extent that people have such attitudes they impose boundaries, and to the extent they do impose boundaries they stunt their moral agency and development as carers. Now, as I have pointed out in the last chapter, it may be the case that carers need to draw boundaries if they are to prevent their caring disposition from being exploited,[111] but there is a further question as to which boundaries are justified. Prejudice and parochialism certainly do not provide justifiable boundaries, nor does their existence prove that the disposition to care itself has boundaries.[112] The degree or intensity of relatedness, by contrast, as well as the type of relationship between carer and cared for, may be seen justifiably to influence the amount and type of care given.[113]

In elaboration of the second point it is worth stressing that the question whether care, sympathy, or benevolence are 'natural' or 'artificial' virtues or moral sentiments is very old and far from decided. I cannot answer it in any detail here, but the following considerations may give an indication of how the question relates to my argument. If, on the one hand, the

disposition to care is general. Note also the fact that the vulnerability of carers to exploitation derives from the same general disposition to care.

[110] See Barrett and McIntosh 1982 for a discussion of familialism.

[111] See Ch. 4 sect. vii.

[112] In fact, it might be argued that the drawing of boundaries and the distinction between 'us' and 'them' is an extension of selfish concerns to others whom one perceives as either one's property (see Aristotle and many after him on the family and paternalist attitudes to subordinates of various kinds) and/or extensions of one's own self (see theories of nationalism, notably Van Den Berghe 1981).

[113] Andy Mason drew my attention to this point. See also sect. vi on the morality of private care.

disposition to care is 'natural', there are two possibilities: either it is natural and generalized, or it is natural but restricted. The first alternative is unproblematic for my argument. The second alternative, pressed by sociobiologists as the latest representatives of a long tradition of argument, may be slightly more problematic. Suppose it were true that the disposition to care were naturally restricted—a supposition which, in view of the varied evidence, I find more implausible than alternative, social constructionist interpretations—it could nevertheless not be concluded that it is morally justifiable for it to be so restricted, that is, that we do not have a moral obligation to transcend our supposed 'selfish genes'. If, on the other hand, the disposition to care is 'artificial', that is, acquired, it raises important further questions about how it might be acquired by all, and this in turn reflects negatively on the sexual division of labour, given that the disposition to care must then be acquired by engaging in caring. If the disposition to care is artificial, in other words, the question of who cares in a society turns into an important issue not just because it raises questions of justice, but also because it raises questions of the possibility of social co-operation and cohesion, and the omission of such discussion in the past would seem rather unintelligible and irresponsible. Hence the objection does not cause any major problems for my account of care: if the disposition to care were naturally restricted this would not imply that there is no moral obligation to generalize it; if, however, the disposition is acquired, there is no deep problem about how people can acquire it through practice.[114]

My second response to the objection based on people's supposed tendency only to care for 'their own' is that relatedness (in the sense defined above) does not necessarily imply good care, nor does non-relatedness imply bad care. It seems to me that the insistence by some theorists on the particularity of caring relationships is at least partly motivated by the underlying idea that care by and for non-related persons cannot possibly be

[114] There may be other factors that prevent people from acquiring it apart from a lack of experience and practice, such as the lack of good care in their own childhood, but again this is not a deep problem because the chain of bad care or 'poisonous pedagogy', as Miller has famously termed it, can be broken, i.e. the existence of such factors is not inevitable and their effect can be overcome individually (see Miller 1990).

as good as care by and for related persons. Two obvious points need to be made in response to this. The first point is that care by and for related persons is not necessarily good care. This is illustrated not only by the now pervasive evidence of physical, sexual, and emotional abuse of children, the elderly, and other so-called 'dependants', but also by the fact that not every person who is related to someone in need of care is necessarily their best carer. Thus relatedness may refer to a history of emotionally involved, but mutually or one-sidedly destructive patterns of interaction between two persons. Such interactive patterns do not allow the kind of attentiveness and responsiveness required for good care, and even less pathological patterns of interaction between persons may still involve systematic biases or blindnesses which prevent care from being given at all, or from being the care that is really needed. Cases in point may be not only sado-masochistic types of relationship, but also apparently less extreme cases such as the completely 'self-centred' friend, the 'insensitive' or violent husband, the 'overprotective' mother or the overly strict father, or a mother not responding adequately to her child's abuse because of her complete denial of her own past abuse.[115] All this, of course, should not be taken to imply that abuse does not take place in the public sphere. But it does go a long way towards debunking the sentimental myth that care by and for related persons is necessarily good care or the only 'real' care on offer.

The second point to be made is that care by and for unrelated persons, i.e. public care, is not necessarily bad or worse care than private care. There are good and bad nurses and doctors as there are good and bad parents and friends.[116] Notice in par-

---

[115] See Miller's argument in *Banished Knowledge* (Miller 1990) that mothers and fathers who were abused as children themselves, whether 'only' emotionally or physically, or sexually, often actively or passively reproduce this abuse on their children, not being able to detect signs of distress or suffering in their children and/or rationalizing it away: their own repression of their past pain leads them to be insensitive and not able to cope with the signs of pain in others and therefore renders them bad carers or possibly even abusers in turn. (Note the most common defence of physical abuse of children: 'It's never done *me* any harm'!— It probably has, but the memory of the pain caused by such abuse is repressed, and the harm done to other children rationalized away.)

[116] There are also a variety of self-help groups which, if functional, may replace and/or complement certain kinds of care by related carers, and which combine properties of both public care (generally accessible) and private care (development of relatedness between members of the group).

ticular the earlier mentioned point that a lot of care if not all care requires skill and knowledge in carers. In so far as professional education involves the acquisition of such skills and knowledge, there is every reason to think that professional carers, in virtue of their training as well as their much more wide-ranging and varied experience, make better carers than 'lay' carers.[117] Their actions and reactions are potentially much more self-conscious and self-reflective than those of 'lay' persons, and it is precisely this informed awareness about their care that may allow them to be better carers. Take the case of a professional counsellor or psychotherapist. Her training will have made her aware of the pitfalls of projection and transference in interaction between individuals and she is therefore in a better position to recognize and work with these emotional phenomena instead of being trapped by them as most untrained people would be. In the same way, indirectly expressed needs or strange symptoms will not be a problem for a nurse because she may recognize the condition underlying the symptoms or the vaguely expressed need for what they are, given her experience with such conditions or needs, while non-professional carers may be at a loss as to what they should do in those kinds of situations. Public care at its best, then, is more informed and hence in this respect better or at least as good as private care.

Lastly, let me venture an explanation of the kind of motivation underlying the definitional restriction of care to care on the basis of relatedness in order to disperse any lingering doubts about the adequacy of my argument. I suspect that the attempt to restrict care in this way stems from the distorted stereotypes we have of private and public care. We hold, on the one hand, an idealized picture of private care by and for those we love, a picture which obstructs the recognition of abuse and bad care as and when it takes place, while we have, on the other hand, a picture of public care which is worse than it need be.[118] More specifically, it seems to me that the reasons why public care is often so bad have nothing to do with the fact that it is care by and for unrelated persons, but relate instead to the chronic underfunding and bureaucratization of the provision of care in the public sector. Thus chronic underfunding perpetuates a condition

---

[117] It may also 'spoil' them in various ways, however: see Waerness 1987, Condon 1992. [118] See Dalley 1988, Ungerson 1990*a*.

of scarcity of resources. For a caring professional not to be able
to care as she thinks necessary because of a lack of time or other
resources must be especially demoralizing, given her commitment to care which implies her wanting to meet needs and avoid
harm. Under chronic scarcity of resources a carer must therefore be immensely resilient if her morale is not to be undermined by constant pressure, and it can easily be seen how such
circumstances would end up producing burn-out and more generally low morale. They also force carers to use further criteria
for the distribution of care which cannot be justified from within the perspective of care.[119] Bureaucratization will be equally
undermining of caring commitment and practice by imposing
constraints extraneous to, and often conflicting with, the imperatives imposed by care.[120]

In conclusion, public care is not necessarily bad if and to the
extent that the causes of its shortcomings are tackled, that is, if
and to the extent that the political will is there, the resources
are committed to it, and the problem of bureaucratization is
resolved. The important point is that these causes do not necessarily derive from the fact that public care takes place between
unrelated persons, while there are, by contrast, some causes of
bad private care that do derive from the fact that it takes place
between related persons. Furthermore, the possibility of abuse
is real in both public and private care because its occurrence is
based on the dependency—and resulting powerlessness—of the
cared for on the carer rather than either their relatedness or non-
relatedness.[121] Relatedness, therefore, may matter emotionally

[119] See n. 99 above.   [120] See Ferguson 1984, Waerness 1987.
[121] The problem with the various forms of abuse of power in care is so intricate mainly because those dependent on care are often, in virtue of their dependency, not taken seriously as persons in their own right, and hence their complaints
are not taken seriously. As a result, abuses of power and bad care are not easily detectable. They will only become systematically detectable and start to be
tackled, first, if those receiving care are given a real voice and their testimony
is taken seriously and, secondly, if carers are made accountable to those they
are supposed to serve and to the wider community. Ultimately, the improve-
ment of care in both spheres has to start with a much more explicit commitment to accept the voices of those cared for as valid voices. This in turn presupposes
a theorization of relationships of dependency, or more generally of relationships
with an inbuilt power imbalance which is not socially created, and of these implications with regard to the rest of social and political theory. One of these implications is the need to rethink independence as an (implicit or explicit) criterion
of personhood.

and subjectively, but it does not necessarily make a difference to the quality of care. Thus one of the points of this section was to show that the appropriate theorization of care is hampered by, and requires the giving up of, various deeply ingrained habits of thought and presuppositions. I conclude, furthermore, that relatedness is not constitutive of care and that there is no good reason to insist on care by and for those related as the only true care. Hence public care is care as much as private care is, even if the constraints in the public sphere may be more severe and may lead to more severe distortions of care than those in the private sphere of care on the basis of relatedness.

(vi) *Care and justice in public and private*

I have reached the following conclusions at this point in the argument: not only do general considerations and hence considerations of justice form part of the practice and considerations of care between individuals who are related (in the technical sense) at least implicitly, but also care does not exclusively take place between related individuals since a lot of care takes place in the public sphere. I argued, moreover, that public care is not necessarily bad in virtue of being public, and that private care is not necessarily good in virtue of taking place between people who know and care about each other. Considerations of care and justice, then, arise in both private and public care. In my argument so far, then, I have stressed the similarity of care in both public and private. In this section, by contrast, I shall explore the differences between care in the two spheres as well as look at how these reflect on the relationship of considerations of care and justice in the two spheres.

The difference between care in the private and public spheres, it seems to me, is best characterized in terms of the presence or absence of relatedness as the ground of care.[122] Thus whilst care in the private sphere is the outcome of a specific pattern of interactions between two individuals based on relatedness, care in the public sphere is an instance of an established function, taking place because both carer and cared for are filling preconceived roles (i.e. the carer is a caring professional, the cared for

---

[122] See my definition of relatedness at the beginning of the preceding section.

is somebody in need with either the money to pay for or the entitlement, *qua* citizen, to the care provided by the caring professional *qua* state employee). Jones's fourfold distinction between private and public roles is useful in elucidating the differences between care in public and private:[123]

1. Private roles emerge in 'face-to-face, one-to-one relationships'[124] while public roles are fixed in advance and to some extent standardized. Private role holders are hence unique and irreplaceable while public role holders are replaceable as long as they meet the requirements of the role.

2. Private roles have a unique set of expectations attached to them which evolve and change with changes in the relationship, while expectations linked to public roles are standardized and determined by the function of the role rather than by the personalities of the role holders.

3. Private roles have a symbolic quality in that they express the particular relationship which has developed between the role holders and in that the actions of the role holders express their attitudes towards each other, while public roles are not supposed to express any particular relationship at all. Public roles, if anything, are expressions of the impartiality of the public sphere and require impartial behaviour from their holders.

4. Private roles are 'organic patterns' which grow and whose 'end is the substance of this pattern rather than aggregation of components combined into this role only because they subserve some external goal'[125] while public roles are clearly and unchangeably defined on the basis of the function they are supposed to fulfil.

Not all of these points of distinction can be applied straightforwardly to the distinction between private and public care, but in elucidating how they do apply the differences as well as the similarities between the two forms of care can be explored further.

Note, to begin with, that there is one major point of difference underlying these various points: what shapes private roles and

---

[123] Jones 1984, esp. pp. 604–9. Jones envisages roles falling into a spectrum ranging from the (ideal-typically) private to the (ideal-typically) public. He takes the roles of friend and lover as 'paradigmatically private' (pp. 603–4).

[124] Ibid. 604.   [125] Ibid. 605.

thus private care is the existence of individualized relationships between people over time, or, in other words, relatedness, while public roles and public care are shaped by the requirement of impartiality, i.e. the non-influence of relatedness (3), and explicit goals (4) which in turn determine the standardized role expectations (2) and the replaceability of role holders (1). Now the reason why Jones's points of distinction cannot be applied straightforwardly is the following: if relatedness is the underlying factor of the distinction in the sense that it implies all the points of distinction that Jones makes between public and private care it implies the endorsement of the claim that relatedness is constitutive of private care. Thus note that the four points of distinction can be understood to follow from such a claim: relatedness can be understood to imply the irreplaceability of private carers (1), the unique set of expectations in private care (2), the symbolic and expressive character of such care (3), as well as the unique organic and evolving pattern of care given and received by people (4). Accordingly, private care would be a completely individualized practice and essentially the kind of particularized activity that particularists ultimately had in mind.[126]

I therefore need to clarify quite how Jones's points of distinction apply to private and public care. While there does not seem to be a problem with regard to the application of the points to public care, there is a problem with the characterization of private care. First of all, and with regard to his fourth point, while private care does form part of an overall pattern of interaction between related individuals which is unique and always open to change and evolution without obvious aim, care itself certainly is not without goal: in fact it has the same goal as public care, namely the meeting of needs. Hence in so far as private care consists of the meeting of needs and has this as its aim, it is in this respect closer to a public than to a private role. It also follows, and this is the basis for my claims about good and bad care in the last section, that it can be evaluated according to how well it meets this aim.[127] Secondly, and with respect to the first

---

[126] See sects. iv and v.

[127] This is a good instance with which to illustrate the difference between a materialist and an idealist conception of care: my materialist conception of care as an activity which meets needs (see Ch. 4 sect. i) focuses on care as a goal-directed practice which is then capable of objective evaluation—as well as a

and second points, private care is not irreplaceable, nor are the
expectations of those cared for unique in all respects. Thus whilst
it is true that relatedness makes people irreplaceable to each
other, and it is also true that private care is given mainly on the
basis of relatedness, it is not true that private carers are irreplaceable. If an infant is not fed by her mother, she can be fed
by her father, by a babysitter, or by a nurse, and her need for
food will be met. None of these instances of care are exactly the
same because they are also expressive of the different relationships between the infant and the carer—because in so far as the
way care is given is expressive of relatedness it is unique—but
one instance can be replaced by any other as long as they meet
the need in the infant.[128] Moreover, and again in so far as care
is expressive of relatedness as well as reliant on different degrees
of knowledge of the cared for, the infant would be right in expect-
ing slightly different care from these different carers. But what
she can equally expect from all of them is that she be cared for.
Private care, then, is entirely private only with regard to Jones's
third point, that is, its symbolic and expressive character, but is
less than private according to the other criteria.[129] The one point,
therefore, that remains and that reliably distinguishes private
from public care, is the expression or non-expression of relatedness as that which determines patterns of caring between persons: private carers care (mostly) *because* they are related and

more 'public' activity—while Noddings's idealist conception of care as an attitude (see Ch. 4 sect. iv) locates care in the subject and thus makes it relatively
inaccessible to objective evaluation because it is strictly 'private'.

[128] This point may need qualifying: it is possible that there are some forms of
care that require such a high degree of trust that carers who have this trust are
not easily replaceable or maybe not replaceable at all. I cannot discuss this point
here, but simply want to note that I am aware of it. It is also worth noting, however, cases where relatedness gets in the way of certain forms of private care
such as intimate physical tending because it causes shame and thus necessitates
professional care by nurses (see Ungerson 1987).

[129] Note that Jones himself suggests that most roles have private and public
aspects. The fact that public care fits the criteria better than private care is not
surprising since public care consists of activities of care defined by a role—that
of a professional carer—while private care is not essentially a role. It may form
part of the interactions between people related in the technical sense, and probably will, but there are no clear or fixed guide-lines of what should happen
between them and whether care should be part of their interaction (the role of
the mother and to some extent that of the daughter and step-daughter are more
explicit with regard to care as an activity than any other (see Qureshi and Walker
1989 and Ch. 4 sect. v above)).

their care is expressive of their relatedness,[130] whilst public carers care because that is the role or function they have and their care must not be influenced by relatedness. Relatedness, therefore, remains the basic factor which is operative in the distinction between private and public care.

Furthermore, and even more importantly, relatedness does not only underlie and explain the actual differences between private and public care, it also provides a criterion for distinguishing their morality. While relatedness justifiably determines interaction and care in the private sphere, it must not make a difference in the public sphere and therefore in public care.[131] Thus a private carer usually cares the more, the more closely or intimately she is related to the cared for. The care she gives, how much of it, and what kind, not only expresses the fact and the quality of her relatedness to the cared for, i.e. has a symbolic quality, but it also reflects the morality of the private sphere in that she is justified in caring for this particular person and not others precisely because she is related to the cared for but not to others. A public carer, by contrast, must not allow relatedness to interfere with her care. A doctor in the public health service cannot allow her mother to jump the long waiting list for hip replacement operations, even if this seems an unbearable restriction, since to do so would be an obvious case of malpractice. Nor must a nurse be seen to provide more and better care for some patients only, except when different needs require different levels of intensity of care. Carers in the public sphere are thus, *qua* participants in the public sphere, subject to the requirement of impartiality, and one of the implications of this requirement is that they must not let relatedness influence their

[130] This point needs qualifying, too, because some private care is given to unknown strangers. This case is interesting in so far as it is even less private than care between related people according to Jones's criteria, but it is obviously not public.

[131] It follows from this claim that there is a valid social and moral distinction between the private and public spheres which cannot be 'abolished'. What earlier feminists should have argued for, I would suggest, is not the abolition of the distinction, but its reconceptualization in non-gendered terms. An early defence of the validity of the distinction and of the specific and irreplaceable value of the private sphere is provided by Elshtain (1981). For a concise and quite different reconceptualization on the public–private distinction see Young 1990: 119 ff. and *passim*. For a radical critique of the 'right to privacy' as conceived by US law, see MacKinnon 1989.

actions: what is appropriate and morally justifiable in private care, namely the favouring of those one is related to, becomes favouritism or nepotism in public care.[132]

I conclude from this that the principles of justice have more force in public care in virtue of its being part of the public sphere than they do in private care. Take the following situation to illustrate the point. I have to choose between responding to a stranger on the street who has to be taken to the hospital and responding to my closest friend who has come to talk a very difficult problem over with me. If I decide to talk to my friend, I do so against the harm minimization principle which would have made me take the stranger to the hospital—the stranger's need being somewhat greater than, but as urgent as, that of my friend. While hoping that somebody else will take care of the stranger, I would thus allow relatedness to qualify and ultimately override the harm minimization principle. Is such a decision justifiable? It is in so far as relatedness implies a certain commitment and obligation to the persons one is related to, that is, in so far as relatedness has moral force, too. My contention is that it does have moral force and that, in virtue of that moral force, considerations of care based on relatedness can come into conflict with considerations of justice in a way that is characteristic of private care but impossible in public care.

One might object to this that my decision is not morally justifiable at all because it is obvious that I should act according to the requirement of justice. This objection, however, misses the point that I have been trying to make about private care, that is, that relatedness does make a moral difference in private care and that, therefore, the taking into account of relatedness is morally justifiable or even required. If relatedness does matter, however, the situation is a moral dilemma rather than a simple case: the choice of either alternative is equally justifiable and equally unsatisfactory. The characterization of this situation as a simple case thus misses the moral character and force of relatedness.[133] Hence what this example illustrates is how relatedness matters morally in private care in ways which are

[132] See Jones 1984: 608.

[133] See my discussion of Barry's position in sect. vii. I understand Blum to make essentially a similar point about the morality of particular relationships although his argument is mainly directed against impartialist accounts of their morality as well as against the Williams/Nagel position that particular relationships involve non-moral rather than moral values (see Blum 1986).

inadmissible in public care. It furthermore illustrates that considerations of care based on relatedness can conflict with considerations of justice in private care in a way that is specific to private care because generated by the morality specific to it. Public care, by contrast, in virtue of being constrained by the impartiality governing the public sphere, does not generate the same conflicts and thus brings out more clearly the two principles of justice, 'undisturbed' by relatedness, that I introduced earlier.

Distribution of care in the public sphere should thus follow both the harm minimization principle and the principle of equality in that both principles express as well as satisfy the requirements of impartiality in the public sphere: the harm minimization principle implies that, in the calculus of harms, everybody's need is to count for one and nobody's need for more than one, whilst the principle of equality requires that everybody's needs be taken into equal consideration and to some extent be met.[134] Distribution of care in the private sphere, by contrast, follows patterns of relatedness and therefore the two principles of justice in a rather weak fashion: the principles of justice are satisfied if compatible with considerations of care based on relatedness. The principles of justice are compatible with such considerations, however, only in cases where relatedness is equally strong or weak between the carer and the prospective beneficiaries of care. Thus in cases of equal relatedness, the two principles of justice serve as tie-breakers (as illustrated by the example of the mother finding the compromise solution of spending time with both her sick child and her healthy child), while they are qualified in all other cases exhibiting circumstances of justice by differences in relatedness (as illustrated by the example of my deciding to stay with the less needy friend at the expense of the more needy stranger).[135]

---

[134] For further explication of the two principles see sect. ii; see also n. 48 above for the distinction between the weak interpretation of equality implied by the harm minimization calculus and the stronger principle of equality of consideration.

[135] The original Noddings example of Ms Brown having to decide between staying with her child and going out with her husband is ambiguous between three possible interpretations if relatedness is taken into account (see sect. ii above): (1) Relatedness is equal between Ms Brown and her husband and children and her child's need is stronger. (2) Relatedness is not equal, and (2*a*) She is more related to her children than to her husband: this easily clinches the decision in favour of her staying with the child. (2*b*) She is more related to her husband: this is the most difficult case because she now has to balance the strength of relatedness against strength of need and hence considerations of care based

It might be thought that I am contradicting my earlier claims about the role of principles of justice in care in this section since I seem to be taking back much of what I claimed earlier. Note, however, that when I derived the two principles of justice in section ii I did not make any claims about their status or force. In fact, I could not have done so because I had to choose specific cases (cases of equal relatedness) in order to be able to point at the force of these principles. The minimal claim I made, therefore, was that these principles form part of the considerations a carer engages in under circumstances of justice. I had to await the discussion of care and justice in public and private in this section before I could provide a more detailed analysis of the differential status and force of principles of justice. What I argue in this section, therefore, is consistent with what I have claimed before.

In conclusion, the main difference between private and public care is the extent to which relatedness matters both actually and morally. This difference, in turn, has implications about the force that considerations of justice and, more specifically, the two principles of justice which I have introduced above, have within considerations of care. As an outcome of the impartiality constraint on care in the public sphere, and as an expression of this constraint, the two principles of justice override relatedness in the public sphere. In private care, however, the two principles are qualified by relatedness and have full force only in the special case of equal relatedness between the carer and those in need of care.

(vii) *Considerations of care and justice reconsidered*

I have spent most of this chapter arguing against various versions of particularist objections to the prospect of conceiving of

on relatedness against considerations of justice. On balance, the child's need must be great enough to outweigh her commitment to her husband and to going out with him. Case (2*b*) is obviously the most difficult one for Noddings because it is dilemmatic. Noddings, however, has no further analysis of the grounds of its dilemmatic character. My analysis of the role of considerations of care based on relatedness as pitted against considerations of justice provides a valid interpretation of why it might be dilemmatic (see my discussion in sect. ii above for another interpretation—unfortunately, Noddings's presentation of the example is not detailed and informed enough to allow for further discussion between the two interpretations).

considerations of justice as part of considerations of care and an ethic of care. This focus was forced, first, by the unfortunate association of the ethic of care with particularism that has been typical of the ethic of care debate as well as, more particularly, of course, of the particularism debate.[136] It was forced, secondly, by the corresponding association of justice with impartialism and what I have called strictly principled types of ethics. While these associations can to some extent be traced back to Gilligan, they certainly took on a life of their own in the particularism debate by focusing the discussion on a metaethical level which then made considerations of justice and care seem incompatible because of their association with incompatible metaethical positions. This focus moreover prevented a detailed discussion of how considerations of care and justice are related at the level of the content of the two ethics. More specifically, it also prevented an enquiry into how considerations of justice could form part of an ethic of care. I have thus also tried, in this chapter, to redress this balance by deriving the two principles of justice in care and by looking at their differential force in private and public care. In this section, I shall draw the different threads of the argument together and draw some conclusions with regard to the 'ethic of care vs. ethic of right and justice' debate.

Note, then, that I have systematically avoided giving any answers to the question which metaethical model an ethic of care does or should follow. I have done so mainly because the most important task seemed to me to make the case for considerations of justice as part of an ethic of care at a less abstract level. I have therefore discussed the question of how considerations of justice relate to considerations of care by looking at examples taken from the practice of care instead of discussing, at the metatheoretical level, what the relation between the two ethics in question was. On the basis of this more concrete discussion, I have argued, first, that considerations of justice had to be part of any responsible practice of care, and therefore of an ethic of care based on this practice, and, secondly, that there are various metaethical models that an ethic of care inclusive of principles of justice could adopt. The metaethical question—the particularism debate—is therefore at least to some extent independent of the question of how considerations of care and

---

[136] For the distinction between the two debates see sect. i.

justice are related. It is not, however, completely independent. Thus it seems to me unlikely that an ethic of care theorist would endorse a strictly principled type of metaethical model such as those endorsed by Kantians, utilitarians, or contractarians simply because the ethic of care is too closely linked to a practice and hence fits more easily into a virtue-based metaethical model such as Aristotle's than into a strictly principled one.[137]

Regardless of what conclusions about metaethical models one might want to draw, however—and I leave those to other ethic of care theorists—what should be of interest to the metaethical debate is that the outcome of my substantive discussion in this chapter may be used in evaluation of such metaethical models. Thus my derivation of the two principles of justice in care has allowed me to draw quite a detailed picture of the place these principles have in an ethic of care: how they are related to other considerations and how these relations are differentiated by the public/private divide. On the basis of this picture, it is now possible to return to the metaethical discussion and evaluate some of the metaethical positions with regard to whether or not they can accommodate such a differentiated picture. I shall thus use the outcome of my substantive discussion to throw a critical light on the particularism debate.

In fact, there are two opposite positions in the particularism debate that can be ruled out on the basis of my discussion. These are the positions:

1. Considerations of care have strict lexical priority;[138] i.e. whenever in conflict, considerations of care override considerations of justice.

2. Considerations of justice have strict lexical priority; i.e. whenever in conflict, considerations of justice override considerations of care.

The two positions are not formulated as metaethical positions, but on the basis of the conclusions they draw with regard to the relationship between considerations of justice and care. They coincide, however, with two opposed metaethical positions in the

---

[137] In fact, as I have indicated above, Nussbaum's interpretation of Aristotle's ethics would seem to provide a very suitable model since it contains enough flexibility to accommodate particularist concerns whilst also leaving an important role to general considerations and principles: see Nussbaum 1986, 1990.

[138] For the concept of 'lexical ordering' see Rawls 1971: 42–3.

particularism debate in so far as these metaethical positions were —and they usually were—interpreted as implying the more concrete claims which I have used to characterize these positions.

Position 1, of course, is that of Noddings and of what I have described as the 'pure' or 'Noddings-type' carer in the last chapter. It is an explication of the particularist interpretation of the ethic of care. This position is illustrated by Noddings's barricades example: if considerations of justice and care pull in different directions, care overrides justice, and hence the carer will not fight against her bigoted relatives in the name of justice.[139] Note also, and in a similar vein, the 'carer's burdens' case where considerations of justice are dismissed with the argument that anybody who follows principles or rules too strictly is suspect as a good carer.[140] Position 2 is an explication of what I have called a strictly principled type of ethic or any impartialist theorist, most strikingly illustrated by an example of Brian Barry's intended to explicate the priority of impartial justice.[141] If your son is wanted for an offence and he is hiding in your home you must not deny his presence should the police knock at your door. Justice thus overrides care, according to Barry, and it overrides care whenever they may be thought to be in conflict.[142]

Given the results of my discussion in the last section, it is obvious that both positions are implausible because they are too simplistic in their structure to accommodate the differential relations between considerations of care and justice in private and public care that I have argued obtain between them. Thus

---

[139] Noddings 1984: 109–10; see also Ch. 4 sect. vii.

[140] Noddings 1984: 13; see also sect. ii.

[141] I heard the example in a seminar presentation in November 1990 at the London School of Economics. In his discussion of the ethic of care in *Justice as Impartiality*, Barry uses a different example which is much more obviously biased in favour of considerations of justice (it is located in the public rather than the private sphere and involves a person in a public role) to motivate his contention that 'principles of justice win' (Barry 1995: 251). In his view, there are no genuine dilemmas involving considerations of care and justice precisely because justice as second-order impartiality 'determines the choice' as and when it applies, so that considerations of care are only valid when 'the decision is left open by the structure of rights and duties' (p. 250; cf. p. 253). Barry thus continues to provide an example for position 2.

[142] It has to be assumed, of course, that there are no good reasons for resisting the justice system such as corruption of the police or judiciary or the inadequacy of the penal system. The only reason for resistance, then, would be considerations of care such as that the son really needs your love and attention

Noddings is not only unable to acknowledge the role of principles of justice in the practice of care, but she also clearly models her ethic on private rather than public care. She therefore comes up with a framework that cannot make sense of the different morality in the public sphere, nor of the different moral constraints on public care.[143] She thus also bars the possibility of expanding the ethic of care beyond the confines of the private sphere into a public and/or political morality.

Barry, on the other hand, models his position on a contractarian public morality which is unable to account for the moral force of particular considerations of care based on relatedness that I have argued is specific to the morality of private care. Nor is he therefore able to appreciate the moral dilemmas that carers encounter in their practice, such as in the example above which, to an ethic of care theorist, would be clearly dilemmatic whilst it looks like a straightforward case to Barry.[144] Barry thus illustrates very strikingly the chill of a strict insistence on, or superordination of, justice and impartiality, which is well captured in the old saying *fiat iustitia pereat mundus*. It is that chill that has turned feminists and some moral theorists against impartialism.[145] This, however, should not have been taken to imply that particularism was the answer, especially not a particularism without considerations of justice.

In so far, then, as these two positions can be taken to reflect much of the 'ethic of care vs. ethic of right and justice' debate in its stress on formal contrasts—care being understood as particularist and justice as impartialist—it would seem obvious that the discussion could not advance much. Much of the argument between the different positions was geared to show the

and that he will be much worse off in prison. (I do not know which reasons Barry had in mind and therefore have had to reconstruct what would be considerations of care in this situation.)

[143] See Noddings's discussion of education which is clearly a form of public care (Noddings 1984, ch. 8) (if it is care at all according to my definition). Her discussion is remarkable in that it manifests, yet again, her failure to appreciate the moral force of considerations of justice and specifically the impartiality requirement of the public sphere.

[144] See also my discussion of the dilemmatic decision between caring for a stranger versus one's less needy friend in sect. vi above for another example of a dilemma that Barry could not appreciate, and n. 141.

[145] By 'impartialism' I refer here to first-order impartialism and second-order impartialism of the type endorsed by Barry (1995).

implausibility of one position and then conclude that, therefore, the other position must be correct. If, however, both positions are implausible and flawed, the correctness of one cannot be concluded from the implausibility of the other. What both sides of the debate thus overlook is the possibility and plausibility of a more complex alternative, consisting of the position that neither considerations of care nor those of justice take lexical priority and that the picture is more complex than either of the opposite positions would have us believe. I have started to develop such a position in the last section by pointing at the differential role of considerations of care and justice in private and public care: while justice overrides relatedness and hence considerations of care based on relatedness in the public sphere, relatedness and hence considerations of care based on relatedness qualify considerations of justice in the private sphere. The main flaw of the two opposite positions thus lies in their oversimplicity which, in turn, is linked to their endorsement of the metaethical contrasts with which the whole debate has been riddled.

Progress, therefore, in the ethic of care debate lies in the direction of detailed discussion rather than that of programmatic and simple oppositions. I shall leave the discussion of the ethic of care debate with this conclusion and move on to more practical conclusions in the last chapter.

6

Outlook

In the preceding chapters I have argued, in the first three (Part I), that conceptions of women's work proposed in the literature either could not accommodate the claim that women were exploited specifically as women through the unpaid work they do (Chapters 1 and 2), or, if they did contain such a claim, came with a faulty story of women's exploitation (Chapter 3). I then developed my own conception of women's work as care and argued that it is as carers that women are specifically vulnerable to exploitation and often exploited (Chapter 4). In Chapter 5, I argued that an ethic of care which derived from the practice of care could and indeed must incorporate considerations of justice and that, consequently, the particularist interpretation of the ethic of care which opposes it to the impartialist or universalist ethic of right and justice is mistaken because it eclipses just such considerations of justice. It is now time to draw the strands of my argument together. Whilst I have discussed how considerations of care and justice are related to each other in an ethic of care, I have not yet addressed the claim that an ethic of care can function as an oppressive ideology that serves to perpetuate women's part in the sexual division of labour by making women continue to care even when such care is clearly exploitative. In so far as the claim that women are specifically vulnerable to being exploited as carers is a consideration of justice, then, I have to address a further way in which considerations of care and considerations of justice are related to each other. I shall do so by reconsidering first the three myopias that I claimed constituted grave problems in Noddings's version of the ethic of care as well as in any version of the ethic which claims to be particularist and fails to discuss the role of considerations of justice within and in relation to it.

(i) *Noddings's myopias reconsidered*

In my argument so far I have addressed two of the three myopias I claimed arose from the type of caring (as an activity and as an ethic) that Noddings describes. First, and with regard to the first type of myopia—which concerned the distribution of the benefits of care to those in need—I have argued that just such distributive considerations arise from the practice and perspective of care and therefore form part of the ethic of care.[1] The two principles of justice that I derived as part of this argument can moreover be applied not only to private and public care, but also to considerations of social justice more generally. Thus a general concern about the distribution of care to those in need follows from the simple step of expanding the range of persons included in considerations of care: if all human beings are included in the scope of considerations of care and hence also considerations based on the two principles of justice—instead of only those one is related to and those to whom one is physically proximate, as Noddings suggests—general requirements of social justice result. Such a step seems to me to urge itself on anyone holding an ethic of care.[2]

Moreover, given that this step is so straightforward, the ethic of care crosses very easily the private/public divide and can be further developed as a public morality.[3] What becomes clear when one looks at the distribution of the benefits of care at a social level on the basis of my discussion of private care[4] is that as long as the distribution is based on relatedness and to some extent proximity, i.e. takes place in the private sphere, it is bound to be uneven and hence unjust.[5] Hence the only way to achieve a just distribution of the benefits of care in a society is via social and public institutions which assure the equitable if not equal meeting of needs,[6] whether by supplementing private care or by

---

[1] Ch. 5 sect. ii.

[2] This step is in fact implied by the ethic of care if the disposition to care is general with regard to its recipients, as Noddings agrees it is; see Ch. 5 sect. v.

[3] For an argument that private morality has to be different from public morality see Elshtain 1981. For cursory suggestions—partly very different from mine—about how the ethic of care could be applied to the public sphere see Friedman 1987b: 103–4. [4] See Ch. 5 sect. vi.

[5] See Ch. 4 sect. vii.

[6] See my discussion of the joint application of the two principles of justice in Ch. 5 sect. ii.

taking it over to some extent or both. The extension of the scope
of the ethic of care thus provides a very simple but (on its own
terms) strong argument for welfare state type public institutions
which remedy the distributive injustice produced by the pattern
of private care. Even more generally, then, such a general ethic
of care will be a needs-based type of morality and could be
developed in various directions.[7] In contrast to Noddings, then,
I conclude that an acceptable version of the ethic of care such
as I have developed in the last chapter can easily address and
satisfactorily deal with questions of distributive justice with
regard to the benefits of care.

Secondly, and with regard to the third type of myopia[8]—which
I called the 'anti-abstractionism' in Noddings and which can now
be understood as her mistaken interpretation of particularism—
I have argued in various sections in the last chapter that there
are no grounds for holding on to Noddings's claim that the practice and ethic of care are antithetical to the use of general principles or rules. Carers must, and do, have recourse to—and the
ethic of care must therefore comprise—principles of justice as
well as other types of general considerations, standards, and
rules. It seems to me that it is at this point that Noddings's particularism does greatest harm. She dangerously prejudices the
further development of the theory and ethic of care with regard
not only to the public sphere but also more generally in various
directions by not acknowledging the potential for generalization
implicit in the practice and perspective of care. Furthermore, as
a consequence of her anti-abstractionism, she also rules out any
more systematic discussion of the relationship between considerations of care and other moral considerations. Thus even though
her version of the ethic of care is meant to apply very generally,
presumably there are parts of the moral realm that are not
mapped out by considerations of care. Hence there are other
moral considerations whose standing with regard to considerations of care has to be discussed. As I illustrated in the last
chapter,[9] Noddings's position is that considerations of care have

---

[7] I cannot develop any of these suggestions any further here, nor can I indicate how such a morality would be related to various other types of moralities.
Work on these issues would be an interesting area for further research. See
Sevenhuijsen 1993 for thoughts along similar lines (pp. 143–4), and Wiggins
1987, Braybrooke 1987, and Thompson 1987 for recent work on needs.

[8] I shall take up the second type of myopia presently.   [9] Sect. vii.

lexical priority over considerations of justice, and one may reasonably conclude that she thinks something similar with respect
to other moral considerations. I have argued that this position
is implausible given the complex nature of the relationship
between considerations of care and justice, and a similar evaluation suggests itself with regard to the relationship between considerations of care and other moral considerations. The third
type of myopia, then, while being a grave problem in Noddings's
particularist version of the ethic of care, can be circumvented by
a more adequate understanding of the role of general considerations, rules, and principles in the ethic of care. Such an understanding also allows for a much more sophisticated discussion
of the relationship between the ethic of care and other types of
moralities or moral considerations.

Lastly, having addressed and resolved two of the three myopias
plaguing Noddings's version of the ethic of care, I need to look
in detail at the second type of myopia, which concerned the distribution of the burden of care to carers. This is certainly the
most problematic case for any ethic of care because it involves
a straightforward contradiction between considerations of justice and considerations of care. Take the case of a carer who is
exhausted from the double burden of caring for her children as
well as for her very demanding frail mother-in-law (not to mention servicing her husband).[10] Note, first, that this is an instance
of the 'carer's burdens' case that I discussed above as one of the
points where Noddings fails most appallingly to realize the relevance of considerations of justice.[11] According to Noddings,
what a carer needs to do in this situation is, in the short term,
recover herself or make others care for her, and, in the long term
and more generally, strengthen her self-image as a carer so that
she is not so easily vulnerable to exhaustion. Noddings's treatment of the case thus eclipses considerations of justice from the
picture altogether and illustrates her myopia perfectly. Note, further, that this case is also an instance of the worst case scenario
which, as I had argued earlier,[12] may make women question
why it is they are doing all or most of the unpaid caring in the
first place and, ultimately, the justice of this distribution of
the burden of unpaid care. While self-identified carers do not

[10] For a discussion of care and service see Ch. 4 sects. i and viii.
[11] Ch. 5 sect. ii.   [12] See Ch. 4 sects. iii, vi.

necessarily come to question their caring, the kind of situation where they may start to do so is certainly the kind where their burden of care is obviously heavy, obviously exploitative, and hence obviously unjust.

Our carer, then, may realize when considering her situation that her unremunerated burden of care is unjust. Now, if she took these considerations of justice seriously, she would have to conclude that she must either try to reduce her burden of care or try to obtain remuneration. Assuming, furthermore, but realistically, that the latter is not forthcoming, nor that she can successfully appeal to other people's help, the only way to change her situation is to care less herself. As a carer who endorses the ethic of care, however, she will not be in a position to do so because this move motivated by considerations of justice is in plain contradiction to the considerations of care deriving from the ongoing demands for care that she encounters. This dilemma, which I shall call the exploitation dilemma, is lived day by day by many carers more or less consciously and is one of the main ways in which carers are trapped into an exploitative, unjust burden of care.[13] It is crucial to this discussion because it sheds light on possible limitations of the ethic of care. What makes this dilemma so interesting is, first, the fact that for any carer it is heavily weighted towards ceding to the considerations of care at the disregard of the contradictory considerations of justice, and, secondly, that this fact in turn explains its central role in women's exploitation as carers: it is its inherent bias in favour of considerations of care which explains why those carers who endorse an ethic of care are so easily exploited. Hence the dilemma also explains why, given the sexual division of labour, women are exploited as carers.

Why is there such a bias in favour of caring? Recall that the result of not caring in these dilemmatic situations is that the person in need incurs harm. The consequences of ceding to considerations of justice are therefore invariably negative and may be fairly grave. The consequences of ceding to considerations of care, on the other hand, may not be as grave. Being exploited, unlike not being cared for, does not imply harm, since it may

---

[13] It is also known as the 'caring trap' in the social policy literature. See Ungerson 1987 and various papers in Maclean and Groves 1991, especially those by Land and Baldwin and Twigg.

simply mean that the carer enjoys fewer benefits than she is entitled to.[14] Being unjustly treated, in other words, may be a moral
wrong, but the wrong of injustice is morally less compelling than
the wrong of actual harm. This last claim may be contested, of
course, but the point is that whilst it may be contested by those
endorsing an ethic of justice, it will certainly not be contested
by those endorsing an ethic of care. Given that it is not, those
holding an ethic of care will be compelled to care by considerations of care as against considerations of justice. Moreover, they
will be compelled to care even though this implies their own
exploitation.[15] Thus while, in principle, carers have a choice
between not caring (or reducing their care) and continuing to
care (and being exploited) in such dilemmatic situations—and
thus may be said to 'choose' being or remaining in an exploitative situation—their choice is pre-empted by their endorsing the
ethic of care.[16]

What this analysis of the exploitation dilemma shows, then,
is that Noddings's myopia about considerations of justice with

[14] Of course, exploited people may also, as a result of their being exploited,
not be able to meet all their needs or have all their needs met, but the link
between exploitation and actual harm is contingent, whilst the link between not
being cared for and actual harm is necessary (cf Ch. 4 sect. i).

[15] They will not be similarly compelled to service others, hence they will
not be similarly vulnerable to exploitation on the basis of considering servicing
others. The problem with many actual self-identified carers, as mentioned above
(Ch. 5 sect. viii), seems to be that they do not see the difference or else see those
they service, especially their husbands, sons, and fathers, as less competent at
and capable of meeting their own needs than they in fact are, hence more as in
need of care and less as wanting service (a proclivity which is part of what is
otherwise known as the infantilization of those cared for by carers). There is, of
course, a grey area where it is not clear whether people are in need of care or
wanting service. Consider a husband who has never learnt to cook and who
'needs' a home-cooked meal to be able to relax and unwind in the evening: if
his wife wants to take up paid work and cannot consequently cook his dinner
anymore, does she have to teach him to cook in order to rid herself of her caring duties, or could she just insist he wants her service and she will not feel
obliged to indulge him? In response to this grey area we might think of some
activities as having elements of both care and service, as neither exactly care,
nor exactly service. Correspondingly, considerations about such activities would
have more moral force than considerations of service, but less force than considerations of care.

[16] The 'choice' for carers between caring or justice may look similar to that
of workers between an exploitative work contract and starving in that both are
systematically vulnerable to exploitation because they do not have a real choice.
Carers, however, are specifically vulnerable in virtue of their morals (and, of
course, other factors such as their gender socialization, their material dependence

respect to the distribution of the burden of care to carers is not specific to her version of the ethic of care. It is, in fact, inherent in any version of the ethic of care because it is generated by the very value that the ethic of care is based on, that is, the avoidance of harm by meeting needs. Hence it points up a dangerous limitation in any ethic of care: the ethic of care renders carers vulnerable to exploitation because they do not have the 'moral resources' within their caring perspective to deal with this problem. It also points up an important respect in which considerations of care are irreconcilably opposed to considerations of justice. It might be objected here that the problem of exploitation can be solved from within a perspective of care by including the carer herself in the scope of those whose needs are given equal consideration by her, that is, by using the principle of equality that I have argued forms part of the ethic of care. Certainly Gilligan and possibly Noddings might respond to the exploitation dilemma like this, even if Noddings would not agree that such an inclusion were based on considerations of justice.[17] However, whilst this move may assure that some or all of the carers' needs are met, it does not assure their being justly treated nor their not being exploited. As I have pointed out above, carers' exploitation may not imply their needs not being met, it may 'merely' imply their being deprived of benefits they are entitled to, given their caring burdens. Hence the demands of justice as far as the exploitation of carers is concerned cannot be satisfied from 'within' the ethic of care.

I therefore conclude further that while some considerations of justice are compatible with considerations of care and indeed arise from within a perspective of care, at least one type of consideration of justice is not and cannot be reconciled with the ethic of care. This conclusion, however, is crucially important because it concerns the exploitation of carers and moreover, as long as the sexual division of labour persists, it concerns the

on a breadwinner, lesser earning capacity, etc.—see Ch. 4) while workers are vulnerable in virtue of their material needs (and, of course, other factors such as their work ethic, their dependence on work for their self-esteem, their having to support dependants, etc.).

[17] See Ch. 5 sect. i and Noddings 1984, 1990; see also Baldwin and Twigg's very similar suggestions from a social policy perspective in a very perceptive discussion of the social policy literature on women and care (Baldwin and Twigg 1991).

exploitation of women. The very ethic, then, that has been hailed as 'women's moral voice' is thus not only in Noddings's, but in any conceivable version, a crucial factor in women's continued exploitation.

(ii) *Outlook: conclusions and openings*

What are we to make of this diagnosis? Further conclusions, but also, as always, new openings, suggest themselves at two different levels: first at the more theoretical level concerning the further understanding and evaluation of the ethic of care, and secondly at the more practical level of thinking about women's exploitation as carers. The main conclusions at the theoretical level are that the scope of any ethic of care is limited and that the ethic of care is therefore in need of (some) complementary considerations of justice which it cannot generate by itself and which, indeed, are incompatible with its very foundations. At the practical level, there is a solution to the exploitation dilemma which consists of the systematic prevention of the type of situation where carers find themselves trapped by such dilemmas. The exploitation of carers can thus be abolished. I shall discuss the two levels in turn.

First, then, I would like to consider in more detail and defend my conclusion that the ethic of care, in whatever version we might imagine it, is limited in scope and hence in need of complementation. What the discussion of the exploitation dilemma has shown is the fact that there are moral and political considerations which are important and should be taken seriously (not only by feminists but by all moral and political philosophers) but which are not compatible with the ethic of care. This relatively restricted result should make us wonder whether there may be other moral or political considerations which may turn out to be incompatible with certain or even all possible versions of the ethic of care, but which are thought to be equally important. The question, in other words, that the exploitation dilemma has raised is what exactly the power and scope of the ethic of care is, and how much of the moral realm it can make sense of, given the moral and political concerns we have and certain preconditions we might want to impose on any acceptable

version of it (such as that it not function as an exploitative ideology for women). I can obviously not answer this question here,
but it seems important enough to have arrived at this question
and to realize what an answer to it requires. One of the traps
for enthusiastic ethic of care theorists, it seems to me, is the idea
that the ethic of care may represent a new paradigm which feminists can endorse as a 'cure-all' to all the problems and weaknesses of mainstream moral and political theory that have been
criticized by feminists in the past. It is undeniable that the perspective of care, including more specific perspectives such as
mothering, has been more than productive in the last ten years
and has inspired some of the most interesting and innovative
work within feminist theory.[18] There is also a need, however, to
be aware of possible limits. One such limit is thrown into relief
by the exploitation dilemma, but there may be others. The import
of this realization, however, should not be to stop discussing the
ethic of care, but to be aware of this possibility whilst continuing to explore from many directions and on the basis of many
different questions or problems what such an ethic might look
like. This more detailed exploration, as opposed to the programmatic and much too general discussion characteristic of the
particularism debate, has only just started, and it is only through
such detailed discussions that the various versions of the ethic
of care in their strengths and weaknesses, possibilities and limitations, can start to take shape. Far from concluding, therefore,
that the ethic of care must be rejected because it cannot deal
with the exploitation dilemma, I consider it important to continue the exploration whilst being aware of other possible limits. In this sense, my conclusion opens up space for further
discussion of the ethic of care, whilst also imposing caveats.

It might be objected to this conclusion that it is premature and
that I have not really explored the possibility that the exploitation dilemma *can* be dealt with from within the ethic of care.
Thus it might be argued that the ethic of care that I have been
discussing so far is extremely specific and that since, as I have
suggested myself, it is open to generalization it may be further

[18] In the field of moral and political theory, the following seem to me especially noteworthy: Noddings 1984, 1989, Ruddick 1989, Held 1993, Tronto 1993,
Hirschmann 1992.

generalized to an extent which would permit the inclusion of the considerations of exploitation that I have claimed are incompatible with it. More specifically, it might be argued that the carer's basic concern with meeting needs may be generalized to a concern with other people's welfare. The reason why justice in general and exploitation in particular would form an important part of such a generalized ethic of care, then, is that part of what determines the welfare and flourishing of any person is their being paid equal respect, and their being justly treated, hence their not being exploited, is an expression of such equal respect. The inclusion of considerations of justice *in general* could thus be derived from a general concern with the welfare of others, and considerations of exploitation be included as part of the considerations of justice.

Whilst I have no objections to this argument as such, and whilst it is certainly possible to argue that a concern with justice ultimately derives from a concern with the welfare of others, I do not see how this generalized morality is still recognizably an ethic of care. In other words, the level of generality that is required in order to make considerations of justice in general compatible with considerations of care empties the latter of their *specific* content. Thus a concern with the welfare of others, it seems to me, underpins most if not all moralities, hence it fails to be specific to the ethic of care, and in so far as it does, it forces the ethic of care theorist to abandon any of the more specific features that made it distinctive as an ethic of care. One of these more specific features, surely, is the special motivating force that the perception of needs in others has for the carer. If this force is recognized, however, the exploitation dilemma continues to be a problem. If it is played down, the exploitation dilemma can be dealt with, but then one of the most distinctive features of the ethic of care is lost. A solution to the exploitation dilemma within the ethic of care, in other words, is purchased at the price of abandoning what is distinctive in the ethic of care.

In order to illustrate this point, let me, for argument's sake, distinguish three levels of generality:[19]

---

[19] One could imagine many more levels of generality. I only use these three to give an idea of what I have in mind.

1. The ethic of care as derived from the practice of both private and public care and applied to questions arising about care generally: this is the level at which, for example, my own discussion has been pitched;
2. The ethic of care as derived from the practice of care, with its central concepts, values, and principles being applied more widely to various issues or problems and in various areas of private and public life: for example, the ethic of care as a distinctively needs-based political morality;[20] as a basis for discussions of democracy, equality, liberty, war and peace;[21] as a basis for discussions of traditional concepts and issues in moral philosophy such as that of evil;[22]
3. The ethic of care as a general, all-embracing moral outlook, perspective, or *Weltanschauung*.[23]

If we consider these three levels, it seems to me that the first two levels of generalization leave the ethic of care recognizably intact as an ethic of *care*, but that the third level is too much in danger of losing any specific content. Quite where and when its distinct features are getting lost is, of course, a matter of more detailed argument, but as the exploitation dilemma illustrates, some general features may only be achieved at the price of losing important and distinctive specificity. Hence the ethic of care is best understood as more specific and limited in scope and generality. While levels (1) and (2) of generality seem unproblematic, the interesting question then is just how far the ethic of care can be generalized. Rather than assume it can, ethic of care theorists should therefore probe the ethic of care with respect to its general potential and limits. The implication of this conclusion is, of course, that the ethic of care does not map out the entire moral domain and, more specifically, that considerations of justice will occupy an important place in the moral domain, both inside and outside the ethic of care. Furthermore, other moral considerations may be found similarly located, both within and without, if investigated.

---

[20] See my suggestion in sect. i above.
[21] See Tronto 1993, Held 1993, Ruddick 1989.
[22] See Noddings 1989.
[23] Noddings often presents her version of the ethic of care as embracing this most general level as well as the more specific ones (Noddings 1984).

One last point needs to be made before bringing this discussion of the potential and limits of the ethic of care to a close. The recognition of the limits of the ethic of care may be disappointing, but it should not lead to premature withdrawal from working on it, nor to a loss of trust in its potential, but rather to a detailed exploration of both its strengths and weaknesses. What can be observed in some of the recent literature, unfortunately, is evidence of such a loss or lack of trust in the potential of the ethic of care. Thus Tronto introduces the need for considerations of justice on the basis of the problems she finds with the ethic of care, notably its supposed parochialism,[24] whilst Held calls for principles because she sees a danger that carers may be too 'capricious or domineering' in their practice.[25] Both arguments, it seems to me, derive from a lack of trust in the potential of the ethic of care to deal with those problems by drawing on its own resources. They are also mistaken since it is arguable that these problems only derive from a mistaken conception of the practice of care as more contextual and unreflected or 'unprincipled' than it actually is.[26] If, instead, they had explored the potential of the ethic of care more—in these respects, as they have done in so many others—they might well have found that at least some considerations of justice and even principles of justice arise organically from within the practice of care and are far from opposed to it or a corrective of it.[27] Hence, on the basis of such a more realistic appreciation of the actual potential of the ethic of care, they would also have had to conclude that the idea of justice or principles as a counterbalance to dangerous tendencies within the ethic of care cannot be generally upheld and that the picture is more complex.

In conclusion, then, whilst the exploitation dilemma has pointed up an important limitation in the ethic of care, this should not be taken to imply that considerations of justice in general are needed to counterbalance limits in the ethic of care or that the ethic of care is not worth much more thought. The acknowledgment of some limits can very well go hand in hand with the further exploration of the as yet very sketchily discussed potential of the ethic of care as an alternative to mainstream moral

---

[24] Tronto 1993: 155, 170–1.   [25] Held 1993: 75.
[26] See my argument in Ch. 5, especially sects. ii–v.
[27] See my argument in Ch. 5 sect. ii.

and political theories. In this sense, my conclusions represent also a true opening towards more work on the ethic of care.

I move on, then, secondly, to the conclusions at the more practical level of argument about women's exploitation as carers. Given, as I have argued above, the irreconcilable tension between considerations of care and considerations about the exploitation of carers captured in the exploitation dilemma, and given that there is no solution to the dilemma within the ethic of care, the solution has to lie in the application or social realization of considerations of justice. Now, one possible solution—which, since it is obviously silly, I mention only to make a certain point about care—would be to abolish the ethic of care altogether by re-educating carers into fighters so as to deliver them from their vulnerability to exploitation as carers. I take it, however, that this solution is not desirable and that the ethic of care is here to stay. To begin with, care as a practice is bound to continue since there will always be needs that persons other than those in need have to meet. Care as necessary labour, in other words, cannot be abolished precisely because it is necessary labour and will always have to be performed in any human society, whether this is 'officially' recognized or not. Furthermore, given the need for, and practice of, care, there will always be people who endorse an ethic of care—assuming that it is the most likely and the most fitting ethic to hold for those who engage in caring as well as the most beneficial ethic for those cared for.[28] In other words, it is not only necessary that care continue to be performed, but it is also desirable that the ethic of care continue to be held by people. Given, however, that people who hold the ethic of care are vulnerable to exploitation because they do not have the moral resources to prevent their own exploitation, and that social justice demands that nobody be exploited, another solution to the problem will have to be found.

It might be thought, conversely, that the answer to the problem is simply that everybody should care, hence that fighters be re-educated into carers. This, to me, seems an excellent idea for various reasons, not least because the abolition of the moral division of labour would make men and thus societies more humane

---

[28] Compare a Kantian duty-bound carer with a carer who holds an ethic of care: it seems obvious to me that the latter would be more likely to have the required skills and the right 'touch' (see Ch. 5 sect. iv) than the former.

and liveable. The exploitation problem, however, would not be solved by this change either, since it would merely end up making everybody vulnerable to exploitation. While this might be preferable to the situation where only some, mostly women, are vulnerable to exploitation, given that it abolishes the gendered aspect of the moral division of labour and thus spreads the risk of being exploited more evenly, it does not abolish the exploitation of carers as such. The actual burden of care might still be rather uneven because some are faced with more demands on their care than others, simply in virtue of the chance distribution of people with needs which make heavy demands on carers and the uneven distribution of patterns of relatedness. Hence exploitation dilemmas may still arise, and the re-education of fighters into carers, whilst spreading the burden of care as well as the risk of exploitation more evenly, does not present a solution to the exploitation problem, although it certainly represents an important and desirable change.

In order to get closer to the solution, then, we have to look again at the situation which gives rise to the exploitation dilemma. The crucial aspect in this situation is the fact that not caring results in harm. If it did not, the carer could freely decide not to care and would therefore not be vulnerable to exploitation. Accordingly, if a carer had systematic access to care provided by others—'third parties'—the dilemma would not arise and exploitation would cease to be the systematic result of carers' endorsing an ethic of care.[29] However, such access cannot be provided privately, either unpaid or via the market, without raising further problems about the uneven provision of such access and the exploitation of badly paid carers. Unpaid care is not always available, especially in the age of the nuclear family where other members of the family who might have helped may live too far away. Reliance on the unpaid care of others, at any rate, just passes the problem of exploitation on to other unpaid carers. Leaving the problem to the private market will result in further injustice, as this creates a new class of badly paid carers

---

[29] Of course, some carers might care nevertheless and therefore enter or remain in an exploitative situation, but the point is that under these circumstances such a decision would be unforced. It is impossible to prevent people from freely entering arrangements which are exploitative. But it is possible to abolish social institutions or structures which subject some people systematically to exploitation.

who work for those who can afford to 'buy themselves out' of their caring burden. The more inequality there is in society, the more likely this pattern is to occur. The badly paid carers in turn will not be able to afford to pay for care, hence have to care themselves, and so will those who cannot afford to pay for care. These two groups thus clearly remain vulnerable to exploitation as carers. Hence private provision of care does not solve the problem, since it merely shifts the problem of exploitation to other vulnerable groups in society. The only possible conclusion, therefore, is that a just society has to take it upon itself to provide care for carers to take up as and when they are in danger of becoming overburdened. The practical solution to the exploitation dilemma thus is the systematic social provision of care to replace that of carers where needed.[30] The solution requires, however, that carers' exploitation is seen as a problem of social justice.

This solution recommends itself on various grounds. First, it allows people to endorse an ethic of care because it is safe for them to do so.[31] This seems to me very important not only because, as I pointed out above, the need for care is permanent— because care is necessary labour—but also because a society in which people can endorse and act according to an ethic of care will be a much more humane society. Secondly, given that it implies the conception of the exploitation dilemma as a *social* problem, it allows further questions to be asked and observations to be made about the distribution of the burden of care at the social level. I shall point to various such avenues in what follows.

First, it allows us to ask whether the sexual division of labour

---

[30] Nothing is implied here about the form such provision would take, that is, whether, for example, the state would organize such care provision or merely fund it, who would be recruited for such provision etc.; see my discussion of various scenarios below.

[31] Brecht's play *The Good Person of Szechuan* deals with a structurally very similar problem: the one morally good person in a morally corrupt society ends up having to double up as her wicked (male) cousin in order to put to a halt the typically self-destructive situation she finds herself in. (Interestingly enough, the cousin starts appearing only at the point where the good person has to make provisions for her baby to be born.) Brecht thus didactically leads his audience to the conclusion that the world needs changing so that it is safe to be good: a move from the individual to the social level exactly parallel to the one I am proposing.

which makes women provide most of the unpaid care is justified itself, even if the problem of the exploitation of carers can be solved. Thus note that, although I have developed this solution in general terms, that is, for carers in general, it is a solution that will mainly benefit women, given the sexual division of labour. It thus contingently solves the problem of women's exploitation because it solves the problem of carers' exploitation, but it does not address the further question of who should care in the first place. While it takes the exploitative sting out of the ethic of care and therefore out of the sexual division of labour between carers and fighters, it does not provide an answer to the following further question: even if it is safe to care, is there not something objectionable for some to get away without caring, especially if the universal distribution of care is in itself desirable and probably immensely beneficial? This question can now be posed clearly and, furthermore, more distinctly because unrelated to the question of women's oppression. As I argued above, the abolition of the moral division of labour which goes hand in hand with the sexual division of labour, whilst in itself not a solution to the exploitation problem, may be an important part of an overall aim for change because it demands from men equally what women have always been expected to provide. The focus of the problem to be solved, in this aim, is correspondingly shifted away from women and onto men: instead of asking ourselves whether women care too much we will ask ourselves why it is that men do not care enough?

Secondly, focusing on the social distribution of care provides an answer to the problem I had to leave unresolved when I discussed the question, in Chapter 1, how women could be freed from their 'slavish relationship' to women's work. The answer is that the sexual division of labour has to be understood as a social institution which can be changed rather than as a natural given. It is this different understanding that will allow, first, the analysis of the mechanisms which enforce the division of labour[32] and, secondly, conscious social decisions about how to change it. The liberation of women from their 'slavish relationship' to care thus implies, most importantly, the realization that this

---

[32] See my theory of care in Ch. 4.

relationship is socially constructed in the first place, and this in turn implies reflection on the distribution of care at a social level.

Thirdly, the further question can be posed to what extent care should be understood as a private responsibility, and to what extent it should be seen as a public and social responsibility. Note, in particular, that one of the main reasons why Delphy and Leonard's conception of women's exploitation was unsatisfactory was that they conceived of care as work which has to be provided privately, by the family, and more specifically, whose provision it is the duty of the head of the household to ensure. Thus the focus is on the husband and head of household, rather than men in general, as those who benefit from women's exploitation, and the general implication is that heads of households should do more caring themselves. As I argued above, however, a redistribution of care between men and women is by itself no solution to the exploitation of carers. The crucial theoretical move in the solution of the problem, by contrast, is from the micro-level of individual caring relations and provision, such as in households, to the social level. If this theoretical shift is made, it then becomes possible to ask at what level the responsibility for care lies, and to see the fact that it is the very relegation of the responsibility for care to the private sphere, combined with the sexual division of labour, which enables women's exploitation in their own homes. Delphy and Leonard's more or less exclusive focus on the micro-level of the household, however, not only leads to their implausible micro-level theory of women's exploitation, it also leaves them with no way out of the problem.

Fourthly, different scenarios of the distribution or provision of care, at both public and private level, can be thought out, analysed and evaluated. Some models may recommend themselves more than others not only on the grounds that they are less exploitative of carers, but also on other grounds such as that they provide a way of abolishing instead of reinforcing the sexual division of labour, that they encourage the learning of caring skills and the endorsement of the ethic of care or that they are less exploitative of large families' care for many more children or individual carers' unwavering endorsement of the ethic of care and thus provision of care in the face of huge demands on their care. I shall sketch three such scenarios to indicate what kind of discussion I have in mind.

First, we might imagine a society where the burden of care is socially recognized as an important task in society and distributed equally to all able members of society. This would certainly abolish exploitation, but it would also require that no care be provided privately, based on patterns of relatedness or willingness to pay, since such private provision—as I have argued above—would invariably be uneven and thus disturb the intended equal distribution. Care, to adopt marxist terminology, would thus be completely socialized. But would anybody want this extreme form of reorganization not only of care, but of all social life as we know it, given that nobody could be allowed simply to care for their friend, partner, or child on the basis of their relation to them?[33] Would it be feasible at all, given that no one can prevent people from liking and caring about and for each other?[34] Hence whatever may be said in favour of this scenario, its disadvantages certainly outweigh its attractiveness in 'neatly' solving the problem of carers' exploitation.

Secondly, as mentioned above briefly already, we might think about leaving the private distribution of care along patterns of relatedness (and to some extent proximity) undisturbed, but with the state providing systematic back-up care to private carers as and when needed. This would equally tackle the problem of the exploitation of carers, but would leave the gendered division of care and morality intact. It might also turn out to be extremely expensive if back-up care is to be well paid and resources for it have to be raised through taxation. Such a traditional state provision solution thus may well be too expensive as well as not radical enough.

Thirdly, then, a more imaginative scenario: rather than follow the welfare state model of social provision, one might conceive

[33] This model is comparable in many respects to the Platonic social model for the guardians in his ideal republic and thus subject to similar criticisms.

[34] This last point, ironically enough, is parallel to Nozick's Wilt Chamberlain argument that nobody can prevent capitalist acts from occurring spontaneously (Nozick 1974: 160–2). I disagree with Nozick, however, in that I think the liberty to engage in capitalist acts is much less central to people's lives than caring about and for others and can be restricted if need be, while caring cannot and should not be restricted.

of care as part of a citizen's obligation to contribute her share to one of the most, if not the most important function any self-governing society has, namely to ensure the well-being of its members. Citizenship would be redefined to comprise care as much as, or even more importantly than, defence as every citizen's obligation.[35] The obligation would be men's and women's equally, and would be discharged by their contributing a certain share of their lifetime to what we might call a 'caring service'. Such a universal caring service may be a better way of providing back-up care for private carers for a number of reasons: it makes care more visible; it gives care the central place and social recognition that has been denied it for so long; it is a 'school for carers' for both men and women and may thus have an important role re-educating fighters into carers by fostering the skills and virtues of care in everybody; it abolishes the gendered division of labour and morality; it may be cheaper than the state provision envisaged in the second scenario.

I cannot pursue this discussion any further, but the point of it should be clear: my presentation of women's work as care and specifically of the exploitation dilemma enables this kind of discussion in a new way because it directs the view to both private and public, individual and social provision of care and the effects such patterns of provision will have. Hopefully, much more discussion at this policy level will take place in the wake of the more theoretical arguments concerning care.

Last, but not least, and in conclusion of my discussion of care, gender, and justice, the problem of the exploitation of carers and therefore that of the exploitation of women forces itself onto the social justice agenda by being posed as a social problem. The reason why it has not been discussed as part of this agenda is twofold. First, as I mentioned in the introduction, women's oppression and exploitation has mostly not been seen as a problem of social justice.[36] Secondly, as long as care is considered a quintessentially private activity it seems to lie beyond the scope of any theory of social justice. As I pointed out above, however, whether and to what extent care is considered a public or

---

[35] Why should killing and destroying, or preparing to kill and destroy, be more honourable and worthy a citizen's contribution to her society than caring?
[36] See Okin's classic discussion of contemporary theories of justice (Okin 1989).

private responsibility is itself at issue, especially if the relegation of care to the private sphere has such grave consequences.
It would seem, therefore, not only that the ethic of care is in
need of being complemented by considerations of social justice,
but also that the theorization of social justice is in need of being
complemented by a theory of care and of women's exploitation
as carers.

References

ABEL, E. K., and NELSON, M. K. (1990) (eds.), *Circles of Care: Work and Identity in Women's Lives*, Albany, NY: State University of New York Press.

ADAMSON, O., BROWN, C., HARRISON, J., and PRICE, J. (1976), 'Women's Oppression under Capitalism', *Revolutionary Communist*, 5.

ADLER, J. E. (1987), 'Moral Development and the Personal Point of View', in Kittay and Meyers 1987.

—— (1989), 'Particularity, Gilligan, and the Two-Levels View: A Reply', *Ethics*, 100: 149–59.

ALIBHAI, Y. (1989), 'Burning in the Cold', in Gieve 1989b.

ALLEN, S., and WOLKOWITZ, C. (1987), *Homeworking: Myths and Realities*, Basingstoke: Macmillan Education.

ARISTOTLE (1980), *The Nichomachean Ethics*, Oxford: Oxford University Press.

—— (1988), *The Politics*, Cambridge: Cambridge University Press.

AVINERI, S. (1968), *The Social and Political Thought of Karl Marx*, Cambridge: Cambridge University Press.

BAIER, A. C. (1987a), 'Hume, the Women's Moral Theorist?', in Kittay and Meyers 1987.

—— (1987b), 'The Need for More than Justice', in Hanen and Nielsen 1987.

BALDWIN, S., and TWIGG, J. (1991), 'Women and Community Care: Reflections on a Debate', in Maclean and Groves 1991.

BARKER, D. L., and ALLEN, S. (1976) (eds.), *Dependence and Exploitation in Work and Marriage*, London: Longman.

BARON, M. (1991), 'Impartiality and Friendship', *Ethics*, 101: 836–57.

BARRETT, M. (1980), *Women's Oppression Today*, London: Verso.

—— and MCINTOSH, M. (1979), 'Christine Delphy: Towards a Materialist Feminism?', *Feminist Review*, 1: 95–106.

—— —— (1982), *The Anti-Social Family*, London: Verso.

BARRY, B. (1995), *Justice as Impartiality: A Treatise on Social Justice*, vol. ii, Oxford: Clarendon.

BARTKY, S. L. (1990), 'Feeding Egos and Tending Wounds: Deference and Disaffection in Women's Emotional Labor', in *Feminity and Domination: Studies in the Phenomenology of Oppression*, New York: Routledge.

BEBEL, A. (1971), *Woman under Socialism*, New York: Schocken Books.

BECKER, G. (1981), *A Treatise on the Family*, Cambridge, Mass.: Harvard University Press.

BENERIA, L. (1979), 'Reproduction, Production and the Sexual Division of Labour', *Cambridge Journal of Economics*, 3/3: 203–25.

BENHABIB, S. (1987), 'The Generalized and the Concrete Other: The Kohlberg–Gilligan Controversy and Feminist Theory', in Benhabib and Cornell 1987.

—— and CORNELL, D. (1987) (eds.), *Feminism as Critique*, Cambridge: Polity.

BENNHOLDT-THOMSEN, V. (1981), 'Subsistence Production and Extended Reproduction', in Young *et al.* 1981.

BENSTON, M. (1982), 'The Political Economy of Women's Liberation', in Malos 1982.

BERK, S. F. (1985), *The Gender Factory: The Apportionment of Work in American Households*, New York: Plenum.

BLUM, L. A. (1980), *Friendship, Altruism, and Morality*, London: Routledge & Kegan Paul.

—— (1986), 'Iris Murdoch and the Domain of the Moral', *Philosophical Studies*, 50: 343–67.

—— (1987), 'Particularity and Responsiveness', in Kagan and Lamb 1987.

—— (1988), 'Gilligan and Kohlberg: Implications for Moral Theory', *Ethics*, 98: 472–91.

—— (1990), 'Vocation, Friendship, and Community: Limitations of the Personal–Impersonal Framework', in Flanagan and Rorty 1990.

—— HOMIAK, M., HOUSMAN, J., and SCHEMAN, N. (1976), 'Altruism and Women's Oppression', in Gould and Wartofsky 1976.

BLUMSTEIN, P., and SCHWARTZ, P. (1983), *American Couples*, New York: Morrow.

BOBBINGTON, A. C., and DAVIES, B. (1983), 'Equity and Efficiency in the Allocation of the Personal Social Services', *Journal of Social Policy*, 12/3: 309–30.

BRABECK, M. M. (1989) (ed.), *Who Cares?: Theory, Research and Educational Implications of the Ethic of Care*, New York: Praeger.

BRAYBROOKE, D. (1987), *Meeting Needs*, Princeton: Princeton University Press.

BRENKERT, G. (1983), *Marx's Ethics of Freedom*, London: Routledge & Kegan Paul.

BRITTAN, A. (1989), *Masculinity and Power*, Oxford: Blackwell.

BROWNING, G. (1987), *Women and Politics in the USSR*, Brighton: Wheatsheaf.

BRUEGEL, I. (1978), 'What Keeps the Family Going', *International Socialism*, series 2, no. 1: 2–15.

BRYDON, L., and CHANT, S. (1989), *Women in the Third World*, Aldershot: Edward Elgar.

Buber, M. (1970), *I and Thou*, New York: Charles Scribner's Sons.

Bullock, P. (1973), 'Categories of Labour Power for Capital', *Bulletin of the Conference of Socialist Economists* (Autumn), 82–99.

Calhoun, C. (1988), 'Justice, Care, Gender Bias', *Journal of Philosophy*, 85/9: 451–63.

Card, C. (1990), 'Caring and Evil', *Hypatia*, 5/1: 101–8.

—— (1991) (ed.), *Feminist Ethics*, Lawrence, Kansas: University Press of Kansas.

Carter, M. (1975), 'Housework Under Capitalism: Wally Seccombe', *Revolutionary Communist*, 2: 3–24.

Chadeau, A. (1985), 'Measuring Household Activities: Some International Comparisons', *Review of Income and Wealth*, 31/3: 237–53.

Chodorow, N. (1978), *The Reproduction of Mothering*, Berkeley and Los Angeles: University of California Press.

Clark, M. G. L., and Lange, L. (1979), 'Introduction', in M. G. L. Clark and L. Lange (eds.), *The Sexism of Social and Political Theory*, Toronto: University of Toronto Press.

Clatterbaugh, K. (1990), *Contemporary Perspectives on Masculinity*, Boulder, Colo.: Westview Press.

Cohen, G. A. (1974), 'Marx's Dialectic of Labour', *Philosophy and Public Affairs*, 3: 235–61.

—— (1978), *Karl Marx's Theory of History: A Defense*, Oxford: Oxford University Press.

Condon, E. H. (1992), 'Nursing and the Caring Metaphor: Gender and Political Influences on an Ethics of Care', *Nursing Outlook*, 40/1: 14–19.

Connell, R. (1987), *Gender and Power*, Cambridge: Polity.

Coole, D. (1993), *Women in Political Theory*, 2nd edn., Hemel Hempstead: Harvester Wheatsheaf.

Cottingham, J. (1983), 'Ethics and Impartiality', *Philosophical Studies*, 43: 83–99.

—— (1986), 'Partiality, Favouritism and Morality', *Philosophical Quarterly*, 36/144: 353–73.

—— (1991), 'The Ethics of Self-Concern', *Ethics*, 101: 798–817.

Coulson, M., Magas, B., and Wainwright, H. (1975), '"The Housewife and her Labour under Capitalism": a Critique', *New Left Review*, 89: 59–71.

Cowan, R. Schwartz (1983), *More Work for Mother*, New York: Basic Books.

Dalla Costa, M. (1973), 'Women and the Subversion of the Community', in Dalla Costa and James 1973.

—— and James, S. (1973), *The Power of Women and the Subversion of the Community*, Bristol: Falling Wall Press.

Dalley, G. (1988), *Ideologies of Caring*, London: Macmillan.

DANCY, J. (1983), 'Ethical Particularism and Morally Relevant Properties', *Mind*, 92: 530–47.

―― (1992), 'Caring about Justice', *Philosophy*, 67/262: 447–66.

DARWALL, S. (1983), *Impartial Reason*, New York: Cornell University Press.

DELMAR, R. (1976), 'Looking Again at Engels' "Origin of the Family"', in Mitchell and Oakley 1976.

DELPHY, C. (1984), *Close to Home*, London: Hutchinson.

―― and LEONARD, D. (1992), *Familiar Exploitation*, Cambridge: Polity.

DESAI, P. (1983) (ed.), *Marxism, the Soviet Economy and Central Planning*, Cambridge, Mass: MIT Press.

DIETZ, M. (1985), 'Citizenship with a Feminist Face: The Problem with Maternal Thinking', *Political Theory*, 13/1: 19–37.

DWORKIN, R. (1981), 'What is Equality? Part I: Equality of Welfare; Part II: Equality of Resources', *Philosophy and Public Affairs*, 10/3: 185–246; 10/4: 283–345.

EINHORN, B. (1993), *Cinderella Goes to Market: Citizenship, Gender and Women's Movements in East Central Europe*, London: Verso.

EISENSTEIN, Z. R. (1979) (ed.), *Capitalist Patriarchy and the Case for Socialist Feminism*, New York: Monthly Review Press.

ELSHTAIN, J. B. (1981), *Public Man, Private Woman*, Oxford: Robertson.

―― and TOBIAS, S. (1990) (eds.), *Women, Militarism, and War*, Savage, Md.: Rowman & Littlefield.

ELSON, D. (1979) (ed.), *Value: The Representation of Labour in Capitalism*, London: CSE Books.

―― and PEARSON, R. (1981), '"Nimble Fingers Make Cheap Workers": An Analysis of Women's Employment in Third World Export Manufacturing', *Feminist Review*, 7.

ENGELS, F. (1972), *The Origin of the Family, Private Property, and the State*, London: Lawrence & Wishart.

FARNSWORTH, B. (1980), *Aleksandra Kollontai: Socialism, Feminism and the Bolshevik Revolution*, Stanford, Calif.: Stanford University Press.

FERGUSON, K. (1984), *The Feminist Case against Bureaucracy*, Philadelphia: Temple University Press.

FINCH, J. (1983), *Married to the Job: Wives' Incorporation in Men's Work*, London: Allen & Unwin.

―― and GROVES, D. (1983) (eds.), *A Labour of Love: Women, Work and Caring*, London: Routledge & Kegan Paul.

―― and MASON, J. (1993), *Negotiating Family Responsibilities*, London: Routledge & Kegan Paul.

FIRESTONE, S. (1971), *The Dialectic of Sex*, London: Cape.

FISHER, B., and TRONTO, J. (1990), 'Toward a Feminist Theory of Caring', in Abel and Nelson 1990.

FLANAGAN, O., and JACKSON, K. (1987), 'Justice, Care, and Gender: The Kohlberg–Gilligan Debate Revisited', *Ethics*, 97: 622–37.

—— and RORTY, A. O. (1990) (eds.), *Identity, Character, and Morality*, Cambridge, Mass.: MIT Press.

FOLBRE, N. (1982), 'Exploitation Comes Home: A Critique of the Marxian Theory of Family Labour', *Cambridge Journal of Economics*, 6: 317–29.

—— (1994), *Who Pays for the Kids?: Gender and the Structures of Constraint*, London: Routledge.

FRIEDAN, B. (1985), *The Feminine Mystique*, Harmondsworth: Penguin.

FRIEDMAN, M. (1987*a*), 'Care and Context in Moral Reasoning', in Kittay and Meyers 1987.

—— (1987*b*), 'Beyond Caring: The De-Moralization of Gender', in Hanen and Nielsen 1987.

—— (1989), 'The Impracticality of Impartiality', *Journal of Philosophy*, 86: 645–56.

GARDINER, J. (1975), 'Women's Domestic Labour', *New Left Review*, 89: 47–58.

—— (1976), 'Political Economy of Domestic Labour in Capitalist Society', in Barker and Allen 1976.

—— HIMMELWEIT, S., and MACKINTOSH, M. (1975), 'Women's Domestic Labour', *Bulletin of the Conference of Socialist Economists*, 4/2: 1–11.

GERAS, N. (1986), 'The Controversy about Marx and Justice', in N. Geras, *Literature of Revolution*, London: Verso.

—— (1992), 'Bringing Marx to Justice: An Addendum and Rejoinder', *New Left Review*, 195: 37–69.

GIDDENS, A. (1991), *Modernity and Self-Identity: Self and Society in the Late Modern Age*, Cambridge: Polity.

GIEVE, K. (1989*a*), 'And Not to Count the Cost', in Gieve 1989*b*.

—— (1989*b*) (ed.), *Balancing Acts*, London: Virago.

GILLIGAN, C. (1982), *In a Different Voice*, Cambridge, Mass.: Harvard University Press.

—— (1987), 'Moral Orientation and Moral Development', in Kittay and Meyers 1987.

—— (1988*a*), 'Preface', in Gilligan *et al.* 1988.

—— (1988*b*), 'Prologue: Adolescent Development Reconsidered', in Gilligan *et al.* 1988.

—— and ATTANUCCI, J. (1988), 'Two Moral Orientations', in Gilligan *et al.* 1988.

—— WARD, J. V., and TAYLOR, J. M., with BARDIGE, B. (1988), *Mapping the Moral Domain: A Contribution of Women's Thinking to Psychology and Education*, Cambridge, Mass.: Harvard University Graduate School of Education.

—— LYONS, N. P., and HANMER, T. J. (1990) (eds.), *Making Connections:*

The Relational Worlds of Adolescent Girls at Emma Willard School, Cambridge, Mass.: Harvard University Press.

GLENDINNING, C., and MILLAR, J. (1992) (eds.), *Women and Poverty in Britain: The 1990s*, Hemel Hempstead: Harvester Wheatsheaf.

GLYN, A. (1979), 'The Rate of Exploitation and Contemporary Capitalism', *Japanese Journal of Economics*, 30/4: 334–46.

GOLDBERG, E. M., and HATCH, S. (1981), *A New Look at the Personal Social Services*, Discussion Paper no. 4, London: Policy Studies Institute.

GOLDBERG, G. S., and KRENEN, E. (1990) (eds.), *The Feminization of Poverty: Only in America?*, New York: Praeger.

GOODIN, R. (1985), *Protecting the Vulnerable: A Reanalysis of Our Social Responsibilities*, Chicago: University of Chicago Press.

GORBACHEV, M. (1988), *Perestroika: New Thinking for Our Country and the World*, London: Fontana.

GOUGH, I. (1972), 'Marx's Theory of Productive and Unproductive Labour', *New Left Review*, 76.

—— (1973), 'On Productive and Unproductive Labour: A Reply', *Bulletin of the Conference of Socialist Economists* (Winter), 68–73.

—— and HARRISON, J. (1975), 'Unproductive Labour and Housework Again', *Bulletin of the Conference of Socialist Economists*, 4/1: 1–7.

GOULD, C., and WARTOFSKY, M. (1976) (eds.), *Women and Philosophy*, Totowa, NJ: Rowman & Allanheld.

GRAHAM, H. (1983), 'Caring: A Labour of Love', in Finch and Groves 1983.

—— (1991), 'The Concept of Caring in Feminist Research: The Case of Domestic Service', *Sociology*, 25: 61–78.

GREEN, P. (1985), *Retrieving Democracy: In Search of Civic Equality*, Totowa, NJ: Rowman & Allanheld.

HANEN, M., and NIELSEN, K. (1987) (eds.), *Science, Morality and Feminist Theory*, Canadian Journal of Philosophy Supplement, Calgary: University of Calgary Press.

HARDING, S. (1986), *The Science Question in Feminism*, Ithaca, NY: Cornell University Press.

—— (1987) (ed.), *Feminism and Methodology*, Bloomington and Milton Keynes: Indiana University Press and Open University Press.

—— (1991), *Whose Science? Whose Knowledge?: Thinking from Women's Lives*, Milton Keynes: Open University Press.

HARRISON, J. (1973a), 'Productive and Unproductive Labour in Marx's Political Economy', *Bulletin of the Conference of Socialist Economists*, (Autumn), 70–82.

—— (1973b), 'The Political Economy of Housework', *Bulletin of the Conference of Socialist Economists* (Winter), 35–51.

HARTMANN, H. (1979), 'Capitalism, Patriarchy, and Job-Segregation by Sex', in Eisenstein 1979.

—— (1986), 'The Unhappy Marriage of Marxism and Feminism: Towards a More Progressive Union', in Sargent 1986.

—— (1987), 'The Family as the Locus of Gender, Class and Political Struggle: The Example of Housework', in Harding 1987.

HARTSOCK, N. (1987), 'The Feminist Standpoint: Developing the Ground for a Specifically Feminist Historical Materialism', in Harding 1987.

HEARN, J. (1987), *The Gender of Oppression*, Brighton: Wheatsheaf.

HEITLINGER, A. (1979), *Women and State Socialism*, London: Macmillan.

HELD, D. (1991) (ed.), *Political Theory Today*, Cambridge: Polity.

HELD, V. (1987*a*), 'Feminism and Moral Theory', in Kittay and Meyers 1987.

—— (1987*b*), 'Non-contractual Society: A Feminist View', in Hanen and Nielsen 1987.

—— (1993), *Feminist Morality: Transforming Culture, Society, and Politics*, Chicago: University of Chicago Press.

HILL, T. E., Jr. (1987), 'The Importance of Autonomy', in Kittay and Meyers 1987.

HIMMELWEIT, S., and MOHUN, S. (1977), 'Domestic Labour and Capital', *Cambridge Journal of Economics*, 1/1: 15–31.

HIRSCHMANN, N. J. (1992), *Rethinking Obligation: A Feminist Method for Political Theory*, Ithaca, NY: Cornell University Press.

HOAGLAND, S. L. (1990), 'Some Concerns about Nel Noddings' *Caring*', *Hypatia*, 5/1: 109–14.

HOUSTON, B. (1989), 'Prolegomena to Future Caring', in Brabeck 1989.

—— (1990), 'Caring and Exploitation', *Hypatia*, 5/1: 115–19.

HOWELL, P. (1975), 'Once Again on Productive and Unproductive Labour', *Revolutionary Communist*, 3–4.

HUME, D. (1888), *A Treatise of Human Nature*, Oxford: Clarendon.

—— (1975), *Enquiries Concerning Human Understanding and Concerning the Principles of Morals* (3rd edn.), Oxford: Clarendon.

JAGGAR, A. M. (1983), *Feminist Politics and Human Nature*, Brighton: Harvester.

—— (1989), 'Love and Knowledge: Emotion in Feminist Epistemology', in Jaggar and Bordo 1989.

—— and BORDO, S. R. (1989) (eds.), *Gender/Body/Knowledge*, New Brunswick: Rutgers University Press.

JONES, W. T. (1984), 'Public Roles, Private Roles, and Differential Moral Assessments of Role Performance', *Ethics*, 94: 603–20.

JOSHI, H. (1992), 'The Cost of Caring', in Glendinning and Millar.

KAGAN, J., and LAMB, J. (1987) (eds.), *The Emergence of Morality in Young Children*, Chicago: University of Chicago Press.

KALUZYNSKA, E. (1980), 'Wiping the Floor with Theory: A Survey of Writings on Housework', *Feminist Review*, 6: 40–54.

KEKES, J. (1984), 'Moral Sensitivity', *Philosophy*, 59: 3–19.

KITTAY, E. F., and MEYERS, D. T. (1987) (eds.), *Women and Moral Theory*, Savage, Md.: Rowman & Littlefield.

KLAGGE, J. C. (1986), 'Marx's Realms of "Freedom" and "Necessity"', *Canadian Journal of Philosophy*, 16/4: 769–78.

KOLLONTAI, A. (1977), *Selected Writings*, London: Allison & Busby.

KROEGER-MAPPES, J. (1994), 'The Ethic of Care vis-à-vis the Ethic of Rights: A Problem for Contemporary Moral Theory', *Hypatia*, 9/3: 108–31.

KUHN, A., and WOLPE, A. (1978), *Feminism and Materialism*, London: Routledge & Kegan Paul.

KYMLICKA, W. (1990), *Contemporary Political Philosophy*, Oxford: Oxford University Press.

LARRABEE, M. J. (1993) (ed.), *An Ethic of Care: Feminist and Interdisciplinary Perspectives*, London: Routledge.

LENIN, V. I. (1963), 'A Great Technological Achievement', *Collected Works*, vol. xix, Moscow: Progress Publishers.

—— (1965a), 'The Tasks of the Working Women's Movement in the Soviet Republic', *Collected Works*, vol. xxx, Moscow: Progress Publishers.

—— (1965b), 'International Women's Day' (1920), *Collected Works*, vol. xxx, Moscow: Progress Publishers.

—— (1965c), 'International Women's Day' (1921), *Collected Works*, vol. xxxii, Moscow: Progress Publishers.

—— (1965d), 'A Great Beginning', *Collected Works*, vol. xxix, Moscow: Progress Publishers.

—— (1966), 'Message of Greetings to the All-Russia Conference of Gubernian Departments for Work Among Women', *Collected Works*, vol. xxxi, Moscow: Progress Publishers.

LEONARD, D. (1984), 'The Origin of the Family, Private Property, and Marxist Feminism?', *Trouble and Strife*, 3.

LEWIS, J., and PIACHAUD, D. (1992), 'Women and Poverty in the Twentieth Century', in Glendinning and Millar 1992.

LOCKE, J. (1975), *An Essay Concerning Human Understanding*, Oxford: Clarendon.

LOVIBOND, S. (1994), 'Maternalist Ethics: A Feminist Assessment', *South Atlantic Quarterly*, 93/4: 779–802.

LUKES, S. (1985), *Marxism and Morality*, Oxford: Clarendon.

McAULEY, A. (1981), *Women's Work and Wages in the Soviet Union*, London: Allen & Unwin.

MACCORMICK, N., and BANKOWSKI, Z., (1989) (eds.), *Enlightenment, Rights and Revolution*, Aberdeen: Aberdeen University Press.

McDOWELL, J. (1978), 'Are Moral Requirements Hypothetical Imperatives?', *Proceedings of the Aristotelian Society*, suppl. vol., 13–29.

—— (1979), 'Virtue and Reason', *Monist*, 62: 331–50.

MacKinnon, C. A. (1989), *Toward a Feminist Theory of the State*, Cambridge, Mass.: Harvard University Press.

Mackintosh, M. H. (1988), 'Domestic Labour and the Household', in Pahl 1988.

Maclean, M., and Groves, D. (1991) (eds.), *Women's Issues in Social Policy*, London: Routledge.

McLellan, D. (1980), *The Thought of Karl Marx* (2nd edn.), London: Macmillan.

McNaughton, D. (1988), *Moral Vision: An Introduction to Ethics*, Oxford: Blackwell.

McRae, S. (1986), *Cross-Class Families*, Oxford: Clarendon.

Mainardi, P. (1982), 'The Politics of Housework', in Malos 1982.

Malos, E. (1982) (ed.), *The Politics of Housework*, London: Allison & Busby.

Mandel, E. (1975), *Late Capitalism*, London: New Left Books.

Marx, K. (1969a), *Theories of Surplus Value*, part i, Moscow: Progress Publishers.

—— (1969b), 'Wage Labour and Capital', in Marx and Engels 1969a, vol. i.

—— (1969c), 'Critique of the Gotha Programme', in Marx and Engels 1969a, vol. iii.

—— (1969d), 'Preface to the *Critique of Political Economy*', in Marx and Engels 1969a, vol. i.

—— (1972), *Theories of Surplus Value*, part iii, London: Lawrence & Wishart.

—— (1973), *Grundrisse*, Harmondsworth: Penguin.

—— (1975), 'Economic and Philosophical Manuscripts', in K. Marx, and F. Engels, *Collected Works*, vol. iii, London: Lawrence & Wishart.

—— (1976a), *Capital Volume One*, Harmondsworth: Penguin Books in association with *New Left Review*.

—— (1976b), 'Results of the Immediate Process of Production', in Marx 1976a.

—— (1981), *Capital Volume Three*, Harmondsworth: Penguin Books in association with *New Left Review*.

—— and Engels, F. (1965), *German Ideology*, London: Lawrence & Wishart.

—— —— (1969a), *Selected Works in Three Volumes*, Moscow: Progress Publishers.

—— —— (1969b), 'Manifesto of the Communist Party', in Marx and Engels 1969a.

Mason, A. (1993), *Explaining Political Disagreement*, Cambridge: Cambridge University Press.

Mayeroff, M. (1971), *On Caring*, New York: Harper & Row.

Meissner, M., Humphreys, E. W., Meis, S. M., and Scheu, W. J. (1988),

'No Exit for Wives: Sexual Division of Labour and the Cumulation of Household Demands in Canada', in Pahl 1988.

MIES, M. (1986), *Patriarchy and Accumulation on a World Scale*, London: Zed Books.

MILL, J. S. (1985), *The Subjection of Women*, London: Dent.

MILLER, A. (1990), *Banished Knowledge*, London: Virago.

MILLER, J. B. (1988), *Toward a New Psychology of Women* (2nd edn.), Harmondsworth: Pelican Books.

MITCHELL, J., and OAKLEY, A. (1976) (eds.), *The Rights and Wrongs of Women*, Harmondsworth: Penguin.

MOLYNEUX, M. (1979), 'Beyond the Domestic Labour Debate', *New Left Review*, 116: 3–27.

—— (1981), 'Women in Socialist Societies', in Young *et al.* 1981.

—— (1985), 'Family Reform in Socialist States: The Hidden Agenda', *Feminist Review*, 21: 47–64.

MORRIS, L. (1990), *The Workings of the Household*, Cambridge: Polity.

MORTON, P. (1982), 'Women's Work is Never Done', in Malos 1982.

MOSKALENKO, L. (n.d.), *A Russian Lesson For Feminists*, Middlesex University, Centre for Community Studies.

NODDINGS, N. (1984), *Caring: A Feminine Approach to Ethics and Moral Education*, Berkeley and Los Angeles: University of California Press.

—— (1989), *Women and Evil*, Berkeley and Los Angeles: University of California Press.

—— (1990), 'A Response', *Hypatia*, 5/1: 120–6.

NOZICK, R. (1974), *Anarchy, State and Utopia*, Oxford: Blackwell.

NUSSBAUM, M. (1986), *The Fragility of Goodness*, Cambridge: Cambridge University Press.

—— (1990), *Love's Knowledge*, New York: Oxford University Press.

OKIN, S. M. (1989), *Justice, Gender and the Family*, New York: Basic Books.

—— (1991), 'Gender, the Public and the Private', in Held 1991.

O'NEILL, O. (1989), 'The Great Maxims of Justice and Charity', in MacCormick and Bankowski 1989.

PAHL, J. (1990), *Money and Marriage*, Basingstoke: Macmillan.

PAHL, R. E. (1988) (ed.), *On Work*, Oxford: Blackwell.

PARKER, G. (1990), *With Due Care and Attention* (2nd edn.), London: Family Policy Studies Centre.

PARKER, R. (1981), 'Tending and Social Policy', in Goldberg and Hatch 1981.

PATEMAN, C. (1988), *The Sexual Contract*, Cambridge: Polity.

PHILLIPS, A., and TAYLOR, B. (1980), 'Sex and Skill: Notes towards a Feminist Economics', *Feminist Review*, 6: 79–88.

PHILMORE, J. (1982), 'The Libertarian Case for Slavery: A Note on Nozick', *The Philosophical Forum*, 14: 43–58.

PLECK, J. H. (1985), *Working Wives/Working Husbands*, Beverly Hills, Calif.: Sage in co-operation with the National Council on Family Relations.

PORTER, C. (1980), *Alexandra Kollontai*, London: Virago.

PORTER, M. (1983), *Home, Work and Class Consciousness*, Manchester: Manchester University Press.

QURESHI, H., and WALKER, A. (1989), *The Caring Relationship*, London: Macmillan.

RAWLS, J. (1971), *A Theory of Justice*, Oxford: Oxford University Press.

RICHARDS, J. R. (1980), *The Sceptical Feminist*, Harmondsworth: Penguin.

ROEMER, J. (1982), *A General Theory of Exploitation and Class*, Cambridge, Mass.: Harvard University Press.

—— (1983), 'Unequal Exchange, Labour Migration and International Capital Flows: A Theoretical Synthesis', in Desai 1983.

—— (1988), *Free to Lose*, London: Radius.

ROONEY, P. (1991), 'A Different Different Voice: On the Feminist Challenge in Moral Theory', *Philosophical Forum*, 22/4: 335–61.

ROSE, H. (1994), *Love, Power and Knowledge: Towards a Feminist Transformation of the Sciences*, Cambridge: Polity.

ROSS, W. D. (1930), *The Right and the Good*, Oxford: Clarendon.

—— (1939), *Foundations of Ethics*, Oxford: Clarendon.

ROWBOTHAM, S. (1973), *Woman's Consciousness, Man's World*, Harmondsworth: Penguin.

RUDDICK, S. (1989), *Maternal Thinking: Toward a Politics of Peace*, London: Women's Press.

—— (1990), 'The Rationality of Care', in Elshtain and Tobias 1990.

SARGENT, L. (1986) (ed.), *The Unhappy Marriage of Marxism and Feminism*, London: Pluto.

SASSOON, A. S. (1987) (ed.), *Women and the State*, London: Hutchinson.

SAYERS, J., EVANS, M., and REDCLIFT, N. (1987) (eds.), *Engels Revisited: New Feminist Essays*, London: Tavistock.

SCOTT, H. (1984), *Working Your Way to the Bottom: The Feminization of Poverty*, London: Pandora.

SECCOMBE, W. (1974), 'The Housewife and Her Labour under Capitalism', *New Left Review*, 83: 3–24.

—— (1975), 'Domestic Labour: Reply to Critics', *New Left Review*, 84: 85–96.

SEGAL, L. (1990), *Slow Motion: Changing Masculinities, Changing Men*, London: Virago.

SEVENHUIJSEN, S. (1993), 'Paradoxes of Gender: Ethical and Epistemological Perspectives on Care in Feminist Political Theory', *Acta Politica*, 28/2: 139–49.

SHER, G. (1987), 'Other Voices, Other Rooms? Women's Psychology and Moral Theory', in Kittay and Meyers 1987.

SINGER, P. (1980), *Marx*, Oxford: Oxford University Press.

SKILLEN, A. (1977), *Ruling Illusions*, Hassocks: Harvester.

SMITH, P. (1978), 'Domestic Labour and Marx's Theory of Value', in Kuhn and Wolpe 1978.

SPELMAN, E. (1988), *Inessential Woman: Problems of Exclusion in Feminist Thought*, Boston: Beacon Press.

STEEDMAN, I. (1981) (ed.), *The Value Controversy*, London: Verso.

STOCKER, M. (1976), 'The Schizophrenia of Modern Ethical Theories', *Journal of Philosophy*, 73/14: 453–66.

—— (1987), 'Duty and Friendship', in Kittay and Meyers 1987.

THOMAS, C. (1993), 'De-constructing Concepts of Care', *Sociology*, 27: 649–69.

THOMPSON, G. (1987), *Needs*, London: Routledge & Kegan Paul.

TRONTO, J. C. (1987), 'Beyond Gender Difference to a Theory of Care', *Signs*, 12/4: 644–63.

—— (1989), 'Women and Caring: What Can Feminists Learn about Morality from Caring?', in Jaggar and Bordo 1989.

—— (1991a), 'Reflections on Gender, Morality, and Power: Caring and the Moral Problems of Otherness', in Tronto *et al.* 1991.

—— (1991b), 'The Question of Justice and the Nature of Caring in Politics', in Tronto *et al.* 1991.

—— *et al.*, compiled by S. SEVENHUIJSEN (1991), *Gender, Care and Justice in Feminist Political Theory*, Utrecht: Anna Maria van Schuurman Centrum, Graduate School for Advanced Research in Women's Studies, Working Papers.

—— (1993), *Moral Boundaries: A Political Argument for an Ethic of Care*, London: Routledge.

UNGERSON, C. (1987), *Policy is Personal: Sex, Gender and Informal Care*, London: Tavistock.

—— (1990a), 'Introduction', in Ungerson 1990c.

—— (1990b), 'The Language of Care: Crossing the Boundaries', in Ungerson 1990c.

—— (ed.) (1990c), *Gender and Caring: Work and Welfare in Britain and Scandinavia*, Hemel Hempstead: Harvester Wheatsheaf.

VAN DEN BERGHE, P. L. (1981), *The Ethnic Phenomenon*, New York: Elsevier.

WAERNESS, K. (1987), 'On the Rationality of Caring', in Sassoon 1987.

WALBY, S. (1986), *Patriarchy at Work*, Cambridge: Polity.

—— (1990), *Theorizing Patriarchy*, Oxford: Blackwell.

WALKERDINE, V., and LUCEY, H. (1989), *Democracy in the Kitchen: The Regulation of Mothers and the Socialisation of Daughters*, London: Virago.

WARD, B., and DUBOS, R. (1972), *Only One Earth*, New York: Norton.

WARING, M. (1989), *If Women Counted*, London: Macmillan.

WEITZMAN, L. (1985), *The Divorce Revolution: The Unexpected Social and Economic Consequences for Women and Children in America*, New York: Free Press.

WHITEHEAD, A. (1981), '"I'm Hungry, Mum": The Politics of Domestic Budgeting', in Young *et al.* 1981.

WIGGINS, D. (1987), 'Claims of Need', in *Needs, Values, Truth: Essays in the Philosophy of Value*, Oxford: Blackwell.

WILLIAMS, B. (1981), *Moral Luck*, Cambridge: Cambridge University Press.

WOLLSTONECRAFT, M. (1985), *A Vindication of the Rights of Woman*, London: Dent.

Women and Communism (1950), *Selections from the Writings of Marx, Engels, Lenin, Stalin*, London: Lawrence & Wishart.

WOOD, A. (1981), *Karl Marx*, London: Routledge.

YOUNG, I. M. (1990), *Justice and the Politics of Difference*, Princeton: Princeton University Press.

YOUNG, K., WOLKOWITZ, C., and McCULLAGH, R. (1981) (eds.), *Of Marriage and the Market*, London: CSE Books.

INDEX